Asides, Tirades, Meditations

Asides, Tirades, Meditations

Selected Essays

Kiran Nagarkar

BLOOMSBURY
NEW DELHI • LONDON • OXFORD • NEW YORK • SYDNEY

BLOOMSBURY INDIA
Bloomsbury Publishing India Pvt. Ltd
Second Floor, LSC Building No. 4, DDA Complex, Pocket C – 6 & 7,
Vasant Kunj, New Delhi, 110070

BLOOMSBURY, BLOOMSBURY INDIA and the Diana logo
are trademarks of Bloomsbury Publishing Plc

First published in India 2024
This edition published 2024

ISBN: PB: 978-93-56408-88-3; eBook: 978-93-56408-89-0
2 4 6 8 10 9 7 5 3 1

For sale in the Indian Subcontinent only

Typeset in Adobe Garamond Pro by Manipal Technologies Limited
Printed and bound in India by Thomson Press India Ltd

Contents

Introduction by Salil Tripathi vii

PART I ON CULTURE

WRITING

1 Clueless: An Occasional Writer's Journey 3
2 Every Person with a Book Is a Mobile Library 37
3 English and Hinglish: Pidginization the Indian Way 41
4 Memories of Childhood 52
5 On Ageing 69
6 Open Sesame, or The Power of Stories 73
7 Readings, Misreadings and Non-readings: Perils of the Indian Literary Scene 76
8 Shiva's Blue Throat: A Personal Vision of the Artist's Role in the 21st Century 84
9 What Kind of Beast Is This Thing Called 'Style'? 106
10 The Empire Is Dead: Long Live the Empire 108
11 The Role of Memory in *Cuckold* 114
12 The Trees: A Belated Love Story 125

CINEMA

1 The Film Critic and His 'Artiste' 137
2 Bollywood and Me: The Family Connection 141
3 Star Power 149
4 The Other Bollywood 155
5 Film Reviews: Conan's Hedonistic Ode to the Body, One Hell of a Watchable Film, Past the Gates of Hell,

The Brutalization of Indian Cinema in Dacait, The Farther Reaches of Romantic Love 160

PART II ON SOCIETY AND POLITICS

1 Bombay: A Hope and a Prayer 179
2 Bombay by BEST: The View from the Flying Upper Deck 183
3 Climate Change: From Bombay with Smog 187
4 Coaching Classes 190
5 Looking for Gulbadan's Kite 197
6 Ghar (Home) 201
7 Gore Vidal 208
8 How Did We Lose Tomorrow? 215
9 Never Again – For Whom? 222
10 On Memory 228
11 Prohibition's Dead. Long Live Prohibition 241
12 Staying Indian 246
13 The Fine Art of Intolerance 249
14 The Honoraries 259
15 Tuesday, Bloody Tuesday 264
16 We Are All in Batra Lala-land 268
17 A Hindu Festival Called Christmas: Encounters between a Non-practising Hindu and Roman Catholicism 272
18 A Rumination on Frauds: The 'Other' and the 'Artist' 282
19 God-Bothering 297

Afterword: A Personal Tribute by Nayantara Sahgal 313
About the Author 317

Introduction

It was sometime in the early 1980s that Kiran Nagarkar invited some of us to the tasteful home of his friend Rekha Sabnis to listen to the script of his new play, *Bedtime Story*. Sabnis's home seemed familiar – several crucial scenes of Shyam Benegal's *Bhumika* (The Role, 1977) were filmed there. Sabnis was herself an accomplished actor on Marathi stage, and she read the script with Kiran's lifelong companion, Tulsi Vatsal, and his friend, the artist and writer Manjula Padmanabhan.

It was a play that shook your senses. Ostensibly a fresh look at the Sanskrit epic Mahabharata, which Nagarkar described as 'the living epic of our subcontinent', the play reinterpreted it to offer a telling, subversive commentary on our time, of rising fundamentalism, debasement of politics and widespread cynicism. The play showed a mirror to the audience, revealing a lurid version of reality by giving a sharper edge to the myths, stories and fables that we had taken for granted, which lulled us to sleep, where heroes and villains have assigned roles. *Bedtime Story* shattered that trance-like calm we inhabited; it was an individual's cry against our collective apathy and amnesia.

It was no surprise that fundamentalists did not want it staged, when Dr Shriram Lagoo attempted to perform it. When it went to the censor board, what came back had 78 cuts, and attempting to stage what remained would have truly made an absurd play. One board member even asked Nagarkar why he was distorting well-loved original myths. That board member must be innocent of Marathi literary canon then, where reinterpreting classics was a time-honoured tradition: Iravati Karve's *Yuganta* was published in 1967; V.S. Khandekar's *Yayati* dates back to 1957. Nagarkar was part of that great tradition.

His questioning of certainties upset many. Religion, as he writes in these pages, is the world's biggest industry, but for Nagarkar, 'there is only one God, and her name is life. She is the only one worthy of worship. All else is irrelevant.'

Listening to the performance of *Bedtime Story* that day in Sabnis's Girgaum home made us feel as though were part of the *samizdat*, doing what was forbidden. We were accomplices now. Meanwhile, threats multiplied. It was the period after the Emergency, and many artists and writers wanted to exercise the freedoms that had been taken away. In 1995, Sabnis's group, Abhivyakti, staged the play, directed by Achyut Deshingkar, but it had a limited run of 25 shows. It would take years before the play could get published in English.

The play taunted the privileged, the powerful and the upper class and castes. The prejudice the elite had towards those they considered beneath them was glaringly visible – in language, in symbols; it was a bonfire of our hypocrisies. When Draupadi is humiliated after Yudhishthira loses the game of dice, she implores the 'lecherous voyeurs', as she calls the family elders who sit and watch as the Kauravas disrobe her. She calls on Krishna, who comes but is late and yet just in time, like the police in a Bollywood film:

KRISHNA: Stop this demonic game. (*Places himself between Draupadi and the audience.*) No more of this perversion. I will not stand by and watch it.

DRAUPADI: Yet you watched long enough.

KRISHNA: I was waiting for your call.

DRAUPADI: What sort of God are you that needs calling?

Nagarkar was known for his fiction. Explaining why he wrote, he says in these pages, 'I try my best to write simply and compellingly, but without simplifying any of the issues. In that sense I want to be like Coleridge's Ancient Mariner: I want to mesmerize my reader, make him a willing victim. I write to be read.'

Nagarkar's path-breaking modernist novel, deliberately titled *Saat Sakkam Trechalis* (Seven Sixes Are Forty-Three), intended to provoke with its quirky, absurd title. In 1979, in *The Hitchhiker's Guide to the Galaxy*, Douglas Adams had confidently asserted that the answer to the ultimate question of life, universe and everything was 42. Five years earlier, Nagarkar was questioning the mathematics in his Marathi novel (whose English translation would appear only in 1995). *Seven Sixes Are Forty-Three* captured the urban angst and the confused nature of life, where the past, present and future were 'not necessarily in that order', as Jean-Luc Godard would say in another context, when he was asked if cinema should have a beginning, a middle and an end. Godard was upending the grammar of cinema, as the Polish director Peter Grotowski or British director Peter Brook would do with theatre; Nagarkar was doing that to the form of writing, bursting our certainties.

Other brilliant novels followed: in 1994, *Ravan and Eddie*, the precursor of a trilogy (*Extras* came in 2012, and *Rest in Peace* in 2015), which astutely and acutely depicted life in Mumbai's chawls, where two communities might live next to one another without bothering to learn much about the other, and often quietly hating the other and yet tolerating their presence. Tension was ever-present as resources were limited. Nagarkar himself hadn't grown up in a wealthy family, and as he describes chawls in this volume, 'people have to wait for hours in queues for the municipal taps to start spitting out water. Their lives revolve around water.' So water and the wars fought over it are an integral offshoot of

Ravan and Eddie, the story that brought together a Catholic and a Hindu boy. Like Salman Rushdie did with Saleem and Shiva in *Midnight's Children* in 1981, *Ravan and Eddie* pit contrasting duelling characters against one another. Ravan and Eddie were as much about that chawl as about what was becoming to the city and, indeed, India. Once in Chennai, as he recounts here, a reader asked him why he had written a book about Christians and Hindus, when the most important subject was Hindus and Muslims. 'I didn't have an answer to this fiat except to say that I do not write to order and certainly not novels with messages. More often than not, the subjects choose me instead of the other way around,' he writes. As the novel annoyed both Christians and Hindus, Nagarkar said in his characteristically droll tone that in future he might as well write only about ants and insects, though, he added, that too might offend some readers.

With *Cuckold* in 1997, Nagarkar turned to Meera, the princess who danced in temples and who considered her marriage to a king a sham, since she already felt wedded to Krishna. Initially Nagarkar was not much interested in the life of the saint-poet, but as he set about researching her story, he was enchanted, and he made her life vivid, as we discover often in these essays, where he repeatedly returns to the craft of writing that novel and the themes it explores and examines. The chosen medium for the novel is not a third-person narrator, nor Meera, but her husband, whom he only refers to as Maharaj Kumar, and about whom so little is known. That gave Nagarkar the room to imagine. And then, in 2006, he wrote a reflective novel about what makes someone a terrorist, in *God's Little Soldier*. Explaining the complexity that simplistic depictions avoid, he writes: 'We find it difficult, impossible might be more precise, to imagine that the *jehadi* warrior is as much of a human being as we are. We do not seem to comprehend that the human mind is not a logical creature; that it follows its own conscience and if it feels the necessity, it can and will renege even on its own chosen beliefs.'

That, in itself, is a formidable body of work, but Nagarkar did much more than that. With his close friend Arun Kolatkar, he wrote advertising copy – a profession that gave him unique insights into human behaviour. He learned not only what makes us buy products and services, he learned how to stimulate our desire by writing short, pithy texts that lure us into trying something we hadn't or didn't know we wanted it.

In fact, I came across his name first not as a playwright or novelist, but as a creative advertising mind. Nagarkar and Kolatkar were associated with Chaitra, an advertising agency which had a large office at Kemp's Corner, near the apartment I grew up in. My mother used to translate Chaitra's advertisements into Gujarati. And she mentioned Nagarkar to me, recounting humorous anecdotes of when they met at the office. Nagarkar did not have set hours there, and as a freelance translator, my mother popped in and out.

I was in my early 20s when we met, and it turned into a lifelong friendship. He soon invited me to the reading of *Bedtime Story*, about which I wrote in the *Sunday Observer*, then edited by Vinod Mehta, and for *Ovation*, a theatre journal that my friend Sunil Shanbag edited. Like many intellectuals of that era, Nagarkar had taken freedom of expression for granted: he knew that the Indian Constitution placed 'reasonable restrictions' on free speech, but he also knew that you could take liberties, and the law would not outlaw artistic freedom. And yet, the Emergency (1975–1977) changed the rules and made us question our assumptions. In the introduction to *Bedtime Story*, Nagarkar wrote how the play encapsulated his thinking about us and our responses. He realized his own 'callousness towards the terrible injustices perpetrated around me … I had … become conscious of the fact that there is something worse than callousness, an outburst of righteous rage which subsides just as easily as it had risen. My ruminations crystallised into a personal notion of responsibility and accountability, which would become, over the years, one of my basic tenets for practicing that business called life.'

Nagarkar's lifelong commitment to freedom of expression, of supporting banned books and writers and artists and plays, had its origins in his own struggles: his desire to write what he wished, and the criticism his writing received from those who wanted to decide what others could read or see. In this Nagarkar wasn't alone: the Marathi playwright Vijay Tendulkar had to fight spirited battles too (his play *Sakharam Binder* was banned in 1974) to get his plays staged, and Mohan Agashe's Theatre Academy had to get court permission before taking *Ghashiram Kotwal* to Berlin, where the group was invited to perform. Cultural custodians representing Hindu sensibilities had already set the stage for other fundamentalists to demand restrictions: the calls from Muslim leaders for banning Rushdie's *The Satanic Verses* would only come later in that decade.

After my graduate studies in the United States, I returned to Bombay, as the city was still known, and the great editor S. Nihal Singh hired me to be the assistant editor at the *Indian Post*, a daily that was launched in 1987. One of my tasks was to get columnists for the newspaper, and I set about reaching out to the writers I'd like to read. When I met Nagarkar, he immediately said yes: I wanted him to write a column on culture and politics, but he said no; he'd be our film critic for foreign films. I was intrigued and surprised, but of course we agreed. And he wrote rollickingly funny (and sometimes really long) reviews of films. He did not review every film that was screened, but only those he felt strongly about. That perplexed our news editor, who felt a newspaper had to be a paper of record and review everything;

but I trusted Nagarkar's judgement of what was noteworthy: both in terms of what had to be seen and what must not be seen. Life was short, time was precious; some films were too tedious to write about, and not worth reading about either. So be it, Nihal Singh and I agreed.

I left India in 1990, but we met often during my visits to the city that was now firmly called Mumbai. As he grew older, his frustration and exasperation with the fundamentalist turn in politics and in society became more palpable. He kept probing, shaking us out of our stupor, challenging us to shed our apathy and guard our freedoms in our public and private lives. In the essays in these pages, we see all those facets of Nagarkar: fierce commitment to freedoms, desire to speak the truth, interpreting our reality, celebrating imagination, championing the one without voice and provoking us to leave our comfort zones.

At the Chandigarh Literature Festival, where he was a regular feature, I remember him passionately criticizing the simplistic, comical plans of Smriti Irani (who claimed to have graduated from Yale, when all she had done was to have attended a seminar for parliamentarians) to reshape India's educational curricula, leading to India's eventual infantilization. He cared for those with limited means, who tried to make their lives better in this vast adventure, this mega-city of which he was such an essential part. He ran a spirited campaign for Mumbai's public buses. He had profound understanding of the Maharashtrian mind: his descriptions of the Hindu Colony in Dadar, and of Pune, are moving and touching.

Nagarkar was outraged that Gujarat prescribed books by Dina Nath Batra as textbooks at school. Batra was a self-appointed moral guardian who had successfully forced Penguin to drop Wendy Doniger's book on Hindus. Nagarkar wrote then: 'You can't breed the best scientists or economists if they are brought up on a diet of lies and falsehoods, and expect them to contribute innovative solutions. How does false history affect science? If you don't know the history of science and the preceding work on a subject, you will not know where to start. But there is an even more urgent matter. This government's idea of development has two premises. Their role model is the unfettered free market economy and any form of dissent, like Greenpeace or the anti-nuclear movement, has to be scotched … Secondly, right now we are hell-bent on ignoring the gravest problem facing the entire human race: Climate change, but our only hope is to wake up to it at the earliest and act on it forcefully.'

Manichaean divides troubled him; he found the certitude of absolutists ridiculous. Nuance mattered in an era in which the world was increasingly divided into an us-versus-them dyad. Once in Europe, as he recounts in this volume, he attempted to reason with an angry member of the audience who called him anti-Semitic after he criticized the state of Israel, but he realised the futility of reason to argue with those who had faith on their side. Minds open when they learn to doubt, and you learn to doubt by reading everything you lay your hands on. A library, Nagarkar writes, is your personal magic lamp, opening doors.

Unusually, for one with a keen ear for the colloquial who conceived advertising ideas, he was acutely aware of the politics behind the use of Hinglish. In one essay he writes: 'The Hinglish creators are not breaking barriers. They are not inventing a new language. They are merely exploiting the shallowness of the audience, ethnic and communal tics and peculiarities, and using Hinglish to perpetuate and widen the gap between the haves and have-nots, between those who have English and those who do not. They can, thus, be seen to be working not towards an egalitarian society, but reinforcing and reiterating the biases and superiority of the English-speaking super-caste.'

Nagarkar was a familiar feature at cultural events, often turning up unannounced, as he did in 2015 at Kitab Khana, the fine bookstore in Mumbai, when I launched my collection of travel writing. Our mutual friend Shobhaa Dé was in conversation with me, and Nagarkar did me the honour of helping launch the book. Our last meeting was a year or so later, when he was excited about the conversations between the Gujarati poet Narmad and his wife, Dahigauri, which were remarkably candid about sexuality and spirituality, as well as roles assigned to genders by society. I was researching my book on the Gujaratis, and he wanted me to read the original and draw from it to write about Gujarati attitudes towards relationships. I am delighted that Vatsal and Aban Mukherjee are translating that text into English.

In 2018, three female journalists claimed on social media that Nagarkar had behaved inappropriately with them. He strenuously denied the allegations. Some literary figures and festivals distanced themselves from him, and his publisher cancelled the contract on what would turn out to be his last novel. A smaller press ended up publishing *The Arsonist*.

He died of cerebral haemorrhage in 2019. That year, when PEN America held its gala in New York, it flashed the images on screen of writers who had died that year; it felt good to see him remembered in that montage. I admired him as a gifted writer, a champion of freedoms, a friend who saw through the clouds clearly, who warned us about the seductive peril of majoritarianism. He turned to our myths and history, and through the lives of mythical characters from the epics and historical figures like Meera and Kabir, made sense of our time. He made us look at our present with clear eyes so that we do not relive our past.

In his introduction to *Bedtime Story*, Nagarkar warned of the twin dangers of censorship India faces: the higgledy-piggledy arm of the law and the more decisive fury of the mob: 'Legal censorship in India can often be gauche, club-footed and hyper-protective of anything and everything but the freedoms of speech and expression. Extra-legal censorship in the country, however, is fearless and effective.' It is the lawlessness of mob justice that he warned us against so that our internal demons don't devour us.

Salil Tripathi

Award-winning journalist and author of *The Gujaratis*

PART I

On Culture

Writing

Clueless: An Occasional Writer's Journey

(A novel or a body of work must speak for itself. The one person who has no business to talk about his work is the writer himself. Having made that categorical statement, let me proceed to shamelessly do just that.)

WHAT I AM ABOUT to say is likely to shake your faith in writers and put you off my writing for good. Indulge me, take whatever I say with a pinch of salt – sometimes a fistful might be needed.

I have heard of many fine authors who know exactly what their novels are going to be about. They plan their books the way Hitchcock used to plot his movies. They work out every chapter to the last detail. I have heard that Ishiguro, for instance, is one such author. These authors are God's chosen. They obviously can see forever. Unfortunately for me, even on a clear day, I do not think I am able to see too far beyond my nose. There are times, however, when I have been lucky. For instance, it took me about three years to write *Cuckold*, which is 609 pages long. As a matter of fact, I was also working as an advertising consultant at that time so what it boiled down to was that *Cuckold* was produced in three periods, each a couple of months or so. *Ravan and Eddie*, on the other hand, got stalled for almost fifteen years. I wrote the first few chapters in Marathi, and then because of various factors, I did not work on the book for an unconscionably long time. When I got back to it, I wrote it in English. As to *God's Little Soldier*, it took an eternity – eight years.

Much of the way a novel develops for me is fortuitous. I never know when an idea will strike me. I never know why an idea that pops up in my mind is chosen for further exploration. I am sure intuition and instinct play a major role. I suspect they are of moment to other authors too, but I cannot speak for them. There is also something else that comes into play, and that is the element of trust. At some point, almost subconsciously, your mind says, 'Let me try and see if this idea can fly.' Every now and then you may crash-land; but there has to be a willingness to grope, fumble and fall flat on your face; to allow the darkness to slowly reveal contours of character; to get a clue to what motivates your protagonist; and to slowly discover a whole new world: a world which you may believe you are creating. But, if you have any sense, you will give your characters that one dubious gift that the Christian, Jewish and Muslim God seems to have given to his people – the gift of free will. Of course you can dictate to your characters. You can bind them hand and foot, you can take almost all decisions for them, you can make sure that they grow up the way you want them to, but the chances are that what you will find in the end is that they are not flesh-and-blood people but puppets and marionettes. Writing a novel is like flying a kite. You can keep pulling the kite in the direction you want it to go, but it is far more interesting if you allow the kite to go where it will while simultaneously tracking it and keeping an easy but firm control over it.

Seven Sixes Are Forty-Three

Where do books start? Like rivers, they too must have beginnings and sources. In my case, as I suspect with rivers too, randomness and the chance factor must surely play a major role.

I wrote long letters to a professor of mine in my second year at college. Long as in twenty single-spaced handwritten pages. They were hardly letters. For instance, one of them started with the line: 'The undertaker came to get me today', which became the start of my first published story. I wrote maybe five or six short stories in all around that time. I can't claim that they were great stories, but the reason I even bother to mention them is because they exhibited a peculiar trait shared by youthful writers from countries which had recently won independence from their colonial masters but still spoke the occupier's language. Whether they liked it or not, these writers were creatures of a transitional time. They balanced uneasily between the proverbial two stools, their colonial past and their new-found independence. For instance, in India in the 1950s and 1960s, if your medium of instruction was English, then your English literature course reading was selections from Shakespeare, Max Beerbohm and Aldous Huxley. The children's books you read were Billy Bunter, the Hardy Boys and the stories of Enid Blyton. When you started writing, your heroes and heroines as well as their names were English. John, Millicent, William, Alfred, Elizabeth, Jane. The stories were located in some part of England which you most likely had never visited. I took a slightly different route. My stories took place in some nameless land or city. My heroines had western-sounding names which, however, could not be traced to any one country. For instance, the one in my first story was called Schleepa. What, you may well ask, was an undertaker doing in a Hindu writer's story since we do not bury our dead but burn them? The colonizer had left, but the empire was still going strong. It still is. The language of privilege and power sixty years after the British left India is still English.

Oddly enough, the westernized names, the vaguely western land-and-mindscape changed when I started to write *Seven Sixes Are Forty-Three*. In 1966, the poet, critic and short-story writer Dilip Chitre casually mentioned to me that he had been asked to edit an issue of *Abhiruchi*, a one-time famous literary Marathi magazine that had fallen on hard days. I have no idea why, when I got back home, I sat down and started to write. The second puzzling fact is that I switched to a language that was my mother tongue but which I had studied for only the first four years of my primary education. After that my entire education was in English. I had certainly not done any writing in my mother tongue, Marathi, for over fifteen years.

For that issue of *Abhiruchi*, I first wrote a short story about a recalcitrant man and a rather short god whose legs didn't quite reach the ground when he sat on his throne, and before I knew what I was doing, I had switched to writing my first novel, *Saat Sakkam Trechalis,* or *Seven Sixes Are Forty-Three* as the English translation is called. Would I have become a writer of novels and plays if Dilip had not talked in passing about editing an issue of *Abhiruchi*? The gods alone know the answer.

In some quarters *Seven Sixes Are Forty-Three* was critically acclaimed. In traditional Marathi circles it was viewed with suspicion and the kind of sarcasm and scepticism that often greets something which is off the beaten track. Some critics spent a great deal of time on the typographical cover, which was designed by my colleague, the poet Arun Kolatkar. Arun's original cover was a photograph of Mumbai's Chowpatty beach the day after the immersion of the Ganesh images. Perhaps you can imagine the site at low tide. Many of the icons stuck in the sand are exposed. They are badly discoloured and bleached; the limbs and faces of the images are broken and there is a desolate air about them, even though the previous night's frenetic drumming and dancing still resonate in the air. After having shot the photograph, the publisher suddenly discovered that he had no money for a four-colour cover. So Arun decided to switch to a typographical treatment.

We Indians suffer from a kind of schizophrenia. We have two sets of standards, one for Indian writers and another for the western variety. The critics lambasted me because I had had the impertinence to quote three well-known writers on the cover: a philosopher, a literary theoretician and a controversial novelist. They could not stomach such self-aggrandizement. This is curious and inexplicable considering that many of them must surely have read several English novels whose covers are packed with extensive quotes and blurbs. When the traditional critics were not damning the book for the blurbs, they spent their time debating what kind of beast the book was. It was so fragmented and disjointed a narrative that nobody in his senses would call it a novel. If it was neither short stories nor a novel, then they wondered what the fuss was all about. It was a mere nothing.

I have been told that *Seven Sixes* is fatalistic, that it is dark and intensely pessimistic. As the author, I do not think the book is about resignation at all. If there is a theme, it is: What difference does it make? Throughout the book the narrator insists that what you do with your life does make a difference, whereas his lover, the person called 'you', consistently maintains that it makes no difference whether you are alive or dead. Yes, when in the end he is beaten black and blue by his cellmate, he does remember his girlfriend's words. Since the narrator is no superman, there are no heroics for him when he has been brutalized. He is merely being honest about his state of mind under extreme stress.

Critics who liked *Seven Sixes Are Forty-Three* thought it was a landmark in Marathi literature. They felt that not only was the content very different, the language and syntax were so unusual that they were almost a reinvention of Marathi. My relationship with Marathi after *Seven Sixes Are Forty-Three* has not been a particularly happy one. Both *Ravan and Eddie* and *Cuckold* were written in English. When the Marathi translation (by Rekha Sabnis) of the former was published, I was told that it was so good that it felt like the original, and the English, a translation. However, not a single newspaper or magazine in Marathi thought it worth a review. By ignoring the book, what the media did, in effect, was to make certain that it was stillborn. *Cuckold*, which was published in 1997 and won the national literary prize, the Sahitya Akademi Award for the Best Novel of the Year in 2000, could not find a Marathi publisher till 2008, even though the translation, again by Rekha Sabnis, had been ready since 2002.

When I received the Sahitya Akademi Award, one of the leading Marathi newspapers wanted to interview me. The interviewer had two long sessions with me, each of an hour and a half. He had only one question to ask: 'Why have you stopped writing in Marathi?'

You Cannot Choose Your Parents But You Can Choose Your Ancestors

Every writer is asked time and again which authors have been his role models. It was Coleridge who wrote something to the effect that one would have to be a stone not to be influenced by others, but the trick is to assimilate these various influences and, hopefully, find one's own voice.

I have little doubt that there are many authors who have, in one way or the other, helped to give shape to my sensibility and writing. But if you were to ask me exactly how those influences are reflected in my work, I would be stymied for an answer. Besides, it's not only writers or artists who influence one. There are one's teachers, the chance encounter, an off-hand remark and who knows what else. Indeed, one of the most underrated and understudied phenomena in art criticism is the role of accidental factors and sheer happenstance.

But there's something else that has proven to be just as important to my writing: one of the lessons I've learnt in the course of my literary life is that while you are not at liberty to choose your parents, you can choose your ancestors. The bond between me and my chosen forefathers has been one of kinship and not of conscious study and emulation. I discovered that we believed in many of the same values: irreverence, a dislike of solemnity and a pathological aversion to self-righteousness, a subtle subversiveness, a compulsive need to question received wisdom, and an egalitarian abhorrence of caste and class distinctions.

My first ancestor was an aspect of my own culture that we now mostly disown. I've often railed against the Indian obsession with our 'glorious' past, and yet there is a facet of our heritage that I identify with deeply. What I'm talking about is the openness of a mindset from an earlier Indian epoch. There was a time when the West rather superciliously equated Indian temple sculpture and other kinds of art with nothing but erotica. Thank God our artists and their patrons rejoiced in the full range of sensuality and did not subscribe to the artificial dichotomy between the material and the spiritual. They endeavoured to encompass the entire human project – the spiritual, the physical and the intensely philosophical. What is remarkable is that this earlier culture is utterly devoid of shame, guilt and self-consciousness. Unfortunately, hypocrisy and sanctimoniousness have replaced this wonderful openness, and we now persecute our artists if they paint a naked goddess or write something which purportedly gives offence and can be turned into political capital.

My second forefather was the rich and bawdy legacy of the folk theatre in Maharashtra called *tamasha*. My exposure to this variety of theatre was limited to a single play called *Gadhavache Lagna* (*The Donkey's Wedding*). The British may have disapproved of our heathen gods, our elaborate treatises on sex, etc., but the tamasha in my state was killed by the hypocrisy and prudery of the middle class and the government-sponsored censor boards that were created after Independence. The tamasha form is a loose mix of various theatre traditions, song and dance, political commentary and the follies and foibles of mankind. Its staple is humour of every variety: broad farce, double entendre, satire, outrageously tasteless sexual innuendo, bawdy and sharp wit and improvisation. Nobody is spared, not political leaders, not saints, not frauds, hypochondriacs and quacks, philanderers and misogynists. Political correctness is altogether missing, and the women get it as good as the menfolk. The tamasha writers, improvisers and actors have a whale of a time sending up the gods and exposing their shenanigans, especially those of Lord Krishna who has sixteen thousand wives and mistresses. But you never for a moment forget that they can take such liberties only because their faith is unshakable and they are at ease and peace with their gods.

My own predilection, as seen from the beginning in my very first novel, *Saat Sakkam Trechalis*, was towards acute black humour, though I tended to switch constantly between the tragic and the ebulliently comic. And when I followed it up with my play, *Bedtime Story*, it became even clearer that what I shared with the tamasha tradition (and, come to think of it, with one of my French ancestors, none other than Rabelais) was a joie de vivre and an appetite for life that bordered on sheer and sinful gluttony. Nothing that dealt with human life was taboo – it was open house for sex, bodily functions, friendship, human relationships, the works. Political correctness was a no-no. The only precondition was that whether it was erotica, meditations, farce, or what have you, it had to be germane to the characters and the situation and never something imposed from the outside.

The third of my kindred souls is rather different. It's the notion of *Bhakti* or a personal and mystical equation with God. It's all those wonderful mystical saint-poets of the subcontinent, and in truth from all over the world, regardless of their religion. It still takes me aback to find that a feckless and irreligious person like me feels so close to them, and to rediscover almost daily how significant and relevant they are to our times. And yet I have to confess that I had no idea what intense emotions they could arouse in me till I started writing *Cuckold*. Not even in my remotest fantasies had I envisaged that I would write what, at least superficially and only superficially, is a historical novel. But far more far-fetched than that was the risible idea that I would write about Meera, the royal princess of Mewar in the current state of Rajasthan, a woman-saint who bored the pants off me. Well, dear Meera made me eat my words. I wrote a 609-page novel about her husband, but throughout she is at the dead centre of it. And how grateful I am to her for showing me that I too am a victim of stereotypes. And then I wrote *God's Little Soldier* where, in one section, I tried to reimagine very briefly the life of Kabir, one of the most remarkable mystic poet-saints of India.*

One of the most disheartening developments associated with the 20th century, and recorded music in particular, has been the commercialization of spirituality and mysticism. Regardless of the Fortune 500 companies, God has been and will always be the world's biggest industry, but that kind of cynical exploitation cannot sully the likes of Kabir, Rumi and other mystic saints. In truth, it has long been my secret ambition to get Kabir sung as pop music, perhaps by A. R. Rehman, the composer of *Slumdog Millionaire*, so that even Hindu fundamentalists and the Taliban will have Kabir on their lips and realize that 'There is only one God and her name is life. She is the only one worthy of worship. All else is irrelevant.'

On the face of it, one can hardly think of two more dissimilar cultural traditions than tamasha and Bhakti. But look at them a little closer and you will realize that they are in many ways blood brothers, however differently they may

* Nagarkar's last novel, published in 2019, is *The Arsonist; Reimagining Kabir.*

manifest themselves. They have a one-to-one relationship with God, whatever name he or she goes by. God is father, mother, brother, friend, guide and lover. Both Bhakti and tamasha are rugged, robust and earthy. They are life-affirming; they are against any sort of hypocrisy and fearless in exposing chicanery and hocus-pocus. They stand for tolerance, and they remind us that the rich and the down and out, the pretentious and the profane, the privileged and the deprived all share the same legacy: they cannot escape their humanity.

I have no idea whether my chosen ancestors will have me in their fold, but I cannot seek better company than theirs.

The Writing of *Ravan and Eddie*

Every book, I'm sure, has a history, perhaps even a moment of conception. I'm afraid I've forgotten the birth dates of my two children, Ravan and Eddie. This is an unforgivable crime on my part; I can see a Kafkaesque fate awaiting them. Since they do not have birth certificates from the Mumbai municipality, nobody will believe that they were born. They will never get admission to school and, of course, nobody will give them a job since there is no proof of their birth. And they will never be permitted to die, quite understandably, since how can anyone who is not born possibly die? All their lives will be spent trying to prove that they are alive.

As usual, I'm going off at a tangent. *Ravan and Eddie* started with an image. And the image was that of a child falling from a great height. For some reason that I can't quite explain, I knew that the child wouldn't die. This kind of thing, as you well know, does occur in real life. At least once a year a newspaper headline announces, 'Miraculous escape – Child falls from the 11th storey and survives.' But barring the practitioners of magic realism, no novelist who has read his Aristotle would ever let this happen in fiction. After all, hadn't Aristotle said very clearly, though not exactly in these words, that the realm of fiction is the probable and not the possible? Which meant that if Ravan fell from a fourth-floor balcony and survived the fall, he would be contravening the Aristotelian axiom. My own way out of this dilemma was to make someone else pay the price for his lucky escape. In this case, that someone else was Eddie's father, Victor.

The other contributing factor to the birth of *Ravan* and *Eddie* was the Catholic secretary in the advertising agency where I worked. During a Sunday lunch at her home, she casually mentioned that the first four floors of the chawl where she lived were occupied by Hindus and the top fifth by Catholics. I don't think that this fact made much of an impression on me at the time, but it must have been tucked away in a fold of my memory, for right from the start, I had a clear idea of not only the geographical location of my protagonists in the city of Bombay, but also of the breach in their psyche. The schism in their souls was the one that divided the Hindus from the Catholics.

Unlike the relationship between Hindus and Muslims, the one between Hindus and Catholics in India, especially after Independence, has been, by and large, peaceful. Yet what I learnt about my secretary's complex of chawls was that while there was no antagonism between the two communities, they might as well have been living on two different planets. They lived cheek by jowl but led parallel lives. 'And parallel worlds can only meet in a geometrical utopia called the horizon.'

When I started writing *Ravan and Eddie* in Marathi, the idea was to tell the story of these young children and their relationship as it evolved over the years, but I gradually realized that obliquely I also wished to paint a portrait of post-Independence India through the lives of its two protagonists. When I switched to writing the novel in English, I realized that the book gave me ample opportunity to go off at a tangent and write commentaries about different subjects which were at times related to what was going on in the book; and hardly at all in other places. These asides, tirades, meditations or disquisitions deliberately interrupted the narrative flow. But I knew that if I could make them short and readable, they would add to the texture and density of the novel. Let me cite a few examples. The first one is called 'The Great Water Wars'. Most futurologists warn us that by the middle of the century, wars are going to be fought over water. The rich will have water, and the poor most likely won't. Unfortunately, the city of Bombay has been familiar with this problem since the 1950s. In the chawls, people have to wait for hours in queues for the municipal taps to start spitting out water. Their lives revolve around water. So water and the wars fought over it are an integral offshoot of the story of *Ravan and Eddie*.

Another aside deals with cinema, which has such a unique hold on the imaginations and lives of Indians. And especially on Ravan and Eddie. The title of this particular essay is 'A Not So Short and Utterly Unnecessary History of Romantic Comedies in Hindi Films in the 1950s and 60s'. It occupies a full six pages and makes no bones about the fact that the reader is entirely free to skip the article. Incidentally, this particular history has been dropped from the German version since the publishers thought the German audience would not be so interested in Hindi movies. I was unhappy about this at the time, and as luck would have it, Bollywood has become very big in Germany. So perhaps I was right in not wanting to drop the essay.

I first wrote *Ravan and Eddie* as a screenplay after a well-known film director approached me for an original script. But he soon realized that my children did not tell his kind of story. He was an over-earnest sort of person who wanted something dripping with high seriousness; something shocking and violent that would jolt people out of their seats. I was the wrong writer for him. I can't take myself that solemnly. I then wrote the first eighty pages of the book in Marathi. After this, for various reasons, one of them being the business of making a living, there was a long gap of ten years. When I took up the book again, I switched to English.

In the original Marathi version, the Hindu child protagonist was called Maruti, better known as Hanuman, the monkey-god from the Ramayana, and the loftiest symbol of devotion in Hinduism. To this day I have no idea why I finally christened him Ram, the embodiment of integrity and righteousness. When, to avert the evil eye, the baby's mother, Parvatibai, changes her son's name from Ram to Ravan after he flings himself out from the fourth-floor balcony and is saved, the ironies pile up. Ravan, the ten-headed demon king of Lanka or Sri Lanka, as it's known today, kidnaps Ram's wife, Sita. As in all epics, the forces of good are now ranged against Ravan's villainous hordes. There is the mother of all battles, and in the end Ram vanquishes Ravan. My Hindu child protagonist's journey from Ram to Ravan then is fraught with all kinds of ambiguities and dilemmas. Is he Ram or Ravan? Is he good or evil? Is he the epitome of light or of darkness?

Ravan and Eddie has got, over the years, a fairly secure following, especially in Bombay. But as with almost all my work, it has also elicited strange responses. I was invited for a reading to Chennai. After the reading, a lady asked me, 'Why have you written a book about Christians and Hindus? You should write about Hindus and Muslims. That is the most important subject in India.' I didn't have an answer to this fiat except to say that I do not write to order and certainly not novels with messages. More often than not, the subjects choose me instead of the other way around.

The second time when I was invited to the same city, it was by a group of active Chennai socialites. The day before I was to leave for the reading, the secretary of the organization called up frantically and said please don't come. Many of the members had read the book and were appalled at its frankness.

I seemed to have given offence to both Catholics and Hindus. I'm now thinking of writing a novel about ants and other insects. But maybe I will have to rethink this also. In India, everybody gets upset about everything. I'm sure if I write about ants, the Society for the Prevention of Cruelty to Animals and Insects will file a suit against me.

Cuckold

My third novel, *Cuckold*, was written almost against my conscious wishes. From the time that I was old enough to think for myself, I had decided that two subjects were out of bounds for me. The first was incest and the other was the most famous saint-poetess of India – I am of course, talking about Meerabai. To this day she is the subject of much kitsch art. There are innumerable plays and movies depicting her life. As to her songs, they have been on everybody's lips for the last three hundred and fifty years. Clad in white, strumming that one-stringed instrument called the ektara, looking inward, perhaps contemplating her God, Lord Krishna, Meera was, for me, the quintessential holier-than-thou, humourless, one-dimensional saint. Neither she nor her beloved Lord Shri Krishna, that most philandering of Indian gods, had the least interest for me.

Then somewhere around 1991, or perhaps it was 1992, I was in Delhi on a cold cold night sitting in a rickshaw with a friend of mine. We had finished seeing the sixth movie of the day at the Indian International Festival of Films and were on our way back home. The wind blew nastily. As a Bombayite, I was not equipped for the Delhi winter, and the open three-wheeler only made matters worse. What happened then was completely out of context. It suddenly occurred to me that whilst Meerabai was perhaps the most well-known woman on the sub continent, nobody knew anything about her husband. He was a void, a black hole, and a hiatus in history. On the rare occasions that he was mentioned, he was either the villain, the man who made various attempts to murder his wife, or was depicted as a nincompoop. Nobody, however, seemed to have ever been struck by the appalling dilemma of the man.

It was a passing thought and it passed right out of my mind; at least that is what I supposed. But over the next year or two I could not get rid of Meera. Without any intention of writing even a short story about her, I began, first of all, to read Meera's poetry and then search for her husband in the books on her. I went through standard texts like Tod's *Annals and Antiquities of Rajasthan*. Tod mentions Meerabai, but he was convinced that she was married to Rana Kumbha, the king of Mewar who had died long before Meera was born. Contemporary comic books like Amar Chitra Katha not only got the timeline wrong but had no qualms about disseminating disinformation. Though the Mughal Emperor Akbar ruled over much of India after she was dead, he's shown visiting her and presenting her a pearl necklace.

Finally, I managed to learn the missing man's name. He was heir apparent to the most powerful Rajput kingdom of the 16th century, Mewar. His name was Bhojraj. All that the history books and other material said was that he was born, that he married Meera and died. By this time, even if the thought had crossed my mind that I might write about Bhojraj, I could at the most think of a book of 100–104 pages in rather large type. My conception of him was limited, if not pathetic. I saw him as the typical macho Hindu husband. His way of dealing with the problem of a wife who was in love with a god, as far as I was concerned, would be at best to lead a life of debauchery or, far more likely, abuse her constantly.

I remember the night I started writing the novel. It must have been 9–9.30 at night. I had no idea of what I was going to write except one thing: at some point in time my prince would paint himself blue. People keep talking about the importance of starting out on the right note. The first sentence and the opening sequence are held to be crucial. I could see their point but I hadn't given either of them a thought.

The most inconsequential and irrelevant snippets from real life can influence and pop up in fiction in unexpected places. At the time I started *Cuckold* I was fighting a case in the *Small Causes* Court in Bombay to keep my rented apartment, which is why, for all I know, the opening scene occurs in a law court. Chance, coincidence, serendipity, happenstance, the stray remark, not to mention the ups and downs in one's own life, yes, all these certainly play a role in the business of writing. While there is no gainsaying the primary contribution of conscious thought and planning, it is the subconscious processes of the mind and that strange chemical laboratory called 'gestation' whereby at times things seem to fall into place by themselves and tricky problems get resolved.

Superficially I may have been clueless, but some major decisions must have already been taken unbeknownst to me. For instance, even as I wrote the first sentence of *Cuckold,* I knew that I was not going to use archaic language. My characters would employ a contemporary idiom but without indulging in slang. I also knew that I would use modern terminology so long as the concepts were familiar to 16th-century India. For instance, ordnance and weapons technology would not have been a new concept in those days, nor the notion of a school for military training. So I just went ahead and thought of my characters as real people leading just the kind of lives that we do. Initially this would be unsettling for the reader because of the dissonances. After all, we don't associate a National Defence Academy or the Institute for Advanced Technology with 16th-century India, and we do not think that people in those times talked about hours and minutes or miles and acres. But my calculation was that such dislocation would have desirable side effects.

In a sense the past is always unreal for us. We rarely think saints, kings or common men sat down to drink a cup of milk or lassi, and had intense conversations, as we do, about politics, music or the stars in the heavens.

I recall reading Boswell's biography of Dr Johnson, the 18th-century Englishman who single-handedly wrote one of the very earliest dictionaries in English. What stayed with me was that this same Dr Johnson and his friends and acquaintances like Burke, Goldsmith, Sheridan, the artist and caricaturist, Hogarth, the Shakespearean actor, Garrick, the portraitist Sir Joshua Reynolds and others sat in coffee shops the way people today sit in Starbucks and talked about every conceivable thing: Newton's laws of physics, the political theories of Hobbes and Locke. They discussed Shakespeare, poetry, current poets and playwrights. They gossiped, they joked, they remarked on political events. Boswell, the sedulous disciple, must have taken copious notes, for we get a lively portrait of each of the major characters along with a vivid picture of 18th-century English society. I guess somewhere in my mind I must have noted that the only way to make the past as urgent and immediate as our own lives was to write about it as if the characters in my book were contemporaneous with us and in a language that my readers themselves talked.

The Business of War

As I got into the book, one of the factors that I had to come to terms with was the fact that since I was writing about a Rajput royal family, I would willy-nilly have to deal with wars, a subject about which I was completely ignorant. I have always been wary of war novels. There is much camaraderie in them, tragic loss of friends, swearing, boredom, the usual time spent thinking about girlfriends at home, and having sex in brothels outside the military base. Then, of course, there is the war itself. At this point, generally the book begins to get unreadable. There are all kinds of arcane details about weaponry, attacks, sorties and incomprehensible war plans.

I did not think about it consciously, but one thing was clear to me: if I wrote about war, it would have to grab the interest of the reader and make sure that it stayed grabbed. The tactics, the deceptions and the outcomes would all have to be cliffhangers. Naturally, I did a fair amount of reading on the subject. But most of the time, I used my own imagination to devise the strategies which would reflect the Maharaj Kumar's frame of mind and his war philosophy. I would sit with paper and pencil and work out entire battles with diagrams. As I have already indicated, I did not have much of an idea about what this prince was going to be and how he thought. But gradually I got to know him. He turned out to be a deeply introspective and reflective man, yet he was also a man of action. Slowly it became clear that I was writing an epic story in the original sense of the word 'epic'. Epics, as you know, shun the introspective mode. Their heroes are doers. That was also the code of the powerful warrior clans, the Rajputs of medieval India. The centre and periphery of Rajput life were war, chivalry and honour.

My protagonist then was going to be a misfit. He believed in the 'dharma' of a Rajput, but he did not adhere to the Rajput code of honour. His first and foremost objective was, if possible, to win a war without having to fight it. If that was not possible, then his greatest concern would be to sacrifice as few men as possible. To achieve this goal, he would be willing to be called a coward, to put his tail between his legs and run; to fight guerilla warfare – anything and everything that a Rajput warrior should never be willing to do. What that meant was that the Maharaj Kumar would have to be a thinker. In terms of form, this was the crux of the problem: How to combine a novel of action with intense introspection?

Was I being unreasonable and far too ambitious? Was my hero going to be larger than life and impossible to give credence to? I don't think I spent time debating this, but in retrospect I can see that I need not have worried on this score. At the back of my mind, I must have had a fine role model for my prince in Akbar, the 16th-century Mughal emperor. Akbar was truly a renaissance figure. It is suspected that he was dyslexic, but that did not prevent him from being interested in almost everything under the sun. He loved architecture. He had the finest musicians in his court. He constantly fought – and won – wars. A Muslim emperor in a Hindu country, he founded a new faith called 'Din-e-Ilahi', which tried to combine the loftier features of different religions.

Halfway into my book, I came to know Babur, the small-time king who would establish the great Mughal dynasty in India, and discovered that he was an amazing (I use the word advisedly) man. He was an audacious statesman and a superb warrior who could handle both defeat and victory with equanimity. He was a keen student of architecture. He was not merely interested in natural history but was a minute observer of birds and plants and trees. And he was a superb writer. His *Baburnama* is one of the finest autobiographies written. Hagiography was alien to him. He was as unsparing of his father and others as he was of himself. I was on solid ground. My Maharaj Kumar then could afford to be a complex character.

Like many an author who has allowed his characters to lead him by the nose, instead of putting them on a tight leash and leading them, *Cuckold* took me to unknown places in the hearts, minds and souls of my characters. The Maharaj Kumar I could invent from scratch. But it was Meera who made me fall flat on my face. If I had thought of her as insipid, it was because I had bought into the kitsch stereotype of the woman. As I stayed with her, I realized that she was a woman with a mind of her own. A woman who was intelligent, stubborn, astute, sly, wilful and also very competitive. Most important of all, she was a princess, and the way I saw her, she was a woman of the world who had been trained in the martial arts and statecraft. Just like the Maharaj Kumar, I too fell in love with her despite putting up a colossal amount of resistance.

I have often been asked why my protagonist in *Cuckold* is never called by his name but always referred to as 'Maharaj Kumar' or 'Prince' and his wife as 'Greeneyes', 'the Little Saint' or 'Princess'. The reason is that the name Meera carries far too much baggage. What I wanted to do was to start with a blank slate, so that in one single stroke I would be able to get rid of all the preconceptions, clichés and other accretions that have become attached to her name like barnacles over four hundred years. Since I had decided to start afresh, I did not see any point in calling Bhojraj by his name either. In a sense, I too was perhaps doing him a grave injustice. He had been a void all these years and would continue to be so – even though I was resurrecting him – because I too had left him nameless. I think, on the whole, this strategy has worked out all right.

In an aside, I must confess that I was disappointed that the German title of the book *Krishnas Schatten* (*Krishna's Shadow*) deviated completely from the English one because I did not want Krishna's name to appear till about page ninety in the book. The other reason for my dissatisfaction was that the book would be slotted in many people's mind as a Hare Rama Hare Krishna tract. The latter worry was not unfounded. In my reading tours I came across Krishna buffs who instantly either embraced me as one of their own or were incensed that I was not respectful enough about Lord Shri Krishna and Meerabai.

Let me tell you one strange incident which occurred after I finished *Cuckold*. I woke up one morning and said to a friend half-jokingly, but I suspect half-seriously too, that while almost nothing was known about Meerabai's husband, everything I had imagined about his life had indeed happened exactly the way I had narrated it. Then a few years later, I met the well-known academician, critic, poet and novelist, Makarand Paranjpe, for the first time. We must have spent about ten minutes together when he said to me 'You did not write the book, did you, Kiran? It just got written.' *Cuckold* was no cakewalk, but I think Makarand was right. There are times when you feel that you cannot take the credit for a work that bears your name. I am grateful that *Cuckold* is considered a classic in some quarters. I can only think of myself as the medium through which it got written.

Form

I am unable to think of form as existing in isolation. Form and content, for me, are inseparable. *Seven Sixes Are Forty-Three* played considerably with form. The only threads that run through it are: (1) the first-person narrator, (2) the 'you' character to whom the narrator keeps talking throughout the book, and (3) the peculiar style of narration. The last is a bit like a handheld movie camera. The action shifts suddenly from one subject to another; from deep focus to dead close-ups. The language is highly condensed, and often the book feels like a car speeding down a steep gradient with the brakes not working. If there is a sense of panic, it merely seems to increase the exhilaration.

I did not set out to experiment when I wrote *Seven Sixes Are Forty-Three*. The material seemed to demand it. The search for originality leads nowhere but to a blind alley. The trouble with always wanting to be original and insisting on playing with form, whether your subject demands it or not, is that you may very often get trapped in a device which ultimately becomes a linguistic mannerism. I would have been a fool had I repeated the form of *Seven Sixes Are Forty-Three* in my later novels.

One of the obvious variations in form in *Cuckold* is the switch between the first and third-person narratives. But there is another one, one that is hardly visible. One of my favourite axioms about art is Oscar Wilde's observation, 'True art lies in concealing art.' The epic genre on the one hand, and the psychological novel of introspection and probing on the other, are really mercury and water. That is what I set out to do in *Cuckold*: to meld and blend the two so inextricably that they form a third entity – a novel of far greater scope than either.

Transparency and Velocity

In a recent review of the third and final volume of Norman Sherry's monumental biography of Graham Greene, David Lodge mentions that Greene was denied the Nobel partly 'because of the implacable hostility of one Swedish academician, Arthur Lundkvist, but also because the other members of the Academy thought he was more of an "entertainer" than a "serious" writer'.

How can the first purpose or raison d'être of literature, which is to entertain and engage the audience as Homer, Sophocles, the authors of the Mahabharata, and Shakespeare did, ever be forgotten or denigrated? I cite Greene's case deliberately to draw attention to his unique strengths which were considered weaknesses or flaws by the academics. First of all, Greene called a considerable body of his work, entertainments. But even in his most substantial novels he was not averse to using the modalities, techniques and strategies of the spy genre, of thrillers, adventure stories and even the detective novel. In his best work, and there is much of it, Greene is telling you damning stories of the human soul and the human condition, often creating a Greeneland where the protagonists live beyond hopelessness. It is a singular vision expressed in a unique style and language that is so seamless that you can only marvel at the man's slyness and superb unobtrusive control over his material.

I have long held that transparency of language and lightness of touch are not an index of shallowness or slightness. Quite the contrary – transparent waters can run so deep, it is impossible to see the bottom. Again one of the most underrated features of fine detective fiction is speed, or as Professor Monika Boehm-Tettelbach calls it, velocity. I have often been told that *Cuckold* reads like the wind, like a thriller. Maybe people mean it pejoratively, but I take it as a compliment.

I've always had only one audience in mind, the whole world. I do not say this facetiously. I may fail miserably in my aims. Let alone the whole world, I can't even get most Indians to read my books. But that doesn't change the fact that I would be happy to sit down at Churchgate railway station and read to the peak-hour rush. Even when I write about complex subjects like religion, human relationships, war, matters of life and death, I try my best to write simply and compellingly, but without simplifying any of the issues. In that sense I want to be like Coleridge's 'Ancient Mariner': I want to mesmerize my reader, make him a willing victim.

I write to be read.

God's Little Soldier

Did I know what I was in for when I started writing *God's Little Soldier*? Would I have abandoned the project if I had foreknowledge of what seemed to be insurmountable difficulties? It's good to ask these questions after the book is done and published, and however good or bad it is, nothing you do or say can change its fate.

Time and again I've been asked whether I decided to write *God's Little Soldier*, or *GLS* for short, because terrorism is a hot issue, and I was hoping to make the most of a bankable subject. Ah, if only I was that pragmatic and sure of instinct,

I might have been a successful writer who made millions. Moreover, *GLS* is most definitely not about terrorism, though some critics have been disappointed because they preferred to think that it was. It is about extremism.

I started writing *GLS* in 1998, three years before 9/11. There were several reasons why I was drawn to the theme of fanaticism of one sort or other; about those who take it upon themselves to defend their God or ideology and commit violence ranging from murder to holocausts and genocides. India won independence from our colonial masters as no other country in the world had, most notably through one man's unique political ideas and pragmatic strategies: non-violence as a philosophy against the might of the British Empire, and a strategy that revolved around active resistance through peaceful non-cooperation.

Had Mahatma Gandhi, that wispy little old man who could fast for three and four weeks at a time to cleanse the nation's conscience, deluded us into believing that we had it in us to oppose injustice, naked force and the ubiquitous power of the state with nothing but the ideal of ahimsa or non-violence? Because as we were about to begin shaping our own future, fortune and destiny, we plunged into such an orgy of violence that it is considered perhaps the bloodiest partition in the history of mankind.

There are times when it seems that violence is the only form of dialogue left in the world. And there is a new and terrifying wrinkle to it. In the past when the Crusades were fought, or the Allies went to war with the Axis powers, the enemy was clearly defined and so were the objectives of both parties. The advent of modern terrorism, however, has changed the dynamics of mass murder once and for all. The idea is to kill as many people as possible, and to create mayhem and a media event. As a consequence, keeping up with the Joneses becomes mandatory; every terrorist organization feels obliged to constantly up the ante if it is to garner attention. What matter then if the victims often include your own people?

The picture gets even more murky when the violence is state-sponsored. The immediate trigger for *God's Little Soldier* was an event that occurred in 1988. As I had discovered with my first play, *Bedtime Story*, the precondition for exercising textual censorship is that you have not read the work in question. Salman Rushdie's *The Satanic Verses* had just hit the bookshops in India when a Muslim member of Parliament who wanted to revive his political fortunes brought many parts of the country to a standstill, claiming that the book was an act of blasphemy against Islam. Riots broke out, four people were killed, and before you knew it, the government had banned the book.

Change of scene. Now that India had shown the way, the supreme head of the state of Iran, not a layperson but the very highest-ranking religious authority in the country, issued a fatwa to kill an individual from another country without even pretending to go through the motions of a judicial trial. The curious thing was that not just Iranian Shi'ites but Shi'ites across the globe felt compelled to execute the fatwa. It was then that I asked myself the question 'What kind of person would feel duty-bound to commit such a deed?'

There seems to be an unshakable template for the Islamic fanatic or jehadi warrior amongst most of the non-Muslim world, perhaps amongst many Muslims too. He comes from a poor conservative background, has been educated in a fanatical madrasa where he has sat on an earthen floor and rocked himself back and forth memorizing the Koran. He has closely knit eyebrows, a dense overgrown black beard, a low forehead partially covered by a crocheted white skullcap and wears loose trousers that narrow down at the bottom and don't quite reach his ankles. The geometry of stereotypes is two-dimensional. Its planes and angles and theoretical propositions are reassuring because they offer such clear choices. Black is black and white is white. There's no room for doubt, and all conundrums and complexities are ironed out. The world is once again a comprehensible place. You know who the bad guys are, and your innate modesty prevents you from mentioning who the good guys are.

Unfortunately, oversimplification, as we all know, often has dangerous repercussions. Lacking a three-dimensional perspective rich in nuance and depth, you get a skewed view and misinterpret the situation, sometimes with tragic consequences.

There is no denying that the majority of the holy warriors of Islam are nurtured by the fundamentalist madrasas, but it would be singularly short-sighted and self-defeating if one did not grasp that all strata of Muslims are deeply unhappy, hurt and alienated by the blinkered vision of the majority of the western countries, but especially at what they view as the rank injustice of western, and especially American, bias towards Israel. As a result, even the well educated and the well heeled, including those who were not particularly deeply religious, felt compelled to assert their religious identity and stand with their disaffected brothers.

One of my very first decisions as I started working on *God's Little Soldier* was to locate my protagonist, Zia, in an affluent liberal Muslim family in Mumbai. The Khans, that's their surname, belong to that class of Muslims who have contributed over the centuries to the enormously rich intellectual Islamic culture without which western medicine, astronomy, science, architecture and philosophy as we know them today would have been inconceivable. The younger of two sons, Zia, is something of a mathematical prodigy but his aunt Zubeida wants him to be a good Muslim and urges him to become an apostle of Islam without ever imagining that Zia will not only take this injunction seriously but twist and distort it, as he does with everything, to its extreme.

Zia is a purist. He views the world in absolute terms. There is no middle ground for him. He abhors that space which the Buddha called the Golden Mean. From the very start, I was seized by the problem Zia would pose for me. He has some wonderful qualities. In a world where the only values we worship appear to be money, rapacious consumerism and a total lack of fellow feeling, fair play and compassion for the downtrodden, Zia is an idealist, one who is willing to put his life on the line for his convictions. As his name suggests, he could have been a beacon of light.

What I wanted to examine was the great divide between what he set out to achieve and what he ended up perpetrating.

When Ayatollah Khomeini proclaims the fatwa against Salman Rushdie, Zia, who's studying in Cambridge, UK feels duty-bound to pick up the gauntlet. Early in his search for the blasphemous author, his girlfriend and disciple, Vivian asks him, *'But have you read the Satanic Verses?'*

'No, I have not. And I don't intend to.'

'How can you condemn a book without reading it?'

It is at this point that Zia crystallizes his rationale for pursuing Rushdie.

> 'On whose authority do you or I take God? God is not $E=mc^2$, or the quantum theory, that you can check him out for yourself if you are so inclined. Nor can different gods subsist side by side as Newtonian physics does with Einstein. God is faith and must be taken on faith. That is the essence of God.' Zia spoke as if he was hewing the words out of stone ...
>
> 'No Rushdie can affect Allah, nor can blasphemy or heresy touch the Almighty. Allah does not need protection from Satan but a true believer does. It is I who must defend the honour of God or else I, not God, will be defenceless against Satan. If I am to lead my people and perhaps even

non-believers to Allah, then I must prove myself worthy of Him …'

As it turns out, Zia's attempt to murder Rushdie is foiled at the very last minute by his brother Amanat. From that moment Zia turns into a jehadi warrior. It is Amanat who goes to the heart of the matter. 'You are a good man,' he tells Zia, 'gone terribly, terribly wrong.'

And that was for me the crux of the problem as a writer. If Zia turned out to be such an unsympathetic, perhaps hateful, character, the result would be to turn off my readers altogether, instead of making them look closely at the man, and perhaps even try to understand him.

For a considerable time, I thought I could walk this tightrope and manage to keep the delicate balance between portraying Zia with ruthless honesty while still retaining an ambivalent sympathy for him by using humour and the occasional bawdiness. Laughter would take the edge off his appalling actions, and his bawdy sex life would make him more human and likable. I finished my first draft sometime in May or June of 2000. There were some good bits in it, but I had to admit it just did not work. It took many more rewrites and two or three years to get the hang of where I was going wrong. On the one hand, making fun of Zia was not just too easy and pat, it ended up trivializing the man and the enormity of his malfeasance. On the other, it also did him an injustice. One would be a fool not to take Zia seriously.

The Abhimanyu Dilemma

In the Mahabharata Abhimanyu, the brilliant young son of the great archer Arjun, penetrates a highly complex enemy maze with astounding courage and bravery and against all odds but then finds himself unable to negotiate his way out. It is a dilemma that I suspect almost every author has had to confront some time or the other. Abhimanyu never made it back. For years I thought neither would I.

After the initial setbacks, I was able to gradually get back on track when Zia wrote that brutal and heartless letter to his mother. The sex and the randy escapades went out of the window, and Zia remained true to character, single-minded, humourless, and untainted by doubt. But as yet I had no idea how the closure of the book would come about. I had made my way to the centre of the maze but had no clue how to get out. I groped around blindly, I tried every trick in the book, and many which were not there. I tried this, that and the other and knew in my heart of hearts that I was lost in an endless darkness, and nobody but nobody was going to extricate me.

Then it happened. Yunus, Zia's most trusted assistant who betrays him in Kashmir, came to my rescue. It struck me that perhaps Yunus would have a son who would hate his father for betraying his hero, Zia, and ultimately Allah himself. What if Nawaaz Irfan, the son of Yunus, was the mirror image of Zia and met him long after Zia had repudiated Islam and become a devout Christian? I finally had a denouement. Does it work? That's up to the reader to say.

The Ambivalence of Betrayal

GLS, however, also forced me to confront several issues that have lain submerged in my subconscious. For instance, the notion of betrayal and the glib judgements we pass on so-called villains have always troubled me. I recall reading an article about Isaac Babel which criticized him for having confessed and perhaps 'betrayed' his friends under torture. Even as I write this, I am incensed at the self-righteousness of our species. How would any of us know what Babel went through? Is there such a thing as a fixed breaking point just as there is a boiling point for water? Or does it differ from person to person, the time of the day, the chemical balance in the body? Who knows?

The universal symbol of treachery is of course Judas. He is the epitome of the traitor but if he had not betrayed Christ, as the Son of God had foretold time and again, that too would have been a betrayal of the Lord. I am not trying to be facetious or perverse, nor is it my intention to glorify traitors, but there is something heroic about the cross Judas had to bear. What an unbearable burden he has had to shoulder over the centuries.

In *GLS*, when Zia discovers that it is Amanat who has foiled his attempt to execute the fatwa against Rushdie, he stabs and nearly kills him. Years later, when Amanat looks back at the incident, he wonders whether it was *he* who had betrayed Zia. Wasn't Zia following the dictates of his conscience and defending the honour of Allah when he tried to carry out his mission? After all, whose authority except his own conscience had Amanat followed? On the other hand, surely Zia was betraying humanity itself when he decided to take another man's life. Again, was Zia right or wrong to seek vengeance when he stabbed his brother? Do ethics and morality really boil down to nothing more than one's point of view?

9/11

Then came 9/11. It was notable for many reasons: a new and untried but highly effective and visually stunning method of creating havoc and fear, together with the monumental scale of the destruction and loss of life. Secondly, it occurred in America, and that set it apart. Thousands are massacred in Sri Lanka or Darfur and many other places, but these events do not have the self-importance that the one superpower in the world thinks is its due. The American media monster immediately transformed the terrible loss of life into an annual ritual.

But perhaps the most far-reaching consequence of 9/11 was that it eliminated all nuance from the discussion of extremism or terrorism. Discernment and the ability and willingness to discriminate between different causes and goals had gone out of fashion. Everybody you wished to vilify was called a terrorist. The Taliban, Al-Qaeda, the Palestinian Hamas, the Tamil Tigers and others were clubbed together and painted with the same brush.

Since 9/11 was not the central event in my book, it made sense for me to refer to it only obliquely. Since Zia feels that he has been in some way responsible for the tragedy of 9/11 and goes into deep depression, the Abbot, Reverend Father Augustine, brings him back to the Abbey. And at one of the Monday morning introspections, he tells his community of monks:

> Many of you have come to me and asked that we fly the American flag. I know you mean well and wish to show solidarity with the people of our country. But the flag of God is not that of America. He does not fly any flag but the flag of all those who are good and compassionate and will eschew all forms of violence.

Zia's Religion

One of the themes of *GLS* is supposed to be religion. But Zia's religion is neither Islam nor Christianity, and it certainly is not Hinduism as some critics and readers tend to believe. Nor is it some ideology like Marxism, the free market or rampant anarchism. Zia's true religion is extremism. Whatever the faith he embraces or the 'ism' he propounds, he always takes a stand at the rabid outer limit of the religious or political system.

Think about the idealists of the 1930s – John Dos Passos, Arthur Koestler and so many other Marxists of the time, thirty thousand foreigners in all – who went to Spain to fight the civil war on the side of the Republicans. Many went home disillusioned, first with the victory of Franco and later with the atrocities perpetrated by Stalin. When they turned their backs on 'The God That Failed', many of them swung to the other extreme and became fervent rightists and capitalists.

Benito Mussolini was not merely a card-carrying Marxist, he was secretary of the local Socialist party and then a little later, editor of the official Socialist journal *Avanti,* and became, by all accounts, the most forceful labour leader of the socialist movement in Italy. And yet by the end of the First World War, look what he had become: the founder of Italy's National Fascist Party. The rest is history.

Perhaps all polarities are identical twins, and Zia was following an honourable, or dishonourable, tradition, depending on your point of view.

Guilt and Remorse

I have a confession to make, a rather bizarre one at that. Fifteen months after *God's Little Soldier* was published in English, I added a new chapter of close to fifteen pages towards the very end of the book for the new European editions. The scene is set in Afghanistan, immediately after the Afghan leader Nawaaz Irfan offers Zia a blank cheque to supply him with nuclear weapons. For once, the thought of this radioactive money seems to paralyse Zia.

Why, you may well ask, had I felt the need to add a new chapter to a book that was already published? The answer lies in the question the Trappist monk Father Paul puts to Zia: 'Why did Zia decide to become Lucens?' In short, why did Zia abandon Islam and become a Christian? We know of Christian soldiers who have returned from Vietnam and of late from the war in Iraq who are unable to live with their past and to adjust to civilian life. The maladjustment can take two forms. The first occurs in *First Blood*, the novel in which Rambo is the protagonist. As we all know, from the book as well as the Sylvester Stallone movie, something like a moral synapse in Rambo's psyche seems to have snapped, and he finally goes on a killing spree on his return from Vietnam. The same kind of thing occurs in Philip Roth's *The Human Stain,* where in a subplot a soldier with memories of war becomes dangerously dysfunctional.

The other way in which a war veteran malfunctions has recently been the subject of many studies and is described in the memoirs of soldiers who have returned from duty in Iraq. The way it manifests itself is through recurrent nightmares of the horror of war and the appalling things the soldier has done or witnessed. The mind seems to go into shock with the crippling guilt and remorse, and is no longer able to relate to even the closest members of the family. Life loses all meaning and a return to civilian life seems impossible.

Malfunctioning soldiers are abhorred by any war machine, whether it is the western model or any other one. But since the First World War, western medicine, science and psychology have tried to grasp the enormity of the damage and put into place systems and mechanisms to study the toll taken by carnage and violence and generate rehabilitation therapies for the victims. They might not always be effective, but there is at least a serious attempt to come to terms with the condition. Christianity, with its emphasis on repentance and the possibility of forgiveness, gives succour and hope to some affected soldiers.

But what of the jehadi warrior? Does he suffer from guilt and remorse? What an absurd idea. Aren't the two tantamount to blasphemy? How could guilt or remorse assail the holy warrior when he's doing Allah's bidding and fighting Allah's war? Sadly, neither the non-Islamic nor Islamic mind is able to get away from this oversimplified and fixated way of thinking in the current climate of distrust. We find it difficult, impossible might be more precise, to imagine that the jehadi warrior is as much of a human being as we are. We do not seem to comprehend that the human mind is not a logical creature; that it follows its own conscience, and if it feels the necessity, it can and will renege even on its own chosen beliefs.

The tragedy is that the rare jehadi warrior who wishes to turn his back on his vocation of relentless violence is also trapped within the stereotype. And that is Zia's dilemma. He dare not even admit to himself that he is choking on guilt and remorse and that he yearns for forgiveness and absolution. Instead, he believes that he is letting his God down and tries to compensate for his failings by escalating the level of violence. And here is the paradox: the only person who can liberate him from his terrible dilemma is the one who will betray him.

The new chapter then is about Zia's descent into hell and the absolution that must come from betrayal. It is perhaps the one and only time that the adult Zia slips up and shows his human side. There's a crack in his unassailable and absolute certainties, and we begin to suspect that even he is not beyond redemption.

Every Person with a Book Is a Mobile Library

PERHAPS THE MOST MEMORABLE sentence I have come across about poverty and hunger was in the autobiography of Malcolm X. He and his siblings used to be so hungry, he wrote, they could have eaten the hole in a doughnut.

My family and I were never that poor. Ours was a genteel poverty, a hand-to-mouth job, a lifetime of failing to make the proverbial ends meet, a never-ending cycle of borrowing and debt, and come the last week of the month, a frantic scramble to see if my mother had managed to save some small change that might just help us make it to the 31st of the month until my father got paid.

As with most Indian parents who can barely keep their noses above water, education for their children was priority number one for my parents (in fact, many working-class families are prepared to borrow huge amounts to put their children in English-medium schools). Happily though, education has never exercised either our national or state governments, except when it's election time and exorbitant promises of quotas for the Dalits or depressed classes are parlayed into votes.

My parents saw my brother and me through college and post-graduation. But given our precarious financial condition, books were mostly an unattainable luxury.

Libraries today are an endangered species. For most Indian children they are never-neverland. There was a token library in my school, but it was almost completely empty.

Barring one or two occasions, none of my friends or I ever borrowed a book from it. Which is why I knew nothing of Beatrix Potter, A. A. Milne, Enid Blyton and Roald Dahl, or the Hardy Boys and Billy Bunter.

The most extensive and underrated library in the world, especially in the poorer countries, however, is the institution of the grandmother. So-called notions of progress and independence might have made her obsolete in the West today, but she is the mother of all libraries, the largest archive of the oral tradition. In India she is the repository of the stories from the epics, from the Panchatantra and from mythology. She is the one who transmits oral history from generation to generation and is the fount of traditional wisdom. Unfortunately, both my paternal and maternal grandmothers died much before I was born.

My first (and only) brush with a real library was when I moved from Bombay to Pune to join Fergusson College, one of the oldest and most prestigious academic institutions in the country. I didn't know a soul there and was lonely as hell. The library was my only refuge and sanctuary. I was there the moment my classes got over and borrowed a book. I got back to my room, read the rest of the day, returned the book the next morning and borrowed another one. I read indiscriminately. I went through the whole of O'Neill, I read James Barrie, Boswell's biography of Johnson (I wish I could tell you I finished it in a day, but it took close to a week, maybe more), Alan Paton, Sterne, Harper Lee and God knows who else. It was a time in my life when I managed some sustained serious reading.

This was the time I read Ayn Rand's *Atlas Shrugged*. Indians love her books. In a recent poll of 'Books That Changed My Life', she hovered between number one and number two with the majority of readers. Most of our judgements are coloured by the weight of the past and the current literary climate: reviews, what's in and what's out, and the peer group we belong to. I suspect most of the time I am no different. But at least this once I made up my own mind: I loathed her total disregard for the wretched of the earth, for the deprived and the downtrodden. Most of all, I detested her 'me, me, me' self-righteousness.

I came back to Bombay to do my master's. The library building downtown is a beautiful Victorian structure with perhaps the most famous clocktower in the city attached to it, the Rajabai Tower. But I didn't find it a hospitable place and had to develop my own library system, one that people who are not exactly flush with money must resort to.

My libraries have been people, people who have been one, sometimes two-book libraries for me. These are people to whom I owe incredible debts which I have no intention of ever repaying. They introduced me to authors, lent me books, sometimes gave me their own copies, and at times even bought brand new books for me. Sudarshan Chhibber introduced me to Camus, Sartre and Kafka. Dr Patankar gave me his copy of Graham Greene's *The Heart of the Matter*, my friend Srinu gave me Camus' *The Plague* as a birthday present, Dilip Chitre lent me his copy of *Journey to the End of the Night* by that warped literary genius, Louis-Ferdinand Celine, whose outrageously funny but unstintingly black vision defined much of 20th-century literature. And my South African friend the late Jeewa sent me a copy of *Catch-22* which had me rolling and roiling in bed with laughter while my father wondered if his son had gone mad. I could go on and on, but you've got the drift.

You will find my Parnassus strangely empty of some of the gods in the literary pantheon. It chills me to the marrow in my bones to know how poor and unread I am. No Molière, no Balzac, no Stendhal, no Beowulf, no Saramago, no Schiller, hardly any Chaucer. And yet perhaps because of this very lack, how magisterial the lofty peaks of my Himalayas look. Most of the time they are shrouded in mist, and yet every now and then, I can glimpse Tolstoy and Dostoevsky, the mystic saint-poet Kabir, Shakespeare, the Mahabharata, Márquez, Curzio Malaparte, Henry James, Rabelais, Halldor Laxness ...

Who knows, given time I might yet discover new companions for them. And for myself.

English and Hinglish: Pidginization the Indian Way

We were standing in front of the Buddha at Kamakura. It was evening. The sun was winding up for the day. A touch of crepuscular red hovered round the slight smile of the Buddha and glanced off the hair of my friend's Japanese fiancée. Her eyes were cast downward. A moment of undemanding prayer perhaps. The wind stopped, the cicadas ceased their abrasive sawing, the sun hung in there motionless. 'I know nothing about India,' she said, 'except the four things I learnt at school.'

'And what are they?' I asked, more out of courtesy than curiosity.

'That you Indians eat with your right hand, wash your hind parts with your left. You burn your women, and practise Untouchability.'

A brief, succinct and aphoristic cultural, political and sociological history of India. A deadly body blow. The Buddha continued to smile benignly.

I wanted to smile wearily and witheringly. 'You've got it all wrong,' I wanted to tell her. 'A rather one-sided view of India. We Indians gave you the Buddha, the zero, Gandhi and the Taj Mahal.' But how would my protestations alter the truth of what she had said?

We are still lighting up our women but not as frequently. The caste system, despite the fact that it may have gone underground in the big cities, is robust and flourishing.

This paper is about a new caste. A caste whose progenitor was, oddly enough, a foreigner called Lord Bentinck.

In the 17th century, the English East India Company came to India to trade. They stayed behind to rule a vast empire. In 1829, as Governor General of India for the East India Company, Lord Bentinck wrote of the English language being 'the key to all improvement'. Under Bentinck's guidance and with the help of the Law Member of the Council, Lord Macaulay, a series of Acts replaced Persian with English as the language of the high courts and government business. Bentinck further directed that 'all available funds be henceforth employed in imparting to the native population knowledge of English literature and science through the medium of the English language'.

A new super-caste was born. It cut across all castes and classes. The divisions between the haves and the have-nots had rarely been so sharply drawn. Those who had English were the haves, those who didn't were the have-nots.

Jobs in the civil service, economic opportunities, entrepreneurial favour, and status in society for the next two hundred years were a direct consequence of the English language.

When Malcolm Muggeridge came to India in the 1930s, he felt that he had stepped into H. G. Wells's time machine. India, he remarked, was the only place in the world where a strange time warp had preserved Victorian English in mint condition. Coleridge, Dickens, Hazlitt and Lamb would have been at perfect ease in it. Growth, slang and dynamism are the signs of a living organism. What you got in India was a living caricature, a fossilized English that had become timeless.

In 1947, as a result of the only non-violent freedom struggle in the world, the British left India, but they left the English language behind. Independent India declared that Hindi would be the official language. The south Indian provinces, which came to be known as Tamil Nadu, Telangana, Karnataka and Kerala, felt that this was an intolerable northern imposition and protested vociferously. They need not have worried. English had come to stay.

If English opened doors, the old boys' network from any public school like Doon School, Scindia School or La Martiniere or colleges like St Stephens in Delhi admitted you into the sanctum sanctorum. If you had the privilege of studying at Oxford or Cambridge you were, then, one of the chosen, a high priest of Indian business, industry and commerce. The English-speaking brown sahebs made the goods and sold the goods mainly to English-speaking Indians.

It is in the interest of the privileged classes to perpetuate this status quo. But the supremacy of English is also reinforced by the new and fast-growing urban middle class, which goes to great lengths to get their children admitted to English-medium schools. They pay capitation fees, bring ministerial influence, send their three-year-olds for absurd interviews with school boards. Leave alone the middle class, driver Francis Pereira is trying his best to send his daughter to an English-speaking school run by Catholic nuns. Prithipal Singh, who drives an autorickshaw in Bombay, moved heaven and earth and got his son admitted to an English-medium school.

Is there no way, then, to break the barrier between the haves and have-nots, apart from asking for the impossible, which is to make English the medium of instruction right from kindergarten all over India?

Meanwhile, what is happening is that English is being pidginized and indeed further creolized into a full-fledged language drawing from English, Hindi and other sources.

The Random House Dictionary defines pidgin as 'an auxiliary language that has come into existence through attempts to communicate by the speakers of two different languages'. It is 'primarily a simplified form of one of the languages with considerable variation in pronunciation, and with a major part of its grammatical features selected from those common to both of the native languages of its speakers'.

A creolized language is defined as 'formerly a pidgin, but now the native language of a group of speakers, with consequent enrichment of the vocabulary by borrowing and creation'.

Any premeditated or deliberate attempt to invent a language either becomes ludicrous or is doomed from the start, as in the case of Esperanto. In India itself in the early 1950s, several pundits tried to preserve the purity of the Hindi language and also to expand its social and technical prowess through strange and absurd literal translations. A necktie became 'kanth-langot' (loincloth for the neck), an engine 'agni-rath' (chariot of fire), and so on. This endeavour was fortunately quickly terminated since the new vocabulary did not find favour with the common man.

Spontaneity and the dynamics of social intercourse and a pressing need to communicate alone can create a natural hybrid. It is, therefore, impossible to fix a precise date for the pidginization of English in India. What is almost certain is that its first practitioners in post-Independence India were students from schools and colleges. 'Arre, he's hajjar smart' (he's a super-smart guy). 'Gandhi was a Dada, yaar' (Gandhi was one hell of a guy). 'That girl is maha chalu' (she is on the make).

Since the emerging hybrid was mostly a cross between English and Hindi, it began to be referred to as 'Hinglish'. In the print media it occurred for the first time in a big way in a magazine called *Stardust*. It was the country's first cinema gossip magazine. In a column called 'Neeta's Natter', the *Stardust* editor Ms Shobha Rajadhyaksha invented and revelled in this new language. Words and phrases from Hindi were interspersed and incorporated into the English text. They suited the catty, suggestive and just-short-of-slander tone of the magazine.

Here are some samples from the early *Stardust* issues. 'Whenever possible (which is very often), he "maroes chance" with her [makes a pass at her], squeezing her fat leg. Rekha, "shaani" [a smart girl] that she is, asked him bluntly one day, "Do you want to have an affair with me?"'

'Only "desi" booze was going round, and our film folk being used to "phoren maal" [foreign stuff] nobody touched what was being served.'

'But Randhir Kapoor hasn't left off "chadhao-ing" [flattering] Rekha.'

This was just the beginning, but the ice had been broken. *Stardust* took off like a mega-rocket. Clones and copycats proliferated. People enjoyed this new language enormously, but it remained almost copyrighted lingo for film gossip magazines for fifteen years.

Then in the late 1980s, advertising people discovered pidgin. Multi-crore campaigns for consumer products were based on pidgin. By some chance most of these campaigns revolved around food products. One such early example was for a brand of ice cream called 'Go Cool'. 'Go Cool' itself is a play on an Indian word. Gokul is a city where Lord Krishna lived. He was the world's first cowboy, and Gokul was where he and his childhood friends took the cows for grazing. The backbone of the 'Go Cool' campaign was the slogan 'Anything "karega" for Go Cool.' Take the 'Go Cool' jingle:

'Go Go Go Go Go Go Cool

Anything karega for Go Cool (Will do anything for Go Cool),

Diwaana banega for Go Cool (Will go bananas for Go Cool)

Mooh mein paanı laanewala ice cream (the ice cream that makes your mouth water).'

Another case in point is the advertising campaign for Binnie's potato chips. A teaser campaign which was plastered on hoardings across Bombay city said: 'Humko yeh nahi mangta, humko woh nahi mangta, toh Bombay ko kya mangta?' Translated into English the words mean: 'We don't want this, we don't want that, then what does Bombay want?' The answer said: 'Bombay ko Binnie mangta.' (Bombay wants Binnie potato chips.) The response to these campaigns was little short of staggering. For instance, the day-after recall for Binnie chips was an unbelievable 97 per cent.

After the monsoons in 1990, as the weather began to heat up, Bombay witnessed a blitz of advertising from a new soft drink called 'matto'. Divided into four panels, the headline for the press ad gushed: 'Suddenly everyone's talking about it!' A Goanese gentleman in a red bow tie, frilled shirt and black jacket held up a paper pack of 'matto' and said in a mix of Konkani and English, 'Anv tuka sangta, I have switched over to drinking only this.' (I'm telling you I've switched over to drinking only this.) A sweet young thing opined in Parsi Gujarati and English in the next panel, 'After one sip aimne kayu it's sharp and sweet – just like me!' (I told him, it's sharp and sweet, just like me!) A third panel had a gleeful Maharashtrian woman bastardizing a Marathi verb and idiom, 'When I serve suchh a unique drink na it'll really kapofy Mrs Phadke's nose!' (When I serve such a unique drink it'll cut Mrs Phadke's nose. Translated a little less literally it means, it'll put Mrs Phadke in her place.) The last panel with a pack shot mixed Hindi with English: 'Chatpata taste ka wonder!' (A rough translation would read 'a drink with a wonderfully pungent taste'.) The copy at the bottom was brief: 'Matto. An ethnic sensation goes hep! A chatpata new drink of ripe, juicy red tomatoes. With a dash of masala to tickle your tongue. Try it.'

It is perhaps a bit too early to generalize from this limited advertising experience. The bastardizing of English is still at a very early stage. On the face of it, the pidginizing process in India is a laudable attempt. Sometime in the future the vernacular-speaking Indians and the English-speaking ones will meet against the golden sunset on equal terms, shake hands and look forward to an 'equal opportunity' life. But on closer examination, there is something gravely amiss with the pidginization that is taking place in India.

Pidgin may be a confluence of languages, resulting in a third language. But in the colonial context, the ruling class's need for pidgin was limited to giving orders and making itself understood by the natives, so that instructions could be carried out. 'Pankha chalao' for 'pull the fan rope'. 'Ek chhota peg Scotch jaldi lao' for 'bring a small peg of Scotch fast'. 'Memsaheb ko bulao' or 'call the lady of the house'. For the Englishman, it circumscribed the areas of contact with natives. It provided middle ground that said 'Thus far and no farther'. On the other hand, a native needed English to explain delays, to understand technical processes like cleaning a rifle or making an apple pie and custard, or to talk to the children of the English sahebs. And of course the more English words he could assimilate and use, the more status he automatically gained among his peers. Hence pidgin widened his vocabulary, his horizon and his prospects.

History shows us that the creolizing impulse starts with the underprivileged class and hence from the underprivileged language. The colonizers' language is raided, broken, dismantled and distorted to fit the grammatical and speech patterns of the native tongue. What you get then is not a mixture but a compound for a totally new and third entity in which the native language and the superimposed one are inseparable and which takes on a life of its own. But the rules of the dynamics of assimilation are dictated by the needs of the deprived class, those who have been for decades and centuries the underdogs and the have-nots.

Whether the hybridization of Hindi and English will ultimately evolve into a genuine Creole is open to question. What is certain is that the thrust and attempt at hybridization in India has so far come from the privileged classes and not from the grassroots.

Examine the use of so-called pidgin in Indian advertising and you will realize that there is a strong class bias to it. It is exactly the same patronizing and tolerant attitude as the British sahebs or nabobs, as they used to be called, displayed when they condescendingly ordered a chhota peg or a burra peg.

At heart, advertising pidgin or Hinglish is a caricature, a good-natured, haw-haw belittling of the underprivileged class and its idiom. For instance, the Binnie chips campaign is not in Hindi nor is it in a dialect of Hindi like Bombay Hindi. It is specifically the Hindi variant which Goan Catholics and even Parsis are supposed to use when addressing the menials in their home. I underline the words 'supposed to use'.

Barring Anglo-Indians, the Parsi community felt closest to the British rulers in India. To this day they are teased about 'Aapri Rani' (our queen), a phrase that indicates their sense of possessiveness towards and loyalty to the queen of England. After the Portuguese left India in 1961, Goan Catholics also felt an emotional wrench at the loss of the Portuguese connection, and hence a certain distance from other Indians. But these communities have assimilated into the Indian rubric and have contributed substantially to the growth of Indian culture. By using phrases like 'Hum ko yeh nahi mangta, ham ko woh nahi mangta', the audience is expected to smirk and snigger at the inability of Goans and Parsis to speak Hindi correctly. But there is a more disparaging and damaging implication hidden here.

India has some sixteen major native languages. For the majority of English-speaking Indians, English is a second language, so the speech patterns and idiosyncrasies of the mother tongue are very often automatically transmitted into English. Anyone with a good ear can identify the region from which an English-speaking Indian comes. Goan Catholics, by and large, are educated in English-medium schools run by priests and nuns, so they are already one up in the vernacular crowd. But in the pecking order of English-speaking India, they figure pretty low and are as much the butt of fun as Poles in Europe. Their accent, both in English and Hindi, is a constant source of ridicule in movies and plays. The vamp in Indian films is, more often than not, a Goan Catholic. Poor Goan Catholics, the Binnie campaign seems to suggest, they can speak neither good Hindi nor English.

In the Hinglish ads I have discussed, all the Hindi or vernacular words are written in the Roman script along with the English ones. When the main message or slogan itself is a full-fledged Hindi sentence, the only novelty comes from transliterating it. The crucial aspect of all Hinglish advertising is, in fact, novelty.

What and where is the humour of saying 'I will do anything for Go Cool ice cream' or 'it makes my mouth water', or saying 'We do not want this, we do not want that, then what does Bombay want'? In English these concepts and sentences are vapid, and one would be hard put to understand their appeal. Their remarkable success, then, can only be attributed to the dubious thrill of fracturing the language. The humour is forced and generally requires an imbecile's IQ to appreciate it.

For the moment the novelty angle is still working. The 'creative people', who are at a dead end, resort mechanically to Hinglish as a way out of their conceptual dilemmas. But the novelty is already wearing thin, and hopefully one of these days it will stop working altogether.

The urban middle-class consumers who have made Hinglish advertising such a success are the same people who go to see Hinglish plays, like *Bottoms Up*, *Double Trouble*, *Last Tango in Heaven*, which indulge in double entendre, risqué jokes and social innuendo, and often mock and ridicule one community or another.

To see and to be seen at English or Hinglish plays is a sign of sophistication and of social acceptance amongst the nouveau riche. It is, to use a favourite Indian cliché, the in thing. The audience often includes first-generation English speakers whose command of English is a trifle unsure. Thanks to the combination of English, Hinglish, fast action, broad farce, caricature and bad taste, the audience can snigger at the goings-on.

The tickets for plays like these are priced very high by Indian standards but they play to full houses. Very often it is the people whose community is being derided who come and enjoy the fun. Their enjoyment is both smug and awkward, convinced as they are that they have risen above the characteristics or stereotypes of their community.

The trendsetter among these plays was *Bottoms Up* (1989). It was written, as a matter of fact, by Bharat Dabholkar, one of the fathers of Hinglish in advertising. His Amul Butter hoardings, with their mix of the topical/political with Hindi and English have proved enormously popular with English-speaking audiences.

Perhaps the most damning comment on the new Hinglish is that it is only meant for and understood by English-speaking urbanites. It would appear to be mostly incomprehensible to vernacular audiences, and this excludes the vast Indian populace. Its target audience is the well off and the rich. Its strategy is to debase and devalue vernacular languages, thereby confirming the prejudices and contempt of the super-caste for the rest of their countrymen.

The humour, if you can call it that, in 'Anything karega for Go Cool' and 'Hum ko Binnie mangta' is contrived, to say the least. It is not a laughter that cleanses and carries everybody. It can only survive by knocking someone. It is in short a put-down, the equivalent of a white American mimicking Uncle Tom.

By a fortuitous accident, advertising people in India, especially in Bombay, are also the pillars of art and culture. English theatre to a very great extent is in the hands of advertising men and women. They act, they direct, they write plays. They are also heavily involved with films. They are critics of the social mores of our culture. They are thus the crème de la crème. The future of Hinglish rests to a great extent in their hands.

Hinglish advertising may be the product of lazy and flaccid imaginations, but it's important to remember that it is conceptualized and executed by English-speaking Indians. What is really disturbing is not its mechanical impetus and the millions of rupees which are at stake but the cynicism and manipulation that are at the heart of this practice. The Hinglish creators are not breaking barriers. They are not inventing a new language. They are merely exploiting the shallowness of the audience, ethnic and communal tics and peculiarities, and using Hinglish to perpetuate and widen the gap between the haves and have-nots – between those who have English and those who do not. They can, thus, be seen to be working not towards an egalitarian society but reinforcing and reiterating the biases and superiority of the English-speaking super-caste.

Memories of Childhood

EACH OF US HAVE our own notion of space. Link it with memory and the space grows far more personal and complex. If I were to talk about my concept of the memory-space access and how I view and use it as an author, I would have to first cite long passages from my work; then explain their relationship with my own spatial locations and experience and of course the locations in my imagination which, for instance, allowed me to invent the history and ambience of 16th-century Chittor for my novel *Cuckold*.

Instead, I am going to deal with some aspects of memory and space from my childhood.

My brother was born in a chawl next to the fire station at Naigaon in central Mumbai. He was much taken with fire engines. I remember when we were older, my father bought him a 6' x 12' fire engine. It was spanking red, and the chrome ladder could shoot up 4'. My brother should have become a fireman. He did not. What seems to have left a lasting impression on him though is the place where he and my parents lived. My brother was not a sickly child but he was thin and weak, and the doctor advised his parents to give him a raw egg every morning. It was a simple remedy, but it posed almost insurmountable problems for my family. Our home was in a Brahmin chawl, and eating eggs there was as good as eating pork in a 'pak' Muslim mohalla.

My father was an unorthodox man, and he resolved the problem in an unorthodox fashion. My mother would clear out in the morning and see if anybody else was standing in the common balcony, and even more importantly, outside the common toilets. If it was all clear, my brother would be packed off with an egg in a teacup to the toilet. My brother hated raw eggs, but he was an obedient child. He broke the egg, poured it into the cup and took between seven and twenty minutes to down it. Half the time he brought it up and the yolk went down the toilet. The drill was set. Make sure all the bits and pieces of the eggshell were in the pan and not outside. Whatever happens, flush the toilet and then wait to see that all traces of the egg have disappeared. Lastly, do not, come what may, do not ever mention the business of the egg. Because do you know what would happen if you do? They'll throw us out.

My brother, as I told you, was an obedient child. He held his silence. He was four and a half years old.

My brother is older now. Joy or pain, loss, grief, shock or exhilaration, the birth of a son, the death of our father, my brother goes to the toilet, closes the door, swallows a raw egg and flushes the toilet. Whatever turbulence and tremors there may be, his face is shut.

Pop psychology will have us believe that my brother's secretiveness is the consequence of a location in time, the people who lived there and of the egg. Are things ever that pat or simplistic? I don't know. There are no clean and clear equations, no cause-and-effect sequences in matters of the human mind. Only possibilities and likelihoods; ambivalences and ambiguities. Only yeses and nos, simultaneously.

After I wrote *Ravan and Eddie*, people often asked me how I knew chawl life so intimately. Did I do research on chawl or … They hesitate here, then get it out: Did I live there for so many years to be so familiar with them? I don't recall anybody asking me when I wrote *Cuckold* if I had royal blood. Unfortunately, the truth is more prosaic. I grew up in Hindu Colony, Dadar, the heartland of decency. The bastion of middle-class Maharashtrian culture and virtue in this our city of Mumbai.

My parents and my older brother moved to Hindu Colony in 1942, after the bomb explosion in the harbour, when a quarter of Bombay's population abandoned the city thinking that the Second World War had come to India, and flats were going abegging. Hindu Colony is my home. It is the place where I was born.

The structure of memories is molecular. There is no telling what would trigger a memory, but when it comes back you get the whole enchilada: sight, sound or whatever other sensory inputs went into it. There is no separating the elements or blocking them off. What the mind decided to retain, emphasize, underplay or erase, not to mention invent, is highly idiosyncratic. Often the most obvious or the boldest feature of a situation, sight or event is filtered out. But what is archived is preserved in its entirety. When you retrieve a memory, it comes back in mint condition: the stale flowers with their sickly smell, the Beatles on the zebra crossing on the cover of *Abbey Road*, the abrupt thud of a car hitting a body. Since all things human must occur in space, it is the location of an event that is the most common feature of memory.

Hindu Colony, like most other localities, is as much an idea and state of mind as it is a geographic space with architectural artefacts. It is the tension and the interaction between us and our internal and external habitat, be it a chawl, flat, bungalow, palace, colony or ghetto, which in turn shapes the contours and architecture of our minds.

Let me first locate Hindu Colony for you on the time-space axis. You go back fifty years and get off at Dadar TT – TT for Tram Terminus. Walk a little towards Tilak Bridge and turn right on Sir Bhalchandra Road. I'm not quite sure what services Bhalchandra rendered our white rulers for which he was knighted, but it's a straight and narrow road emblematic of the spirit of Hindu Colony. On the left, stretching all the way to the railway tracks are the five arms of Sir Bhalchandra: pahali galli, doosri galli, third lane, fourth lane where Smita Arolkar and her family lived, and fifth lane. On the right Sir Bhalchandra is armless. In the fifth is an unrecognized national institution and treasure: Mr Chaphekar and his classes. Chaphekar wears a dhoti, shirt, dark black jacket and 2½-inch-thick glasses. He used to run a restaurant in London. Now he teaches dull, dazed and indifferent students algebra, geometry, arithmetic, trigonometry ('Don't choke on that word as if it were beef, let me spell it for you, tri-gono-me-try') and English. After the fifth lane, you came to a crossroads where stands King George High School, now named after his Hindu avatar, Shri Chhatrapati Shivaji High School.

Keep going and you are at the junction of Ruia College. The college is still there, but two institutions which are far more visible and prominent in my memory-scape have disappeared. One is Mhaskar shop. This is where my father took my brother and me to buy cotton underpants and 'buniyaans' or 'ganjifrocks' ('ganjifrock', whoever coined that strange hybrid word?) It was a minimalist shop done in brown teak. The shelves reached to the ceiling along three walls. And there were also shelves under the counter. It was dark inside, and the air was the colour of the wood polish and had been still for the last 2,000 years. The shop was sparsely stocked and was lit with three 25-watt bulbs. Behind the counters sat four timeless men. It was not that they were old or young, they were merely beyond the pale of time. Two were bald, one had a thin moustache, and the last was walleyed. What they had in common though was that they were all Chitpavan Brahmins; they all looked like emaciated mummies and were almost as inaccessible.

'He wears size 22 ganjis,' my father told one of the salesmen, and to be on the safe side, added, 'I think it's 22.'

The man did not get up or respond. My father spoke again, 'Could we see size 22 ganjis?' The man gave my father a pained look.

'Make up your mind, its either twenty-two or it's not.'

'I am not sure. It's some time since we bought the last ganjis, and he seems to have grown a bit.'

My father had a temper, the kind that Shiva exhibits when he destroys the universe and all creation. And yes, here he was, pleading with the man. 'I am really sorry to trouble you like this.'

The man gave me a dirty look and got up from his stool for the first time. I realized then that it was all my fault. How could I have had the cheek to grow? Why had I not seen to it that my used vests would not tear? Why did I not go half naked to school? I had humiliated my father, and far worse, I was putting the salesman to untold trouble. I cringed, I squirmed, I thought of Sita. If only the floor of the Mhaskar shop would open up and swallow me.

The man stretched his hand out to the second-largest shelf and brought down a cardboard box with 'Size 22' rubber-stamped on the side and put it on the counter. He took off the lid and picked off the topmost ganji. There were six immaculate white ganjis, pressed and folded one on top of the other, fit to be worn by the god-child himself or if not him, the boy-saint Dominic Savio who looked heavenwards from the wall of my classroom trying to ignore my shenanigans during the P.T. lesson which our midget-sized teacher, Mr Shinde, often held in the classroom since we went berserk on the field. The man across the counter picked up the first vest and held it distastefully against my chest.

'What did I tell you? His size is not 22.' He folded the cotton singlet and laid it gently in its cardboard crib. Shut the lid, put it back on the second-last shelf from where it came and sat back on the stool.

My father was cowed, but to my horror and eternal guilt he still persisted. 'Shall we try size 24?' my father asked. The man looked blank.

I couldn't take it any longer 'No, no. I think we better leave.'

But my shameless father would not give up. '24?' he said again.

'Try the counter across. I have only got up to size 22.'

I dared not look up as my father undertook the crossing and started the search for size 24 all over again. Luck was on my side. When the new salesman finally took notice of my father and his quest for size 24, he did not bestir himself or check whether 24 was there or not. There was neither triumph nor regret on his face. He had started life, found that it was sour and had come to terms with it. 'Out of stock,' he said.

A little farther on Sir Bhalchandra Road to the right is my friend Ramchandra's house. His mother's sitting there in the balcony, her elbow resting on the low wall with her chin cupped in her right palm. She wears gold-rimmed glasses. She is short and enormously round like those weighted dolls that keel on both sides till the head touches the ground but always tock back and find their balance. She is a dense, black, strong woman, but I would advise you not to look at her for more than a nanosecond. She's submerged behind that low wall most of the time, but if you are unlucky, you may see a little more of her. She does not wear anything on top except size infinity bras. She has titanic breasts. I've never looked straight at them and yet they've taken me down, down, down to the bottom of the ocean with them, never, ever to resurface.

Seven minutes from Ramchandra's, you come to Napoo Gardens and to the home of one of my closest friends. But that is Matunga and way beyond Hindu Colony.

The river Brahmaputra runs next to Hindu Colony and separates it from Parsi Colony. Brahmaputra, as you know, is not a *nadi* but a *nad*, the only male river we have in our country and also one of the widest. Most of the time it is a slow, silent river. It moves so majestically and mysteriously, you are almost persuaded to think it is still and stationary. In the middle of the river, called for some obscure reason Vincent Road, are tram tracks. Every fifteen or twenty minutes tram cars come clunking along. The driver presses a metal pedal with his foot, and you can hear a sound like a bell calling you back to school after the lunch recess. It's a good idea to get out of the way when you hear that urgent tolling since the track may be shallow but the tram can still cut you in two. On either side of the tracks, leisurely cars and buses ply. If you are lucky, on an evening you may see a pink 7-mile-long winged Chevrolet Impala with Raj Kapoor slumped in the back.

In one sense you could say my birth in 1942 was a good omen since we had moved from a chawl to a flat. But in fact my birth was the beginning of all the major problems my family went through. I was around three months old when the doctors discovered that I suffered from extremely serious allergies, and warned my parents that I would likely die before I was a year old.

It is something of a mystery that I survived, but it is difficult to fathom what it cost my parents in terms of money which they did not have (my father was a clerk in the Indian Railways, and if I am not mistaken his salary was about Rs 150 a month) and also in terms of non-stop anxiety. I suffered not only from potentially fatal allergies but also from very serious asthma and bronchitis. I would be absent from school for weeks on end. When my asthma attacks were serious, one of my parents would have to take me to Dr Naik's home in Wadala where he would give me an adrenaline injection. By the afternoon, I would have got my second attack, and my mother would take me to Lamington Road where he had his rooms. Come evening, my attack would have recurred, and my father would take me back to Lamington Road. Often Dr Naik would give me an intravenous aminophylline injection and drop us home around 11 o'clock and beg me not to wake him up first thing in the morning. Unfortunately, that's exactly what I did.

The allopathic drugs available for asthma in those days were limited: theophylline or ephedrine tablets – bronchodilators which offered a very short period of relief; and of course, adrenaline and intravenous aminophylline injections for emergencies.

My parents were firm believers in the monotheistic principles of the Brahmo Samaj. But the havoc that my illnesses were causing, and the fact that nothing seemed to work, introduced new elements into their lives. Relatives, friends, distant acquaintances, everybody who had heard of my incurable problems, knew some baba or guru who could cure me in no time. When I was six, my eldest aunt persuaded my parents to take me to Hyderabad to swallow a live fish with its mouth stuffed with some medicine. There were hundreds of people at the place, and by the time my turn came, all the small fish had been used. I was given a 5-inch fish to swallow. It refused to go in.

The number of alternate remedies rose continually. We went to Shirdi; a younger aunt took us to a baba at Khodadad circle in Dadar; my parents took me with one of my mother's friends to see a man in Mumbra who would definitely cure me. Unfortunately, unbeknownst to my parents, all this *babagiri* had a terrible effect on me. I began to see myself as the source of my problems. Anytime I got an attack, I convinced myself that I had not prayed properly or not said some particular shloka I was told to recite. By this time I was studying at Don Bosco, and I persuaded myself that I had to look at the portrait of St Dominic Savio in a particular way during my exams or I was bound to fail. It took me a very long time and a tremendous effort of will to overcome these superstitions that ruled over my childhood.

Few images are as vivid as the one in Malcolm X's autobiography: I was so hungry most of the time I was a child, he says, I could have eaten the hole of a doughnut.

We were not that poor, but poor enough for 10 rupees to make a difference between getting through the last week of the month and … who's to say? I have no idea how my parents managed it but there was always a meal on the table.

My mother was a woman of few words and of great fortitude. In moments of stillness, there was occasionally, a tinge of sadness about her. I wonder if it had anything to do with the never-ending business of making ends meet. But I could be wrong. Every now and then she would make an unexpected observation that would crack me up. She had done her BA in music from the Sayajirao University in Baroda. My father had not made it beyond the tenth grade since he was obliged to get a job to support his family after his father's sudden death. Their marriage had an element of choice in it. They had met just once when my father was visiting Baroda. He said he had fallen for her right away. My mother was much more reticent, and she never spoke about her feelings. My father was a good-looking man, no two ways about it, but not in a rakish or self-conscious fashion, and it's possible that she too liked him from the start.

Mai, that's what my brother and I called our mother, could have got a job, maybe as a teacher in a school, and that would have helped with the expenses. But someone had to cook and look after the children, especially me, since I was a sickly child and needed a good deal of tending. Besides, I don't know if my father would have liked my mother to take up a job.

She must have been fond of music to have got a degree in it. But I don't ever recall her singing even a line from a song.

Home was the ground floor flat in the rear wing of Krishna Niwas. Radha Niwas, Krishna Niwas and Laxmi Niwas, all three buildings had two wings each and were carbon copies of each other. Each was separated from the other by a five-foot wall which curved at the top. The wall was called *kot* in Marathi and all of us children walked on the ridge, some even ran on it, like tightrope artists.

Each wing of the three buildings had six flats; two on each floor, and each flat was two rooms with a separate toilet and bathroom. The front room was a drawing room-cum-bedroom-cum-study while the kitchen doubled as dining room.

There was heavy social traffic and commerce between Krishna Niwas and Radha Niwas but for some curious reason, none with Laxmi Niwas. Both children and grown-ups played seven toiles, cricket, gillidandu and abadhubi. The transition from village to city was incomplete for many of the tenants. In summer, the Sukhtankar children turned up for the games with kerchiefs tied around their heads and reeking of onions. Their grandmother packed sliced onions in their hair to prevent sunstroke. Mrs Kudalkar and Mrs Ranade wore nine-yard sarees at home and covered their breasts, long and heavy like elephant trunks, with nothing but the pallus of their sarees.

Hindu Colony is where the demons and ghouls from my past dwell, a past that was as much a location in space as it was in a culture, class and in the middle-class Maharashtrian version of Hinduism. It is a past that I confront from time to time but am unable to put to rest.

Hindu Colony is a place and a mindset. It is an architectural grid and it is the map of my mind. It is a smouldering underworld full of the vapours of repressed sex and prurience, hidden violence and stifling hypocrisy, corrosive prudery and middle-class gentility.

But the middle class has been too pat and easy a target for far too long. They do not hold a monopoly on high-mindedness or hypocrisy. The poor and the rich are just as open to them. I've therefore to pull myself up sharply and remind myself to consider each event separately and not make blanket generalizations, pronouncements that condemn a whole class, section or subsection of people.

The Arolkars in the fourth lane were my father's childhood friends, or rather Mrs Arolkar was. She and my father had been to school together. Now after twenty years, she had discovered that we were almost neighbours and came to visit us with her youngest daughter, Smita, who was studying in the first grade along with me. We must have got along, for Smita would drop by once in a while, sometimes with another friend.

One Sunday when I was playing with my closest friends, the Shintre children, their father asked me where my peacock feather was. I didn't understand his question and grinned stupidly. 'And the gopis,' he asked, 'where are they?' I stood there, unsure of what was going on while the Shintre senior and the Shintre children laughed amiably.

'This is amazing. How come Shri Krishna doesn't know where his gopis are?'

'I'm not Shri Krishna,' I shouted more in frustration than in anger, 'I'm Kiran.'

'No point pretending. We know you are Shri Krishna, and Smita and her companions are your gopis.'

Soon my friends in the colony were humming doggerel verses about me.

Cock of the walk,
Talk of the block;
Cockadoodle doo,
Kiran, the hens want you.

That's a bad translation and the Marathi original was much more pungent, but my five and six-year-old friends sang it as if they understood the words.

It was not long before I stopped talking to Smita. My parents would ask me to go to her house and play. I refused. If I saw her coming towards me on the road, I crossed over to the other pavement. When she came to see me, I was stubbornly taciturn and frosty. I avoided her in school. When we were cast in a play with only two characters, I clammed up immediately after rehearsals were over. I was embarrassed, awkward and deeply resentful because I liked her, and because she was open and friendly despite my rebuffing her repeatedly.

I lost a couple of years of schooling because of my illnesses, and when I got back I was not only two years behind Smita but also in another school. But Hindu Colony had been a good teacher and I had learnt my lessons well. I had become warped. I could dissemble with ease. I was not just a natural hypocrite, I could even lie to myself.

I would pray that I would run into Smita on Sir Bhalchandra Road or anywhere that I happened to be, and of course, if that ever happened I would feign ignorance, play it cool or be awkward to the point of muteness. Sometimes she came over to our house or I went over to hers. On one occasion she asked if we had only two rooms. I said, 'No, we have two more rooms,' and pointed somewhere in the direction of the bathroom. Of course, she didn't believe me but she let it pass. Perhaps she realized that I was ashamed that we had only two rooms in comparison with her two-bedroom home. And she understood that since I had a quintessentially middle-class soul, monetarily we didn't even qualify for that class, all I ever yearned for and dreamed about was that one extra bedroom.

It was early afternoon. School had closed for the summer holidays. We were having lunch when we heard the first windowpane being smashed, then another and another. A man was screaming somewhere behind our building. In language alien to Hindu Colony, he was invoking everybody's mothers and sisters in abusive terms. My brother and I stopped eating and gathered around my mother. 'Let me go out and see what's happening,' my mother said as she washed her hands. 'No,' I put my foot down, 'if you go, I'll come with you.' My mother must have realized that it was useless to argue with her younger son. She went to the window and we followed her. We could see his back now. He was unsteady on his feet and his words were slurred. 'Who told the police? Bastards, I'll make you pay for it. I'll make it impossible for you to live here.'

Radha Niwas, Laxmi Niwas, and in our own building people were frantically closing windows. That was a mistake. Closed windows were a far easier target than open ones. Glass kept breaking all around us. Sometimes a stone would hit one of the metal grilles in a window and rebound. Sometimes it went in and you heard a scream.

He bent down to pick up another stone. Hindu Colony was always a quiet place, but as his head moved jerkily and he looked around, there was the silence of death. He seemed to be doing everything slowly, very slowly. His hand went beyond his back. The stone sped through the air higher and higher and made contact with the huge glass sliding windows on the balcony of the Karmarkar home. It hung in the air almost suspended, and then the whole glass pane came down with an eerie thin whistle. My mother pulled us down and we lay flat on the floor.

The previous morning a team of four plain-clothes policemen from the prohibition squad had come to the building. They walked straight to the gutters behind my home and forced open the iron lids. Armies of demobilized cockroaches with dark, polished mahogany backs and swivelling antennae scattered for cover. One of the policemen lowered himself on to the ledge four feet inside the first gutter and hefted up a twenty-gallon kerosene can. It was heavy, and the other policeman had to give him a hand. There were two other cans, and they too were brought up. The cans were opened, and batches of new cockroaches struggled over the rims and dropped down on the ground. Some fell on their backs and threw silent tantrums; others ran helter-skelter over the policemen's feet.

A sickly, cloyingly sweet smell rose from the cans. The plain-clothes men tilted them. Dark bubbling liquid with the occasional rotting orange and sweet lime peels and shrivelled berries flooded the ground and seeped into it. It was as if some colossus had been seasick and vomited all over our place. The stench of the fermenting liquor was overpowering. I passed out. When I came to, the men had moved to the next gutter and emptied the three cans which had been stacked there.

Prohibition had been in force in Maharashtra almost since Independence. Everybody, even children like me, knew that for a price country liquor was available everywhere. Every now and then we would see someone in a corner of the colony taking money and pouring a glass from a bottle for a customer. But none of us, including our parents, knew where the stills were and where the liquor was brewed.

The policemen stomped on the cans, stomped on them, and left. For twenty-four hours the flies had gorged themselves on the sudden putrid feast.

Now the man was standing in front of our window staring at us. His eyes were red and there was dry vomit on his shirt front. There was a stone in his hand. He aimed it at my mother when I blurted out, 'Pandu'. It was the servant who worked in the Sirur house on the second floor. He looked at me with intense hatred. The stone fell from his hand. He walked away, stepping into the fermenting fruit. A dark cloud rose, and then slowly a thousand flies settled down again.

The next day the landlord's man came around and replaced the lids on the gutters.

That last is an image which is symbolic of the ruling concern of the middle class of Hindu Colony. The overriding compulsion was appearance, don't rock the boat, get the roaches in and put the lid back.

Sex was not an unmentionable subject in Hindu Colony. It did not exist. Do you remember the work of the great French cartoonist Siné? In one of his cartoons, a priest is taking an anatomy class. As his wooden pointer moves, he identifies the parts of the body: eyes, nose, mouth, chest, stomach, nothing, thighs, knees. Even when our puberty was raging out of control, Hindu Colony treated us as eunuchs, robots and humanoids. We were sexless and innocent. Or it was easier and preferable to think that.

Paradise and the houris lay on the other bank of the Brahmaputra, the Parsi Colony. Ah, ladies and gentlemen, you laugh, you scoff, but even though I was not present, my friends from the colony got a glimpse of unutterably wondrous and celestial things. They were walking on Vincent Road and they had just gone past the Parsi Gymkhana when through the French windows on the ground floor of a building they saw ... Let me switch to Marathi, to the very words of my friends, '*Kay sangu tula Kiran, aai shapath Kiran, cochavar basoon to Parsi manus, hya madheel ek akshar khota nahin, Kiran, ek akshar*.' What was that Parsi man doing? My curiosity had been stretched to the limit and the string was broken. '*Arre, Kiran, to Parsi manus thya sundar baila dabhat hota*.'

Why was I not permitted to witness the glorious sight of the Parsi man squeezing that beauteous woman? There are two kinds of people in this world, those who are God's chosen and those who are not. I knew then that God had closed his eyes when I was born.

What does one do with memories? My erstwhile friends from the Hindu Colony, I suspect, would rather forget them. Others, some of them authors, become single-minded. They make it their mission to bring light to all the dark corners and taboos in their minds and our culture. A third alternative is to refract the material of our memories and transmute them.

There's some kind of routine and schedule to Amanat's sick days. By 1 or 1.30 at the very latest, he's in such a bad shape, Ammi has to take him by bus to Dr Patwardhan's rooms. Dr Pat gives him injection and Amanat is back by 4 p.m. By 9 p.m., he is in a state again and this time Abba accompanies him. Often, Dr Patwardhan drives them back home around 11. He gives Amanat an IV and begs him not to wake him up first thing in the morning. Amanat winces but, needless to say, is at Dr Patwardhan's door at 7.30 a.m. the next day, in need of his morning fix.

From his standard sitting posture, the weight of his breathing upon his arms and hands, Amanat watches his father, mother, brother and aunt. They look washed out but pretend that everything's fine. He knows money's tight, and there's almost always tension in the air...

He's overwhelmed by the weight of his guilt even though he has no idea what he's guilty of. He has a sense that his illness, the spasms that clutch and squeeze his lungs and leave him gasping, is a visitation from a god from another planetary system. He would like to sink his nails and fingers deep into his chest, rip it open and flash-flood his lungs with this incredible and rare substance called air of which all those around him, the ones who are normal and healthy, are blissfully unaware. He sees the look of helplessness in his parents' eyes; he hates himself for what he's done to them and he hates them for not being able to put him out of his misery.

Like a drug addict with acute withdrawal symptoms, his only hope is the needle and the manna passing through it into his body. Ammijaan and the others are always talking about what a brave lad he is taking all those injections. What ignoramuses they are. If he could, he would stab himself with deriphylline or whatever it took, a hundred times a day.*

* Extracted from *God's Little Soldier.* Here Amanat describes the incessant and unbearable bouts of asthma which crippled him from childhood on.

On Ageing

THE FIRST TIME I spotted a white hair on my person was about three years ago. It stared at me from my left nostril like a little flourish at the end of a signature. Apartheid had reached the shores of my body, and the true black or coloured that I am, I hated its presence. They are all over me now, sordid reminders of my age.

I hate shaving and postpone the business for days. Soon I'll have to shave daily. Nothing more seedy and disreputable than white stubs in black stubble.

And now I think if only it stopped with this bleaching of hair. Over twenty years ago I read a long biography of Eugene O'Neill. I had read most of his plays; I was so alone as a paying guest in Pune, I used to finish a play every day, despite the fact that I read as slowly then as I read now. The Gelbs, husband and wife, had written this tome which I had seen in some shop. I went to the forbidding head of the department of English and asked him whether he would buy it for the English department library. He was a man of integrity, solid values and a core of bitterness that could poison Carl Sagan's Cosmos. He had done his bachelor's (or was it his doctorate?) in England, must have been at Cambridge or Oxford, and returned to India. Life, it was assumed by all, had played him dirty. Someone had stuck a knife in his back, and it seemed that he was never going to allow anybody to take it out just in case the wound might heal. He never raised his voice, just thought you and the rest of the world despicable, maybe with good reason. For years, he shrivelled in front of our eyes without losing an ounce of weight. And when he spoke to a rowdy class or a dull or inattentive student, he lifted his light brown-black eyes from his pale, haemophilic face and the class or individual crumbled. And when the wind blew, even the ashes were not to be found. The broken cortisone-brittle bones scattered to the ends of the world for fear of his gaze following them.

English was his subject, English as the Tudors and the Plantagenets and Shakespeare and Sterne and Coleridge spoke and wrote it. Sometimes through de-blooded and wan pallor, would break a half–smile only to be withdrawn in great haste. But it was wondrous rare, and for days we would wonder whether we had imagined it, or the man had actually shown signs of humanity and life. Tristram Shandy broke his pallid resolve to stay unsmiling with indecent frequency. Sometimes, all of two one-eighth smiles in the brief span of sixty-five days. But he liked his subject, and despite his mask of death, it was possible to forgive him his chill negation of life because the cadences of the English language and its great moments stirred within the glacial corridor of his mind.

I see his receding forehead, his thinning hair flattened as close to the scalp as if it were merely an extra lining of skin. The Gelb book was expensive and funds for the English department were minute. And American literature was certainly not his favourite pastime or preoccupation. I must have gone to him with a sense of diffidence and defeat even though I suspected that within the confines of the English honours class, I was tolerated with less distaste than most of the others. He stood still and wearily heard me out. He was patient with me when he spoke. The finances of the college, the fact that O'Neill was not a prescribed author, and the even more relevant fact that an autobiography was not even remotely on the list of urgently required volumes. More than disappointment, I felt a sense of fulfilment of expectations. Resignation overcame my earlier enthusiasm without too much of a fight. The Gelbs' biography of Eugene O'Neill which I believed, for totally unfounded reasons, held hidden within it truths and treasures would remain out of my reach, at least for the next few years. When you are young, I've been told, there's forever to live. When I was young, if there was a forever, it meant today, now, this very minute.

Neither as peroration or clincher, but as merely the last sentence of an emotionless monotone, he said that in spite of these constraints and though the odds seemed against it, he would see if the department could accommodate the wayward wishes of an individual student.

The Fergusson Library had an old-fashioned system of keeping track of who had borrowed what book. You chose a book that you wanted to read and took it to the clerk at the main counter. He would open it, and from a brown paper pocket affixed to the inner back cover, remove a card on which he would write your name and the date by which you were supposed to return the book.

If you happened to be a curious soul, you went over the card before you got your book out. Occasionally, you might find that seventy-five or a hundred years ago, one of the greats like the social reformer Gopal Agarkar or Senior Wrangler R. P. Paranjpye had tried to anticipate your own interests. For the many books of O'Neill plays that I borrowed, my name was merely one among many, albeit it was there more consistently than those of others. In the matter of the Gelb book, I use numero uno. I came back one day with the thick hardcover tome, marvelling at what a bright young man I was, quite exceptional really, considering that I was about to read a book that hardly anybody in Pune knew existed. I find the self-congratulatory note today distasteful in the extreme, but I was so full of myself then, it's a wonder I did not go on the road and announce to the world that I had a mind bigger than a dray horse's fart. Today, my mind and brains and body are even fuller of illusions. As you grow older, you stop growing. The sameness of one's own ideas is discouraging and deadly. You shrug your shoulders, you use every excuse not to do the things you feel you were meant to do with your life. Little by little you sell yourself till you begin to believe that hawking is what life is about.

The O'Neill book was dull and informative, maybe the other way round. It's over twenty-two or twenty-three years since I read it, and I do not recall it too well, so it's more than likely that I am being unfair to it. It did trace his family life and his relationship with his father, mother and brother, which formed the subject matter of many of his plays. But it also told of O'Neill's arthritis which grew more and more inflexible and intractable as he aged. His fingers twisted upon themselves. Bent in a frightening fashion, they would not bend to his wishes. His friends and doctors asked him to type his plays now that it was agony for him to hold a pen. That, however, he could not do because he said he thought with his fingers.

I look at my fingers and the slow, warping rigor mortis setting in them; I cannot type either. All that is missing is the body of work that O'Neill built so single-mindedly. (I know that O'Neill is out of fashion now but apart from the fact that he is the father of the unburdening confessional type of play which forms the major genre in American drama, *Long Day's Journey into Night* and a couple of his other plays, I think, will outlast most of the other stuff written after him.) We think of death as a killer. It is, as ancient Indians believed, time that kills. Slowly, like the silent falling of snow on a chill night, I sense the arthritis depositing its soft powder of concrete around my joints. It makes such quiet progress, one is reassured that one's limbs are safe for the next hundred and fifty years. Then, one morning, there is a pain in the bone, and the index finger has assumed the shape of a bow. The imagery, you feel, is anachronistic but that's how you ought to feel because that is what arthritis makes you.

Open Sesame, or The Power of Stories

THAT WAS THE DAY Aladdin of the magic lamp met the five kings for the first time. It was not a happy meeting. He was taking his shower when the five kings walked into the bathroom.

'Gotcha!' they shouted with joy. 'We've been trying to catch you for the last seven years, Aladdin. Now we've got you. Where is the magic lamp? Give it to us right now. Or you're a dead man.'

Each of the kings was poking a long knife into Aladdin's ribs.

'It's upstairs in my office,' Aladdin told them.

'You're lying.'

'Why would I do that? Why would I lie? I don't want five long knives with blades sharp enough to cut my eyeballs into two even if I merely look at them, carving me up.'

The kings looked at each other uneasily. Then suddenly one of them ran up the stairs.

'Thief, thief! Don't let him get away!' The four kings who were left behind screamed and ran up the stairs.

Aladdin quickly dried himself, put on his tunic and pants, slipped a hand into the right pocket, got out the magic lamp and kissed it.

'I'm safe now,' he heaved a sigh of relief and rubbed the lamp against a buttock. No response. He rubbed it again. Nothing. The next time he rubbed so hard, his pants almost burst into flames because of the heat.

At last, the genie popped up from the lamp.

'What's your problem? Can't a genie get even one night's rest?'

'I'm in trouble, Genie ... very serious trouble. Fly me out of here. Now!'

The five kings were standing at the top of the stairs screaming murder: 'Liar! We're going to make minced meat of you once we get the lamp.'

'Genie, save me, get me out of here!'

'Sorry, boss. *Aaj Sunday hai*!'

'What do you mean, '*Aaj Sunday hai*'?'

'Don't you know the Genies' Union has declared Sunday as a holiday from this month.'

And then the Genie disappeared into the lamp.

The five kings were rushing down the stairs, each overtaking the other, shouting: 'The lamp is mine, mine alone!'

And then? And then? And then?

Gotcha.

See, you're hooked. That's what a story does. Once you start, it won't let you go.

But what's going to happen now? Are the five kings about to stab Aladdin in seventy-seven different places? Will the five kings find the lamp and steal it? Will the genie listen to them and take orders from them? Or will the five kings fight over it? And if they do, which of the five kings will get it?

Well, Aladdin's life might just depend on you. Can you save him? How? (Will the five kings fight amongst themselves? Will Aladdin send them on a false trail again and make a getaway? Will the genie change his mind?)

There are, as you know, one thousand and one stories in the Arabian Nights. Scheherazade's life depended on whether she could tell a bewitching story to the king every night.

A library, too, will have thousands of books with thousands of stories. Lucky you. One story for every day for the rest of your life. That's if you become a member of the library closest to you and read every day.

Do you know what a library can do for you? It's your own personal magic lamp. Just say the words 'Open Sesame' and you'll have a treasure greater than any king's fortune. All the books in the world, in Japanese, Chinese, Russian, Maori, Inuit, Spanish, French, Sanskrit and almost every major language in the world will be right there in front of your eyes. Grab the books and become super-rich.

Oh, one last question: Do you know who was the world's very first library? She's right there in your own home, right next to you. Come on, you get three guesses.*

* It's your grandmother.

Readings, Misreadings and Non-readings: Perils of the Indian Literary Scene

I DID MY FIRST READING in public at the age of fifty. Till then I had stubbornly refused to appear even as a mute participant on TV, even when my first novel in my mother tongue Marathi, *Saat Sakkam Trechalis* was being discussed, or when my controversial play *Bedtime Story* had run into serious censorship problems.

Now finally I was making my debut and there were notices put all over the University of Chicago. The organizers (or was it just me?) were expecting between a hundred and two hundred people at the minimum, but the public turned out to be all of four professors from the university who had obviously been coaxed or coerced to come out of pity for an oversensitive author who might be terminally traumatized and take it into his head never to speak or write again. Oh, if only, if only ...

Any other sensitive soul would have lost heart and never dared to go public again, but I must be perverse. At that late age I discovered what a ham I was and how I hungered to let the actor in me come out of the closet. There was no stopping me then. Since that first time the numbers have varied, starting from an audience of one, including myself (the department of English literature at a certain academic institution, best not mentioned, forgot that they had asked me to inaugurate their very first issue of a literary magazine), to four hundred.

My family and friends had a difficult time preventing me from buying my own air tickets to international literary festivals in Iceland, Siberia, the Galapagos Islands, and appearing uninvited on the podium and shoving the scheduled author aside while I read from my own work.

But I must confess that my enthusiasm for lit fests and other such occasions is on the wane of late. My new novel *God's Little Soldier* has been translated into German and I am about to go on a reading tour again, but 'The Hard Knocks School of Life' has taught me a few lessons: that the business of readings is fraught with all kinds of hazards.

It started with *Ravan and Eddie*, my first novel in English. I can't quite recall whether it was in Cologne or at Ann Arbor. After a reading from the novel and after the mandatory question-and-answer session, and after the six or seven persistent readers and non-readers who always want you to read their nine-year-old's 'absolutely marvellous short stories, he's a real prodigy you know, something like the Mozart of literature, the laptop just dances to his fingers', or their own seven-hundred-page manuscripts before you leave town the next day, I noticed a woman who was hanging around in the shadows. The organizers were getting impatient and so was I to get back to my hotel, but I didn't have the heart to disappoint the woman.

'Hello,' I said, 'I'm sorry I made you wait.'

She didn't have time for small talk. 'You've got it wrong, so wrong.'

'You mean the novel doesn't work for you?' I asked enthusiastically. The only thing I'm more keen on than flattery is when people are savaging my work.

'It's okay, funny and all, but I'm talking about something else. That thing that Ravan's mother tries on her husband, it just doesn't work.'

'What doesn't work?' She pronounced Ravan like 'raven', and I was distracted.

'You don't remember your own book? When she holds him and seduces him away from his mistress. I tried it on my philandering husband just like you wrote it, everything she did I did. He seemed happy but the next day he was back with the other woman.'

I didn't know what to say and did my best to look contrite.

'What do you want me do now?' she asked me aggressively.

'Me?'

'What's my next move? How do I get him back?'

Was I missing something here, something pertinent and valuable? I was never going to make money on my writing. Was there a lucrative new career waiting for me as an agony aunt?

The kinds of troubles my next novel, *Cuckold*, got me into were very different.

Cuckold is the story of the husband of perhaps the most well-known woman in Indian history, Meera, the poet-saint whose words, like that of those of the Bible in Europe, are often on our tongues without our being aware of it. Meera cheated on her husband, but unlike the common run of humanity, she did not fall for another man. She fell in love with a god, no less a god than Shri Krishna himself. The curious thing is that while we know a lot about her, almost nothing is known about her husband except that he was born, was married to her and died. There are innumerable plays, movies and thousands of songs written about Meera, but nobody had been interested in her husband. So I decided to write *Cuckold*, a book about the husband. Naturally Meera was very much present in the book but let's just say my treatment of her was not exactly reverential and pious.

Soon after *Cuckold* was published, I got a call from Delhi.

'May I speak with Kiran Nagarkar?' the voice at the other end asked.

'Speaking.'

'I'm calling from The XYZ Arts Centre. My name is Mrs Ram and I am the chairperson of the Centre. We would like to invite you to read from your new novel to a select audience. We were thinking of 7th of December. It's a Friday, and Friday evenings are when we usually get a full house. Does the date suit you?'

Wow, the XYZ Arts Centre, I couldn't believe my ears. I had finally arrived. The world was beginning to recognize my talent and my literary gifts. Friday was okay. Friday was just fine. Actually, I was willing to reserve the whole week for the Centre.

'Let me look at my diary,' I said in what I imagined to be a suave voice, put the receiver down, walked around a bit and then came back. 'Yes,' I said, 'Friday the 7th might be all right.'

'We'll be flying you in and you will be put up in a five-star hotel of your choice. You will be introduced to the audience by the great doyen of Indian literature, Mr C. B. Abracadabra. And we'll pay a fee of ten thousand rupees.'

Ten thousand bucks, give me a break. All these years I had to pay people to come for a reading of mine. Oh man, forget talent and gifts, these folks had grasped my genius. Who knows, they might have already recommended my name to the Nobel Prize Committee. I was too stunned, however, to react. There was a dubious silence at the other end of the line as if the lady was reconsidering the offer.

'If ten thousand is too little, maybe we could raise the sum to fifteen.'

Perhaps I should have extended my silence further. Perhaps she might have raised the sum to twenty, who knows thirty thousand. But I knew when I was on to a good thing, and I was not about to test my luck any further.

'Fifteen should be okay,' I said casually.

'Well, that's settled then,' the chairperson sounded relieved.

Two days before I was to leave for Delhi, the lady called again. Obviously, she was calling merely to confirm my visit.

'Mr Nagarkar?'

'Yes, Mrs Ram.' I recognized the voice instantly.

'I am calling to say that your reading stands cancelled.'

I am not just an Indian, I also happen to be a Hindu, never mind if I am a non-believer. As Indians never tire of telling others, Hinduism is a state of mind and a way of life, and not really a religion. The long and the short of it is simply this: we are fatalists. Didn't I know from the very beginning that the XYZ Arts Centre offer was too good to come through? So it wasn't too much of a shock. Then just as I was about to put the receiver down, I asked, 'What happened?'

'Oh,' she said, 'one of our directors read your book.'

Then *Cuckold* was translated into German and my publisher decided to call it *Krishnas Schaten* (*Krishna's Shadow*). He has always been good and generous to me. But when I begged him on bended knees not to call the book *Krishnas Schaten*, he was pig-headed and would not budge.

Well, you must have guessed what happened at my readings in different parts of Germany. That title attracted every crank, every weirdo, every nutcase in search of spiritual enlightenment. After all, wasn't India the land of spiritual bliss where every second person can lead you to sublime peace and nirvana? So when I was in Kiel and this man fell at my feet even before I had started reading, I knew I was in serious trouble. He had tears in his eyes when he asked me, 'Will you be my guru? Will you be my saviour?'

From agony aunt to guru, I sure was making progress. I might not have made my first billion yet on the literary scene; frankly, I was still looking for that fabled rich young widow to marry, but new careers were opening up every alternate day in front of me. I didn't want to disappoint my would-be acolyte but neither could I tell him that I needed to see a shrink three times a day and that I myself had come to

Germany in search of a guru because the only god even gurus in India seemed to pursue was the one called the Big Buck.

And in Darmstadt a Hare Rama, Hare Krishna woman in a saree turned up in my hotel lobby and told me she could see the light of Krishna flowing from my eyes and would I come to her ashram and give consciousness-raising talks? And I wanted to say yes, yes and yes again, I would be Krishna to all the *gopis* in the ashram. I was about to accept the offer but my publisher, who I was discovering in a hurry was no friend of mine, insisted that I had a reading engagement in Tubingen the next day, and put an end to that prospect.

And yet nothing I had experienced so far had prepared me for what followed the launch of my latest novel, *God's Little Soldier*. The first reading in Delhi was an unprecedented success. And so were the preview articles. Everybody said that it was an amazingly insightful portrait of an extremist mind; that it was a wise book about an idealist who turns into a terrorist; that it did not take sides but made you understand why even a good man can go terribly wrong. But even then I knew that the good times could not last. The ill omens were all there. In my very first TV interview, the prissy interviewer had told the audience breezily that I had written a book called 'God's Little Terrorist'.

Then the first review appeared in a one-time-great-but-now-fading Sunday paper. It was written by a young man who was an apostle of a new school of criticism that is becoming popular today: say anything you want, accuse anybody of anything without substantiating any of the claims or statements. He must have had a desperate need to attract attention, and he had enough toxins in him to poison all the oceans of the world. The good man called me a 'literary terrorist' and many other wonderful things. I pretended I was not upset. I tried to behave abnormally normal while all I wanted to do was to bury my head in the toilet bowl and flush the tank. Or maybe migrate to darkest Africa. What was I going to do? I knew Dubya and Rummy and Dick along with the FBI, CIA and the boss of Homeland Security would already be scouring the whole country looking for me and that there was a solitary cell in the torture section in Guantanamo Bay jail reserved for me.

And then I get this call. The voice on the phone is deep, resonant and somehow sounds dangerous. 'Kiran Nagarkar?' it asks. 'Yes,' I say. 'The author of *God's Little Soldier*?' I would like to say 'no' but for once my mendacity deserts me and I reluctantly say 'Yes'.

'We have not read your book', the voice says, 'but we love it and we have bought a thousand copies of it.'

Oh, my God, there's someone who loves my book, I can't believe it. See, the world is not all bad. But there was more to come.

'You would do us an honour if you accepted a dinner invitation from us for tomorrow night at the Hilton.'

I was so happy I was about to tell him I would pay for the dinner.

The next evening I turned up in my best silk kurta and designer white cotton trousers. I looked around the restaurant. There were mostly couples and families, and in one corner there was a group of seven people in long, flowing white Middle Eastern robes. They looked at me and I didn't like the look on their faces. They looked urbane enough, perhaps a bit too urbane but not exactly nice, not someone I would want my daughter to bring home. But fortunately I was not meeting them. I recalled that the man had said 'us' yesterday but I wasn't sure if it was the pontifical 'us' or two or three men.

The seven men at the table were still giving me the once-over. Then one of them got up and came towards me with an extended hand. 'Such a pleasure to meet you, Mr Nagarkar.'

What had I got myself into, I wondered, but it was too late to do anything about it. There was, however, a silver lining. At least I hadn't offered to pay for dinner.

The dinner didn't go too badly. After dinner, the man who had first shaken my hand spoke. 'We would never have known about you if we hadn't read that review of your book.' I must have looked puzzled. 'You know the review which called you a literary terrorist.'

I could see something was wrong, terribly wrong. But I didn't get a chance to remonstrate and tell my new friends that despite my single-minded terrorist protagonist, I was a peace-loving guy who valued tolerance above all else. 'We are aiming,' he said in a low flat voice which sounded far more threatening than a melodramatic one, 'to start a terrorist chapter in your country. We have been wanting to do that for a long time but couldn't find someone capable and with leadership qualities. Now suddenly we've found you and now you are ours. We are never going to let you go.'

Shiva's Blue Throat: A Personal Vision of the Artist's Role in the 21st Century

THERE ARE MOMENTS IN literature, in the Bible and in mythology when our system goes into shock, and we have to ease ourselves into a chair or lie down and still our hearts. We are staggered by the audacity and depth of the imagination at work. All we can do is marvel at the laying bare of the human condition, and sometimes of the divine one too. What strikes us is the power of an insight that exposes the raw nerve at the centre of our being. We are silenced by the sheer force of the truth; a truth that we cannot quibble about because it will not permit us the luxury of pleading that truth is a volatile substance and each of us can interpret it the way we want to. What we are confronted with is a truth that issues from the act of imagination. There is no arguing or gainsaying such truth.

Each of us will have his own inventory of such moments. Here are a few of mine:

My first moment is from the Mahabharata on the battlefield of Kurukshetra. On one side are the hundred Kaurava princes backed by the vast armies of their allies. Ranged opposite them are the five sons of Pandu – Dharmaraj, Bheem, Arjun, Nakul and Sahadev – and thousands upon thousands of their armed feudatories. The drums should roll now and the bugles blow, but it's time for an operatic moment, the kind where the villain has run his sword clean through the heart of the heroine but instead of dying sensibly and quietly, she has time to sing a fifteen-minute aria and then drop to the floor in a heap.

Instead of joining battle, Lord Shri Krishna who, as you know, is Arjun's charioteer, will keep the troops and their masters gathered for the mother of all battles, waiting till he has recited the whole of the Bhagavad Gita. But we were talking about the moment, the moment prior to Krishna's discourse that will bring our pulse, blood and world to a standstill. The Kauravas have brought great hardship, deprivation and dishonour to the Pandavas by cheating Dharmaraj at a game of dice, then dispossessing them of their throne, kingdom and all their belongings. As if that was not bad enough, they have dared to nearly disrobe Draupadi, the wife of the five Pandavas, before sending them into exile. Now fourteen years later, the Pandavas are back after fulfilling every condition of their banishment but the Kauravas refuse to return their kingdom, Indraprastha. Hence the great war. How long have the Pandavas waited for this moment, this moment when they can redress all the wrongs they have suffered over the years at the hands of the Kauravas? And yet it is at this very moment that Arjun chooses to tell Krishna that he will not fight this battle; that he will not spill the blood of his cousins. Nothing, he feels, neither some mistaken notion of dishonour nor being without a kingdom, is worth shedding a single drop of blood.

It is a heroic moment, a monumental moment for peace that could have changed the history of mankind, for Arjun is that rarest of human beings whose honour lies not in vengeance but in eschewing bloodshed. To no avail of course. The Machiavellian Krishna will dissuade Arjun from his noble purpose. The battle of battles will leave nothing but perdition and annihilation in its wake. Ultimately every single person in this Armageddon, the Kauravas, the Pandavas and even Krishna himself, will come to grief.

My next moment is from the Bible. The Son of God has come down to earth for a specific purpose. We know it, and he himself has foretold it often enough. Now he has been reviled, scourged and nailed to the cross. He is about to fulfil his destiny but chooses that very moment to doubt his father and ask perhaps the most shattering question in literature, or rather in the literature of faith, 'Father, Father, why hast thou forsaken me?'

Let me repeat what I had said at the beginning of this essay. It's not the sheer daring of the writing, it is the artistic and irrefutable truth of it that leaves us speechless. It cannot be; we know for certain that the Son of God does not doubt his father. And yet we also know in our heart of hearts that it cannot be any other way. How utterly lonely and abandoned Jesus must have felt as he was hoisted on that cross on Golgotha. It is truly one of the most human moments ever known to man or God.

The last moment I will touch upon is the one which forms the crux of this paper. We are at the beginning of time when gods and demons inhabited the earth. But more importantly, neither of the parties had yet gained the gift of immortality. Let's pause for a moment here. Who are these marvellous storytellers who had the gall to imagine the whole pantheon of gods: Shiva, Vishnu, Brahma, Agni, Varun and all the others to be mere mortals, hankering like us after eternal life? How can we not doff our caps to these ancients and rejoice in the power of their imagination which could grasp the innermost aspirations of mankind?

But let us return to the gods and demons who are gathered on the shores of Ksheersagar, the ocean of milk. Finally, finally, they have located ambrosia, the elixir of eternal life. There is, however, a slight hitch. It is at the bottom of the ocean. Both the demons and the gods want to lay their hands on the *amrita* or ambrosia. They will indulge shamelessly in chicanery and deceit to drink of it without sharing it with the other party. As usual, the gods will try to get away with murder. But this is one time when they realize that their chances of getting at the amrita are far better if they stand together in this crucial enterprise.

No engineering feat, no technological marvel and no submersible can withstand the pressure of miles of milk and raise the pot of ambrosia. So near and yet so out of reach. It is unfortunate that in the excitement of the moment, the chroniclers forgot to mention who ultimately resolved the problem with a stroke of genius. The gods and the demons would churn the milk with a mountain called Mandara. But what should they use as a rope? No cord, however thick and strong, could take the friction, and it was then that the python Vasuki offered to be the rope.

And so began the Samudra Manthan, the great churning, the gods to the right and the demons to the left. First the gods pulled their end of Vasuki as they leaned all the way back and the demons bent forward, and then it was the other way round. Soon there was a perfect rhythm to the swaying. Back and forth they went, and the waters began to rotate and revolve and the ripples spread wider, and wider and at the very centre, a whirlpool was forming. And now the vortex was whirring madly till it became just a blur, and it was a good thing that the python was mostly submerged in the milk for the heat generated was so great that he would surely have gone up in smoke. And then slowly, one by one, the ocean began to throw up its fourteen *ratnas*, not jewels really, but the most unique objects in its deepest belly. The first to come forth was Laxmi who fell in love with Vishnu, the creator, and became his consort. Kaustubh Mani, the jewel which Vishnu wears in his necklace, was next. Then the flower parijat, which Krishna brought down from heaven and planted for his wife Satyabhama; the wine Sura; Dhanvantari, the physician; Chandra, the moon which Shiva placed atop his braided hair; Kamadhenu, the cow who could fulfil any, but any wish; the elephant Airawat, which Vishnu appropriated as his vehicle; the beauteous *apsaras* who became celestial dancers; Uchhai Shrava, the white horse with seven heads; the bow Sharang; the Shankh or conch shell which Vishnu blows.

And yet there was no sign of the ambrosia. And the gods and the demons began to wonder if there was some foul play for the milk had begun to boil and foam, and they knew that it was a matter of minutes before the python Vasuki collapsed.

Ah finally, there it was. At first merely the rim of the pot was visible. But it was shooting up now like an impatient sun emerging from below the horizon. The gods and demons let out a triumphant cry and they stopped churning and rushed towards the pot. And then they saw it: along with the ambrosia, the ocean of milk had thrown up Halahal, the deadliest poison known either to men or gods. It flew up and fanned out, the livid yellow-green globules, and the rays of the sun got trapped in them, and there they stood poised above the pot of ambrosia. Think about it. The elixir of life was finally within the reach of the gods and the demons and it was about to turn to poison. Can you think of a more dramatic existential moment than this one?

While the droplets hang interrupted midair, the gods and the demons go into an urgent huddle. For the first time they share a common objective. What should they do? The ambrosia needs to be rescued this instant or all will be lost. Who will come forward and do the unthinkable? What a stupid question, no one but no one; neither the gods nor the demons. And all the while the toxic liquid beads that will wipe out immortality itself are making their way downwards. That is when Shiva steps forward and without a word swallows the poison.

The story is not done yet. We'll never know what unbearable agonies Shiva suffered because he won't talk. What we know for certain is that the poison burnt his throat till it turned blue. The fire in his throat will never die. That explains why Shiva always wears a snake around his neck. Snakes, as we know, are cold-blooded creatures and their underbelly is perpetually cold and soothing.

I see Shiva as the role model for the artist. He has witnessed the gods and the demons in action. Both of them want just one thing: immortality. They want it so badly, they will cheat, seduce, kill and use any and every underhand trick to achieve it. But immortality, as we learn from the story about ambrosia, does not come free of cost. There is a terrible price attached to it. No one, except Shiva, is willing to pay it. And having paid it, you would think that he would keep the pot of ambrosia all to himself. After all, he's earned it. But that is not in Shiva's nature. He will share it with all the 33 million gods in the Hindu pantheon and with the legions of demons. And what does he do with the lethal poison? He swallows it.

Everything has a place and a purpose, you told us.
A viper must be true to his creed.
The fang needs sharpening, the lethal venom a victim,
Come my beloved, lie with me today and always.
No telling if poison and ambrosia are the same,
Unless you savour them both.

'Unless you savour them both.' Is there a better creed for an artist than to embrace in his work, both the good and the bad, the light and the darkness, the possibility of happiness as much as of pain and suffering, accept meaning and meaninglessness, the Holocaust as much as the non-violence of Gandhi? And not lose His humanity or compassion? In short, embrace the human condition in its entirety.

It is the iridescent peacock blue of Shiva's throat that has become more and more central to my concept of the artist and his work. What Shiva did was not to vomit or disgorge the poison as quickly as possible. Unbearably painful as the experience may be, whatever its consequences and the nightmares that will follow in its wake, Shiva will not deny them. He will take the responsibility for his own actions and not permit any bastard acts to wander the earth. Instead what he does is to assimilate and internalize the experience.

What precisely is the meaning of 'assimilation' in the context of the artist? Whatever you may be writing about, however alien it may be, it must be deeply felt and lived through. Now you may well point out that it is absurd to expect an artist to have lived the lives of his many characters, good, bad and wishy-washy. In the case of Shakespeare, Goethe, Dostoevsky, Dickens and others, these may well run into dozens, if not hundreds. But that is the crux of the matter. The quality and truth of an artist depend not merely on the precise observation and nuanced mimesis of the lives of his creatures, but on how far he can, through his artistry, undergo every single emotional crisis, betrayal, thought process, dilemma, joy and terror that his characters experience. That is the test of Shiva. The life of the character the writer is depicting must be absorbed so fully that it must burn his throat blue, a blue unlike any other, and result in a voice which is distinctive and unmistakable. In short, the artist must become Shiva.

The reason Shiva is endlessly fascinating is because it is impossible to pin him down. He encompasses the full spectrum of life as no other Hindu god does. He is the great ascetic, the Mahayogi who incinerates Kama, the god of love, with the fire of his third eye for daring to interrupt his meditation. And yet it is perhaps a measure of his engagement with the human condition that he is also the great lover. Unlike Rama, the erotic is not suppressed in him. Shiva's sexually active; hyperactive might be a more precise description. His symbol is the *linga*, the phallus. There is thus constant tension between the two modes in his being.

In the trinity of Brahma, Vishnu, Mahesh aka Shiva, Shiva is the destroyer. He is Nataraja, the Lord of Dance, who dances the *tandav* and annihilates the world. There is a ruthlessness in Shiva that an artist can afford to ignore only if he wishes to jeopardize his integrity and the quality of his work. Authors, like most human beings, get attached to certain pet ideas, themes and styles and are loath to part with them. Shiva can be a severe role model here. What is remarkable about Shiva is that he can kill his own. A writer, not to mention every variety of artist, must have the gumption to scotch bad ideas even though they may translate into popular successes but at heart remain mediocre or worse. There are, however, times when it's necessary to abandon even good ideas when you can't pull them off despite years and years of work. If I recall right, Isaac Bashevis Singer trashed his first two novels when they were scheduled for publication and was silent for the next seven or eight years.

The paradox of Shiva is that while he is the destroyer, he is also the creator and personifies the regenerative cycle of life. The same cosmic dance that destroys the world is also the one that ensures the clockwork precision with which every satellite, planet, star and galaxy functions. In the darkness of the primal void, Shiva, the creator begins to play the *damroo*, his hourglass-shaped hand drum. And the notes and sounds that emanate from the damroo, according to Panini, are the source of every language in the world.

Is there an artist who does not know the terror of the blank page, the stark nothingness of the empty canvas? But that is also the moment when he is closest to Shiva, the only time he can be God, the creator. And like Shiva, and strangely also like the Christian God from the Gospel of John, he must discover that 'In the beginning was the Word. And the word was with God. And the word was God.' Perhaps the artist may realize with a terrible sense of urgency that mankind has lost sight of the power, precision and weight of the Word, especially since the last century. How we have abused and debased this greatest gift of God, this instrument with which we explore, unravel and understand the universe, ourselves and the mystery of human relationships.

It took the good Lord a mere six days to create the world. Being but an over-reaching mortal, a writer will usually take longer, much longer. But the test of his godhood will lie in how self-contained and self-sustaining is the universe he creates. And how good and effective he is in creating an imperfect world.

Shiva is not an easy god to unravel. There are aspects of him that repel and are unsettling in the extreme. He demands blood sacrifices, both animal and human. He frequents the burning ghats and cemeteries accompanied by ghouls and vampires which feed on human blood. He conducts bizarre rituals. In a very real sense then, Shiva will always remain a mystery. And that is the paradox of art.

The first prerequisite of art is that it must entertain. But at a deeper level all art stems from the exhortation of the oracle of Apollo at Delphi: 'Know thyself'. Great literature cuts to the bone and offers insights into what makes human beings tick and why we behave the way we do: why we are cussed, hateful, happy, intransigent, bitter, brittle, enlightened, violent, compassionate, vicious and caring. And yet the life of Shiva is the ultimate cautionary tale. It underscores the inadequacy of explanations and brings home the fact that whole chunks of life fall outside the pale of human understanding. One of the yardsticks of memorable art, we learn from Shiva, is that it deepens the enigma at the heart of human motivation and human relationships.

Let's go back for a moment to the gods and the demons, the *devas* and the *daityas* at the churning of the ocean. The human mind, it would appear, can only comprehend the world in terms of a binary system. Good and evil, light and darkness, night and day, yin and yang, male and female, black and white. It's as if we need to divide the world into antitheses and polarities to negotiate the unknowns of life and our rational and irrational fears. The middle ground or the greys make us uncomfortable. We want certainties and clear-cut divisions even though the world is anything but. As we saw at the churning, the gods and the others are really the same. Both want immortality, both will resort to any means, fair and foul, to get it, and yet one party is called the devas or gods and the other demons or daityas. It's the same as in the Old Testament. Lucifer and company are thrown out of heaven and banished to hell on some flimsy pretext. We cannot be at peace unless we lay the blame on someone or other. Floods, droughts, famines, defeats, plagues, the collapse of the market ... surely the good Lord can't be responsible for our misfortunes. Someone's got to take the rap, someone has to be responsible. The only solution, it would seem, is to demonize the outsider, the misfits and the rebels, those who make us uncomfortable with their alien ways, those whom we dislike or hate; in short, the other. But there is a flip side to all this. The demonized see themselves as victims, and in their view they are the good guys, and no prizes for guessing who in their eyes are the evil ones. One of these days someone's going to write the Bible from the point of view of Lucifer. That will not only be interesting, it will also upset many an apple cart.

Here's a monologue from my novel, *God's Little Soldier*, that deals with the subject. It is the poet-saint Kabir from the 14th century who's talking to his disciples:

> Is Satan not the creation of God? Kabir shouted after them. Are there departments up there, one for evil and one for good? You, Michael, are in charge of all plant life. Gabriel, I am shifting you to the department of plagues and the research institute for the new and more horrific diseases. We haven't had anything grand and deadly since smallpox. And you Lucifer, the portfolio for evil, I'm entrusting it to you. I don't want any dirt to stick to me. You're the bad guy

and I'm the good one. It's very primitive and simplistic but take my word for it, good against evil is the best theatre in the world. People will flock to see us. The bishops, the qazis and rabbis will philosophise endlessly about the tree of knowledge and the doctrine of free will, and how God in his wisdom created polarities and each human being must choose between Him and evil. They will love it, Lucifer. ...

Why does God get all the credit for good, the weaver asked, and why is all evil attributed to Satan? If God is the Creator, he can handle both. You must decide who's in charge here? Only then will you understand that all polarities and divisions are sacrilege. God, if I may use one of these new-fangled academic terms, is the unified theory of the universe. Good and evil, Hindu, Muslim, Jew, Christian, Buddhist are all encompassed in him. He's large enough and wise enough to accommodate all contradictions.

An artist, admittedly, is no God but when he peoples an entire universe in his fiction, he is as close to godhood as a man can get. The boundaries of his world start and end with his own kind. There is no room for demons then.

As any author will tell you, sometimes the artist chooses the subject of his work, and there are times when the subject chooses him. At least that was the way things used to be since the time Aeschylus and the authors of the Mahabharata wrote their great works. But times have changed somewhat. For some authors and their commercial managers, a novel, play or short story is nothing more or less than a product: a product that must be marketable and hence tailored to the demands of the consumer. In recent years, matters have progressed way beyond that. You now have packaging companies for literature just as you have for perfumes. The only difference is that the former not only come up with the formula for a novel, they even help you put the product together, starting at times with the writing itself. And for services rendered they will take as much as 50 per cent of the author's advance and royalties. Around 2005, Kaavya Viswanathan, the Harvard undergraduate, got an advance of US$500,000 from Little, Brown and Company for her chick-lit novel *How Opal Mehta Got Kissed, Got Wild and Got a Life* which she had to share with her packaging company, Alloy Entertainment. In April 2006 the *Harvard Crimson* reported that several portions of Kaavya's book seemed to have been plagiarized from Megan McCafferty novels, *Sloppy Firsts* and *Second Helpings*, and soon afterwards the book was withdrawn. If Kaavya Viswanathan got pilloried for having lifted from another author, surely the heads of her packers, Alloy Entertainment too, should have been on the block along with hers.

Each author must make his own choices when he sits down at his table, and there's no moral judgement attached to it. But the notion of literature as a product does not sit well with Shiva. Playing to the gallery or making compromises is not an option for those who would follow him.

Shiva and the Role of Research in Fiction

Far too often writers today are in a hurry to get their books out. At times the research is incomplete but worse still, undigested. And if current trends are any indication, then the research becomes an end in itself. The danger is that the fiction becomes secondary and often receives slapdash treatment. Here the cart is definitely ahead of the horse.

How did research assume such paramount importance in literature? In rather simplistic terms, what happened was this: the impregnable fortress of God was seriously besieged for the first time by the Enlightenment rationalists. But the actual fall of God took place a good two hundred years later in the 20th century during the Second World War years, and in no time at all technology was declared the new god.

God might be making one of the bloodiest comebacks in history in recent years but the worship of technology has not abated.

In literature too technology has been playing a more and more central role. The result is a new genre where technology is the main protagonist. But to understand the complexities of technology and to convey them to the reader, the author himself has to do a fair amount of research. Frederick Forsyth was one of the early practitioners of this genre. *The Day of the Jackal* was almost a handbook of guns, ammunition and the forging of passports. By the time you were done with the novel, you knew exactly how much of the barrel of a gun had to be sawed off to get maximum lethal impact at various distances from the target. Tom Clancy boned up so well on submarines and other war material, he's compulsory reading at West Point and in the US Navy.

Serious fiction writers too were falling prey to the seductions of research. The starting point for Vikram Seth's *A Suitable Boy* was Jane Austen's oeuvre, but en route he went down various other tracks. What you got in the course of the 1400-page novel were monographs on the curing of leather, traditional Chinese computing techniques and the parliamentary debates in Nehruvian times. The novel is a capacious form and can accommodate a good deal of secondary baggage, but sometimes the strain of packing in so much can retard the flow, and the basic structure gets bent out of shape.

Amitav Ghosh is one of India's most thoughtful novelists. His *The Shadow Lines* is indeed one of the finest novels to come out of post-independent India. He has an uncanny talent for unearthing the intriguing but long-forgotten historical event and has an unerring eye in his research for the arresting fact or story. And yet in *The Hungry Tide* which is both a love story and an account of the terrible tragedy of displaced Bangladeshis in India, there are times when an overload of information about intrinsically engaging subjects like the Irrawaddy dolphin or a GPS system seems to affect the tightness of the novel.

Shiva, I suspect, might demand a little more than research in fiction. The first prerequisite for an artist is clarity: Do you want to write a novel or a research paper? If you opt for fiction, then you owe it to your characters to get inside their heads and not merely use them as a vehicle to showcase your research.

Shiva and the Thesis-novel

Ideology has always been the cradle of polemics. But since the 20th century it has often been the engine driving fiction, poetry and painting. When art and ideology meet, the colour of the fiction can become a little murky.

However desperate the fight against the Axis powers may have been, while the Second World War was on, there was not much time for despair. But once victory was achieved, Europe plunged into terrible angst. The survivors of the war could not make sense of life. The response of many writers to this anguish and overwhelming perception of meaninglessness was to embrace existentialism. It was a strange time when renowned philosophers wrote novels and plays and novelists forayed into metaphysics. Sartre, for instance, wished to negotiate his existential Marxist stance through novels, while Camus who was primarily a fine novelist often crossed over into metaphysical writing.

Later in the 1960s and 1970s, those who were deeply concerned with the disparities and inequities of the capitalist system in India and its disregard for the dispossessed and the wretched of the earth, were also drawn to Marxism, many of them to the extreme Maoist variety. Mao, like most radical thinkers who wish to change the world, had strong, prescriptive notions of what art should deal with and how and the kind of message it must disseminate. Mao had written extensively on the subject, and his followers in India were keen to promote his views amongst creative people so that their work would propagate the revolution.

Now Shiva has no quarrel with anybody pushing and advancing any agenda, whether it be an 'ism', a religion, or what have you. The provenance of art, after all, is the whole human endeavour, the human project itself. And the policy of art is laissez-faire, anything goes. There's just one proviso: everything's okay so long as your characters have free will instead of being programmed in advance to suit your purposes and not theirs. Which means that a protagonist must be at liberty to rebel against his creator's wishes and chart his own fate. Rarely, very rarely will a thesis-novel give you the feeling that its characters are as unpredictable as real-life people. They are almost always mouthpieces. The shape, contour and content of such novels are dictated from high above, from the creator. The direction and the end result of the narrative are not a direct consequence of the protagonists' actions and thoughts or the existing dynamics of the novel but are predetermined. Quite simply the characters and the novel have not earned their peacock blue as Shiva had.

Shiva and Closures

Another related phenomenon in the context of third-world countries and left-wing ideologies is the problem of closures or endings. Whatever the story, comic, 'feel good' or tragic, the artist is expected to end on an upbeat note or at the very least the victim must make a telling or heroic gesture. Whatever the compulsions of the interplay between characters and the forces let loose within the text, the short story or novel must be willing to take an improbable U-turn and give an optimistic pointer to the future.

Oddly enough, the happy or feel-good endings are the one thing that both commercial and parallel cinema in

India share. Shyam Benegal's first film *Ankur* is about a feudal landlord exploiting a mute labourer and his wife with whom he has an affair. In the end after a crisis, the labourer is brutally beaten up and the couple is thrown out. That was the logical end to the movie, but the director felt called upon to suggest a symbolic act of defiance and perhaps a revolution: a village kid throws a stone at the landlord's house and breaks a glass pane.

Shiva's blue throat is about cause and consequence. A god drinks poison and his throat goes blue. He doesn't die only because he has simultaneously drunk the ambrosia. Whatever happens is dictated by the internal logic of the story.

Shiva and Metaphor

When I was twenty-two, a Marathi poet wrote a play called *Dusra Bajirao*. It was much talked about and I thought I must go see it. For some reason, all I remember of the play is the thirty or forty-year-old protagonist playing with his walking stick and talking to it. Many critics went on and on in reverential tones about the significance of the stick and how it was a powerful phallic symbol. Over the years I have heard critics wax eloquent in the most banal terms, about symbols and metaphors. They are so pat and mechanical, you would think they were dealing with some elementary grade-one mathematical equation.

Most of the stuff churned out in the name of criticism is doubtless from the sweatshops of the modern American varsity system of 'Publish or Perish'. But let there be no mistake, I'm not debunking the role of critics. I would be hard put to express my gratitude to the really good and insightful critics who have brought their deep understanding to fiction and illuminated both difficult and superficially simple but layered texts. The best of them infect us with their wonderful enthusiasms, open doors, interpret and unpeel seam after seam of meaning and mystery, and leave us wondering how a simple set of words, sometimes even a sentence, can have so many resonances. They reveal to us that we can never get to the bottom of the great books; that every time we read them, we'll discover new things about the blue of Shiva's throat, and that is what makes them timeless classics.

The Theatre of the Absurd was almost a complete break from the past. It was considered revolutionary and seemed to ring the death knell for the traditional drama of social manners, comedy and high tragedy, farce, musicals and other forms of theatre. But looking back, it's a little surprising that despite the occasional revival, the Theatre of the Absurd is dead and gone while mainstream and fringe theatre show no signs of cardiac arrest. Perhaps one of the reasons for the demise of the Theatre of the Absurd could be that it lacked complexity. In hindsight, the notion of the metaphor seems to have been interpreted rather simplistically by the 'Absurd' playwrights. The path-breaking *Waiting for Godot* created such a sensation when it first hit the stage, and yet one can perhaps be forgiven for thinking that it's a little dated today. You can hardly blame today's younger generation thinking that the metaphorical resonances in the title itself are a trifle obvious: Godot, God, waiting.

Along with Beckett, Ionesco, Albee and Pinter, God alone knows how many others got on to the bandwagon of the Absurd. Life must indeed have seemed meaningless to that generation, but to portray it through one and a half hours of meaningless small talk or to convey the impossibility of communication through gibberish and endless repetition not only became a mechanical and boring exercise but seemed to suggest a terminal paucity of the imagination. (Recall Andy Warhol's *Sleep*, a six-hour-long sequence of a man sleeping.) On the other hand, think of Satyajit Ray's heroine Charulata in the movie of the same name. She has a fine upright freedom fighter for a husband. She respects him, even loves him, but is bored out of her skull. Ray doesn't take a lifetime or even one and a half hours to portray her boredom. He merely shows Charulata moving from window to window of her large drawing room, with opera glasses at her eyes, following a man with his performing monkey. The entire sequence takes maybe fifty seconds, but the audience gets the message loud and clear.

One of the most moving novels of the post-Second World War era was Camus' *The Plague*. The critics never tire of telling us that the plague of the title is the war itself and the blight it brought in its wake. This might be true but the reason we read the novel and accept the central metaphor is because Camus has erased all traces of self-conscious cues. The book is gripping because it tells the story of the plague from the very start. After taking care of the preliminaries in the first chapter, Camus plunges straight into the plague.

'When leaving his surgery on the morning of 16 April, Dr. Bernard Rieux felt something soft under his foot. It was a dead rat lying in the middle of the landing. On the spur of the moment he kicked it to one side and, without giving it further thought, continued on his way downstairs. Only when he was stepping forth into the street did it occur to him that a dead rat had no business to be on his landing ....' There, Camus has cornered you. The fear is already constricting your throat because you have felt the soft fur of the rat under the sole of your foot. From this moment on, you too are in the grip of the plague. Camus does not lose sight of his subject for a moment, but the book is not a horror story, even though it is one of the most remarkably realized tales of a town in the grip of a pestilence that will run its scythe through the greater part of the populace. There is only one reason why Camus is able to pull off the metaphor. He completely forgets it by immersing himself and us in the ambience, the dark corners, the opacity of people and their unwillingness to acknowledge a terrible crisis and, most important, by never losing sight of Dr Rieux's selfless labour and compassion. There is not a grain of self-consciousness in Camus' writing. If it's possible, it's even more straightforward and sly than Daniel Defoe's *A Journal of the Plague Year*.

The wonderful thing about symbols, the ones that are not deliberately and self-consciously planted but are discovered in the flow of a novel or poem, is that they are protean and hydra-headed. They don't have a tight fit and a single equivalent. They are flexible, ambiguous and the best of them can also be mysterious. They are this and that and many, many other things. They are open to interpretation and multiple ambiguities. Only a fool would want to pin them down. Who can enlighten us about the exact and complete meaning of the albatross in the 'Ancient Mariner'? Or Shiva's blue throat for that matter?

What Shiva teaches us is that the power of art is in individual experience and not in some abstract, preconceived metaphor. The symbolism or metaphor will work if it is incidental and arises as an offshoot, perhaps by-product is a more precise word, of the story of one woman or man or a set of individuals. Start with a metaphor and you'll have a stillborn story: a story without heart, pulse or soul.

Shiva and Style

The debate about form and content, about which comes first and is paramount, will only end when there is no more art. But it's almost impossible to talk about form without exploring the subject of style. For Shiva, both form and style are a function of content. No other god is as protean as he is. He's a *bahurupaiyya*, a quick-change artist, and each avatar is different from the other. He has a thousand names. He's Adinath, Bhairav, Bhuteshwara, Gangadhar, Mahadev, Mahakala, Yogeshwara and many, many others.

How then can Shiva have a single form or style? His style, bearing, demeanour change according to the task he sets himself: whether he'll be a destroyer that day or a lover or one who will conduct tantric rites.

A study of two remarkable authors, Márquez and Rushdie, will illuminate the dilemma of style. Both authors are supposed to be practitioners of magical realism, and yet on close examination one would be hard put to find two more dissimilar writers. Rushdie's joie de vivre, exuberance and delirious punning are irrepressible. His language is brilliant, flamboyant and endlessly playful. He hybridizes English with all kinds of unexpected and delightful appropriations from Hindi, Urdu and demotic Hindi film language. He is a virtuoso trapeze artist whose words are always flying and caught in mid-air doing the most incredible turns and twists. How can anyone fail to be carried away by his masterful performance? But neither can we forget that it is a performance. Rushdie then exemplifies the French dictum, 'Le style c'est l'homme.' In his case the style is indeed the man.

Márquez's language, on the contrary, doesn't draw attention to itself. What strikes you from the very start is the richness and fecundity of his imagery, the almost infinite variety of the stories within stories he has to tell. And yet what you remember most are his characters and their fate: the lonely, ageing tyrant in *The Autumn of the Patriarch* incarcerated along with his memories in his palace. All his life he has played one courtier and sycophant against the other, destroyed anybody who he imagined was a threat and must now live in fear of a violent death. The Patriarch will not stop to take a breath or break. Márquez makes sure that the dictator's idiom and style are as dense as his memories. In *Chronicle of a Death Foretold* the reader waits incredulously as Márquez leads him to the 'foretold death' of the title, which could have been avoided at every stage, with the inexorability of fate itself. The prose here is hypnotically sparse and the style diametrically opposite to the magic realism the reader automatically and mistakenly associates with Márquez from his *One Hundred Years of Solitude* days. *Love in the Time of Cholera* is old-fashioned storytelling at its best.

News of a Kidnapping takes a totally different route. Márquez almost dispenses with the notion of style here. He's speaking of real events and does it so artfully, you begin to believe you are a journalist witnessing a kidnapping and its aftermath in action. Stylistically no two novels of his are similar.

However innovative and ingenious Rushdie's style might be, one sometimes wonders whether there is a danger of it becoming a dead end, a trap and a straitjacket. Márquez, on the other hand, has transformed the constraints imposed by content and function into an instrument of liberation. Shiva's own choice, I suspect, would veer towards the Márquez way of dealing with each work of fiction on its own terms instead of sticking to one particular style.

I'm going to do a quick recap by concluding with a medical image: anaphylactic shock. Whatever you eat, drink or absorb through the pores of your skin, the body transforms it into 'you'. But once in a while you will ingest something that your body rejects, sometimes violently. Medical science will tell you that what your body denies and disallows when it has a strong allergenic reaction or goes into anaphylactic shock is called 'non-you'. An artist can never have the luxury of rejecting. There is nothing non-you in the universe for him. Even when he's portraying characters he dislikes intensely, he cannot turn his back on them. On the contrary, he must experience them so intensely that he must be able to project them better than their apologists could ever manage to do.

So what does it all add up to? To be an artist you must first become Shiva. Every time you set out on a new venture, a new novel, you must drink from the glass of poison: assimilate and internalize a whole new world and the characters till your throat has gone blue. That is the only way you can take a shot at immortality. There will be times when you will have to do research. However interesting the facts and stories it throws up, it's worth remembering that the research is not an end in itself. It can never replace fiction. As with the poison, it is a good idea to digest and absorb the research and then use it sparingly. And what of commitment and imparting lofty messages? Why don't you leave that to the gurus and messiahs? But here's the good news: if you stick to the fiction, if your characters have the breath of life, if you tell your story clear and tight, and remember philosophical reflections can also be told with verve, then like it or not, your preoccupations, your idealism and your vision will percolate through. Not didactically but so subtly, that your readers and sometimes you yourself will not be aware of them. But rest assured, that like Uranium-235, they'll be radiating and affecting your reader long after he has put the book down. To be a novelist is a tough but unavoidable balancing act. You have to be true to two parties, yourself and your characters. You take care of the fiction and the metaphors, and the symbols will take care of themselves.

What Kind of Beast Is This Thing Called 'Style'?

A COUPLE OF WEEKS ago a young filmmaker finished writing a screenplay of my novel *Ravan and Eddie* and sent it off to a friend of his whose documentary had recently been nominated for an Oscar. Unlike most people who had got back to him, her reply was prompt and detailed. She had raised many pertinent issues, but the one that seemed to fundamentally question the whole enterprise asked: What was this creature? Was it a comedy, a melodrama, a farce, a tragedy, a naturalist portrait of life in Bombay? She said the ground under the reader's feet seemed to shift constantly. Was it the flaw of the screenplay or of the original book?

As the author of the novel, I can say with some confidence I was the guilty party and that the scriptwriter was merely taking off from the original novel. I can understand the comfort that a clear categorization of genres affords but I seek solace in the belief that *Ravan and Eddie* is a reflection of life, and life can indeed often be exactly the hodgepodge and the potpourri that had flummoxed the documentary filmmaker: a comedy, melodrama, farce, tragedy and many other things, all rolled into one.

The debate about content and form, and along with the latter, the notion of style, will cease only when art itself is dead. Each artist must decide for himself which should take precedence. But the idea that style is a veneer or an independent entity that can be attached to a work of art, conjures up images of a layer of epidermis without the flesh, blood and body, of which it should be an organic and integral part. When seen in this light, style becomes a static concept that imposes severe limitations on the writer and his capacity to create and internalize different worlds and to breathe life into his characters. On the other hand, if you view style as a dynamic force that is protean and can take any shape and form according to the demands of the material, then what you get is the ability of the artist to constantly reinvent himself, not to mention his work. The idea is not to pursue that chimera called originality but to be able to flex your creative muscle and encompass the whole spectrum of the human condition.

The moment style becomes a formal device, one that is imposed from without instead of growing from within, a sameness and staleness seem to set in. What had started out as fresh and vigorous and perhaps even unique turns into a trap, a straitjacket and a dead end. This is why authors like Garcia Márquez cannot be typecast.

My characters Ravan and Eddie come from some of the poorest sections of Indian society. They are ne'er-do-wells but they never give up. If they were mere survivors, their lives would be like hundreds of millions of other Indians, heroic but unexceptional. It would, however, be a mistake to underestimate Ravan and Eddie. They may be down but never out of the game. Whatever cards life might have dealt them, they will improvise on them and rise again. Their lives will always be a roller-coaster ride and full of surprises, not always unpleasant.

What *Ravan and Eddie* demanded is a style and language that is as treacherous and unpredictable as their lives, a supple and volatile idiom that reflected the vicissitudes of their lives and the energy, the verve and pizzazz with which they navigate through these tricky waters.

Ultimately the only thing that matters is whether one can pull it off or not. That, I'm afraid, is up to the reader to judge.

All I can say is that the distance between intention and realization will always remain the same: one of aspiration.

The Empire Is Dead: Long Live the Empire

Any anthology of poetry, fiction or plays, like the list of the best wines or restaurants in the world, is always open to the charge that it is too personal, lopsided or partisan. That is the nature of the beast. If and when someone manages to put together the perfect mix or the ideal anthology, the whole genre will collapse from consensus.

The year 1997 is the year of India. India is celebrating the fiftieth anniversary of its independence, and the western media have decided that India is where the literary action is. *Granta* and the *New Yorker* have devoted entire issues to India. The BBC, the *Times* of London, the *Washington Post,* the *New York Times,* not to mention the rest of the English-speaking western press, speak glowingly of the great Indian literary explosion. A few months ago, Salman Rushdie and Elizabeth West edited the *Vintage Anthology of Indian Writing.* One can't think of a better person to edit such an anthology than Rushdie. When he wrote *Midnight's Children* in 1980, he parlayed the language of our ex-rulers into an instrument that would bring alive the taste, sound and feel of a subcontinent that had refused to be categorized or encompassed all these years. To catch the madness of India, Rushdie invented a mad English and an even crazier imagination. He not only subverted and perverted the language of the empire but radically altered the notion of fiction and literature. Ironically, the ex-empire and the only living empire of the last years of the millennium, the US of A, were delighted to embrace the new iconoclast.

Rushdie's Introduction to the Vintage anthology (reproduced almost verbatim in the *New Yorker*) is the last and definitive word on the subject. Well, at least as far as the West is concerned.

In India, however, Rushdie's Introduction is the subject of much controversy. 'The prose writing – both fiction and non-fiction – created in this period [that's in the last fifty years since Independence] by Indian writers working in English is proving to be a much stronger and more important body of work,' writes Rushdie, 'than most of what has been produced in the eighteen recognized languages of India, the so-called "vernacular languages" during the same time; and indeed this new, and still burgeoning Indo-Anglian literature represents perhaps the most valuable contribution India has yet made to the world of books. The true Indian literature of the post-colonial half-century has been made in the language the British left behind.' (This is the kind of terminal smugness one associates with our regional languages, not with Rushdie, normally.)

Rushdie does not know most, if not all, the regional languages in India. As he himself confesses, he has to base his 'unexpected and profoundly ironic conclusion' on a reading of translations from Indian languages. Again, as he himself admits, the quality of the translations is often inadequate. The truth is that there is no substantial tradition of translation either from one vernacular language to another or to English. Translation is still a very very occasional activity in India, which means that even exceptional and memorable writing in regional languages frequently doesn't get translated.

Many Indian critics believe that Rushdie's profoundly ironic conclusion stems from his profound ignorance. Similarly, his belief that 'Indo-Anglian literature represents perhaps the most valuable contribution India has yet made to the world of books', barring a few 19th-century authors, forces one to infer that Rushdie is unaware of the great earlier writers like Shudraka, Kalidasa, Dnyaneshwar, Kabir and others who constitute the canon of the regional languages in India.

Whatever reservations we Indians may have about Rushdie dismissing regional writing cavalierly, it should gladden our hearts that he does not have double standards, a patronizing one for Indian writing, especially in the regional languages and another for western literatures. If we are damned, it would appear that we are damned by the toughest and finest criteria in the world. At least that is the assumption.

Let us get back to Rushdie's words: 'There is only one Indian writer in translation whom I would place on par with the Indo-Anglians. (Actually he's better than most of them.)' The only regional writer Rushdie includes in his anthology is Saadat Hasan Manto. Whatever your canon and criteria, Manto is indeed a superior author. Curiously enough by Rushdie's own admission, Manto is better than most of the Indo-Anglian authors from his anthology.

After all the fanfare from the *New Yorker* and Rushdie, where exactly does this leave the Indo-Anglian authors? If Manto figures at 'very good' on the standard four-tiered scale of 'excellent, very good, good and poor', then Rushdie has deliberately or unwittingly let slip that the majority of his authors must find a place between good and poor. One can't really agree with Rushdie's assessment since many of the authors in his anthology are mediocre. They write imitation-Rushdie, soap, or thin, watery stuff. Apart from the fact that the Indo-Anglians write in English, is there then such a difference in quality between their work and that of their poor cousins, the regional Indian authors?

Rushdie's relationship to English gets curiouser and curiouser. The *Times of India*, which is the most prestigious and perhaps the largest selling newspaper in India, no longer reviews books by Indian authors who write in English unless they are published abroad. The *Asian Age*, another newspaper published in India and England, too thinks that reviews of books written in English in India are a waste of time. Almost every single Indo-Anglian author selected by Rushdie has been published abroad. Rushdie too then stands with the *Times of India*. Never mind if you write in a regional language or English, you are persona non grata, if you are not first recognized and published abroad.

The Empire is dead. Long live the Empire. Things have come full circle. It is clear that the Empire has fully assimilated Rushdie. What the Empire approves and only what it approves he considers worthwhile.

An anthology offers the reader brief encounters with writers whose work you are not interested in pursuing and with authors who arouse your curiosity, force you to read their entire oeuvre and leave you a marked man. Here are a few brief idiosyncratic footnotes on the authors and their work in the *Vintage Book of Indian Writing*.

If recent Indo-Anglian writing has an original voice, power and seriousness, it is because of authors like Amitav Ghosh. It is a multicultural world we live in where, more often than not, neighbours look at each other in incomprehension. Ghosh is the remembrancer of divided lands of brittleness and Balkanization, of the violence and the bloody blade that is so often the only communication between brothers. *The Shadow Lines* is Ghosh's finest novel to date, sensitive, moving, insightful but never parlaying the sorrow of wounded and divided souls into a commodity. 'Nashawy', the excerpt from Ghosh's sojourn in Egypt, is a quieter version of the chasm between different cultures. (Hopefully it will lead the reader to *The Shadow Lines*.)

When Vikram Seth published *The Golden Gate*, whether you thought it had great depth or not, one thing was clear.

He was a highly accomplished sonneteer with a deceptively easy command over language. Something went wrong, however, when he wrote his opus, *A Suitable Boy*. It seems he wanted to write a novel that would use straightforward English, in contrast to Rushdie's flamboyant verbal pyrotechnics. But Seth confuses triteness (banality) for the rigours of simplicity, long-windedness for epic dimension, and good old soap of the Indian commercial film variety for literature. His character may teeter on the edge of tragedy, but time and again he shies away from it. As so often in his novel, Seth takes aim at easy targets in the Vintage excerpt: poetasters, chauvinism and bad poetry.

Gita Mehta is the author of witty and lightweight commentaries on Indian culture since Independence and a historical novel called Raj. In *A River Sutra* she explored a serious vein and played fabulist to the subcontinent. In the Vintage piece from the *Sutra*, she tells the story of an unsuccessful musician who finds the perfect pupil with the perfect voice, a blind boy. It is a tale told in spare, measured prose that has a compelling pace. It's difficult to understand why Mehta lets go her tight control of the story and opts for an underdeveloped, lurid and botched ending.

There is a school of readers and critics which believes that understatement is the mark of good art. It is supposed to conceal complexities, undercurrents and depths missing in sturdier work. Unfortunately, artists often underplay because what they have to say is modest, vapid and limited. There is no hint of the abyss, no highs and no lows. This world, God help us all, is a doggedly sweet place.

Ardashir's Vakil's 'Unforced Error' culled from his novel *Beach Boy* is, as the name suggests, about tennis. Barring the first self-conscious para, it is engaging and assured writing. The protagonist Cyrus's mother is a delightful and embarrassing portrait of a domineering woman. The game has you as tense as at any final at Wimbledon.

Cyrus's slide from supreme confidence to loss of nerve is documented with verve. Will the rest of his novel hold up to the expectations raised by the excerpt? Who knows? I haven't read it yet.

Anthologies are really a series of trailers. You can rarely be sure whether the trailer packs in the only worthwhile parts of the movie or is just a foretaste of the terrific action and drama to come in the movie. There are thirty-two pieces in the Vintage anthology, some more watery than Delhi dysentery, some compelling. Most delightful and delirious of all is your seventh (or is it the eleventh) rereading of Rushdie's excerpt from *Midnight's Children*.

The Role of Memory in *Cuckold*

I AM GOING TO TRY to briefly explore the role of memory, both collective and personal, in the writing of *Cuckold* and then quote a few ruminations and passages from the novel to comment upon and illustrate the points I'm making.

Cuckold, very briefly, is the story of the Maharaj Kumar of Mewar. The great Rana Sanga is his father and Meera his wife. The throne should rightly belong to him but the succession is not secure since the Rana's favourite queen wants her own son to be crowned. Mewar has four enemies: Gujarat, Malwa, Delhi, and in the distance, the Mughal invader Babur.

If there had been an international competition to locate the one author least qualified to write *Cuckold*, I would certainly have been a prime candidate. Since the time I grew up and started to think for myself, I've found myself out of sync with the archetypal Rajput hero and heroine, and that quintessential Rajput aberration named Meerabai. There were two reasons for my antipathy, and both of them had to do with the collective Indian memory.

The artefacts of collective memory in India, and I include history, legend, mythology, novels, plays and the arts in the word 'collective', give little purchase to a writer if he is cursed with even a slight degree of scepticism. Bad historians, sycophantic chronicles, the Indian craving for monochromatic and larger-than-life heroes without complexity, turned me off popular history a long time ago. They could make the most inspiring, demonic or mesmeric of our leaders into bland, dyspeptic and predictable characters.

What I gleaned from the public perception and memory of Mewar left me cold and exhausted. Instead of a critical analysis of the actions of the Ranas and the Maharanas, there was a blind and unthinking glorification of the Rajput past. The Mewar heroes were all painted with the same paintbrush and had the same specifications. They were all exceptionally brave, never mind how foolish the cause for which they fought. Their wives, daughters, sisters and mothers were just as brave. When Mewar lost a battle and the enemy entered Chittor, they committed mass suicide and jumped into the *Jauhar* fires. Their horses too must have been Rajputs for they too were blindly brave and gave their lives to save their masters. Chetak, Rana Pratap's horse, for instance, is celebrated in sculpture, poetry and film songs.

Here are two comments in *Cuckold* by the Maharaj Kumar about the Indian fixation with the past.

> We are a country of bards and minstrels and story-tellers and troubadours. They never tire of telling stories of the heroic exploits of my ancestors. Of Bappa Rawal, Rana Hameer, Choonda and Rana Kumbha. I think we breathe in less air than we inhale these stories. Our anecdotes are all history. The bedtime stories of our children are about these larger-than-life monarchs and warriors from the past. Our arteries and veins are clogged with them. Sometimes, I think we have no present, only the past.
>
> They paint a rosy picture, these tellers of tales and very sensibly, don't dwell too long or too often on the bad guys. That's not quite true. What they do is far more dangerous. They turn the fratricidal and bloody struggles that always preface the assumption of the throne after a king dies, into a hundred or thousand pretty couplets about heroism and valour. They cannot see death's head above the crown of each king. And nobody calculates the cost of all this insane and internecine bloodshed to Mewar. We are our enemies'

> best friends. For what better chaos and anarchy can they wish upon Mewar than that which we wreak upon ourselves? Only a short-sighted fool will take solace from the fact that the same deadly struggles take place in the kingdoms of our neighbours.

The Maharaj Kumar's second rumination occurs in the context of the writing of his own memoirs.

> The past was with my countrymen every moment of their lives. History for them was that fabled second chance. They could rework the past and get it right this time around.
>
> It was an act of faith and invention where defeats turned to glory; courage, bravery and heroism were chosen above vision or long-term gains and enmity was more precious than alliances. Best of all, you did not have to tot up the accounts and pay for the grandeur of your delusions or the vacuity of your mistakes. To them five hundred years ago was the same as yesterday, an episode outside the orbit of time. The past was never your responsibility. It was not the sum-total of mankind's wisdom, errors and insights. It was not the torch that lit the darkness and choices of today. My memoirs would try to go against the grain and break with tradition. If personal history was an inheritance, then I would leave behind a record that would allow the next generation, including my children, to understand how their fathers and forefathers negotiated the turns and twists of diplomacy and the business of the state; how they failed, what mistakes they made and how they picked up the pieces and started anew.

The other overwhelming reason why I knew I would not have any truck with Mewar was the Meera–Krishna nexus. The Indian or, to be precise, Hindu fascination with the cosmic philanderer Shri Krishna continues unabated even today. If classical dance, painting, poetry, music, our horis and thumris, film songs, the commercial bhajan are obsessed not with the Gita-god but with the playful lover, much of the credit for this must go to Meera. It was not so much Jaidev's *Geet-Govind* or the Pushti Margis' gender-crossing as Meera's madness, her erotic and mystical poetry which caught the public imagination and enslaved us to Shri Krishna.

My one visit to Merta merely confirmed my own knee-jerk reaction to Meera. I had visited Chittor, Kumbhalgarh and Ranakpur, and I now wanted to see Meera's birthplace. What kind of home, people and place could raise and nurture this strange woman, this mutant who shocked and dishonoured the Mewar royal house by claiming that she was married to a god and by singing and dancing in public? But Merta held tight its secret and mystery. It did not offer any clue or inkling about its only claim to fame. My friend Nitin and I drove in around eleven in the morning. We thought everybody would know where Meera's house was. We asked a few passers-by. They didn't think there was anything like a Merta palace but suggested that we take a look at the ruins of a stone haveli half a mile away. Even as a ruin, the site of the haveli was unprepossessing and in a state of terminal disrepair. An ascetic-looking man took us to the adjoining one-storeyed broken temple. 'Was this where Meera prayed?' I asked. He was surprisingly candid. 'I doubt it. But who is to say?'

The local authority on Meera, a schoolteacher, was not in the school but after many false leads we tracked him down to his home. His daughter made us some thick tea while he showed us his Meera artefacts: some poems in the style of Meera; newspaper articles on Meera; and a scrapbook of greetings cards, posters, calendars and other memorabilia with the ubiquitous Meera as the motif. Meera in black and white, embossed, in the colours of the rainbow. As always, she was strumming an ektara. Seated, standing or dancing, her eyes are lowered. I'm informed repeatedly by the teacher that she is looking inward, gazing and meditating upon her beloved Shri Krishna. Nothing will make her look up, smile, scream or shout with joy, not even on the rare occasions when she dances with Krishna or Krishna dances in her heart. I had travelled all the way to Merta to come up short against the crushingly boring, aseptic and sanitized Meera of collective memory. 'God save us from the icons of the world,' I said to myself and dropped by at the comparatively new Meera temple before leaving Merta.

All was not lost. The priest in the temple reminded me of a legend that spoke of Meera disappearing into the image of her beloved at the moment of ultimate samadhi. It was an image and a story that I would play with and alter a little at the very end of *Cuckold*.

Here's a critique of the Indian Krishna fixation from the novel:

> He tried not to listen to the song. The gopis were, as usual, filling their pots with water on the banks of the Jamuna when the god with a thousand names took out a catapult and one by one broke the pots on their heads and ogled at the drenched ladies. How were they to go home with wet, transparent clothes that revealed all? Madhusudana, alias the Flautist, everyone knew was shameless, but they were honourable, decent women, some of them with husbands and children, and all of them had spotless reputations. How were they to face their families and pray, what explanation were they to give?
>
> How he loathed these songs. Didn't the bards of India have anything else to write about? There were thousands of songs about the divine eve-teaser and everyday someone or the other was adding to the genre. In plaintive, vexed or patently false, angry voices, the women complained about

him. They pleaded with him to stop stealing their clothes, implored him not to flirt with them in full public view and spray colours on them during the Holi festival; would he please leave them alone once and for all? No more, no more, no more, they said when they meant more, more, more and please don't stop. If he turned his back on them, instead of rejoicing, they went berserk with grief. They pined, they fretted, they had nervous breakdowns. Frankly, if they were painful when their modesty was compromised, they were unbearable when they were wailing with lovesickness.

Who, he wondered, wrote these songs of soft pornography and suggestiveness, these songs which were keyholes through which peeping toms – that came to almost the entire male population – led a fantasy double life? The voice and persona of the lyrics was that of women but the majority of writers were men. And yet, given half a chance, any housewife who could manage a rhyme, would dash off a song about 'Look Ma, see how the Flautist is undoing my plait and pulling my pallu.' Sure, it was a convention and the poets were working within a framework and the words and images had deep metaphysical significance (a likely story if he had ever heard one), but the curious thing was that the overwhelming majority of the singers were women. Were they too as repressed as the men? What was the lure of this god? It was not just the women who fantasized about him, the entire population of the country carried on one continuous love affair with him. Nobody sang steamy overwrought songs to Rama, Vishnu or Shiva. What was the source of the irresistible attraction of the peacock-feathered god? How was he able to get away with the very things that would land any other man in jail for life? Did the women, in their heart of hearts, want to walk the streets with see-through wet blouses and wait for some dashing young man with a peacock feather in his phenta to tug at their odhanis?

Whatever the ironies and paradoxes, he was convinced the Flautist was wish-fulfilment for both men and women.

For better or worse and, I suspect, without realizing what I was getting into, I began to explore what it meant to be the nameless and faceless void who was married to Meera. I had no alternative but to invent him from the whole cloth. Since it is the Maharaj Kumar who is writing his memoirs, I had not only to invent his persona but to work up his memory from scratch. To put the matter infelicitously, put him together through his ideas, thoughts, emotions, reactions, his debacles, his warrior vocation, his convictions, beliefs, failings and his actions. Since I had very little idea what he was, or how his mind worked, I had to tease him out as I went along. Not chapter by chapter. But word by word, sentence by sentence and paragraph by paragraph. But if he was a voyage of discovery for me, a slow unravelling, so were Meera, Rana Sanga, Kausalya, Mangal, Leelawati, Rani Karmetan, Vikramaditya, Sugandha and Bruhannada. I had to invent them and Prince Bahadur, Mahmud Khalji and most of all Chittor, more or less from the whole cloth too. I say more or less because some of them were historical characters and I had to respect the facts of their lives. To make the point baldly but effectively, I was, for instance, on unspoken oath to make the Rajputs lose the battle of Khanua.

Babur, of course, was the lone exception. Since he left behind one of the finest autobiographies in world literature, I didn't just treat his memoirs as source material but wove them into the life and text of *Cuckold*.

In retrospect, I was fortunate that I did not take the Ved Mehta road to either the narrative or the creation of characters or the locale. Like most of us, the Maharaj Kumar takes his surroundings, in his case, Chittor, for granted. He does not feel called upon (like Ved Mehta) to note every visual detail to prove his bona fides, to reassure us and most of all himself that he was there. Every once in a while, he will glancingly dwell on the colour of a phenta or choli, speak of the rains of Chittor but there's no compulsive inventory. Perhaps, and only the reader can be the judge of this, Chittor and its people are the more real because of this unstudied way of talking about his city.

> I'm doing a three hundred and sixty degrees swivel. The township within the fortress walls is slowly coming to life. It's always the women who wake up first and come out to fill water. If someone were to ask me what is Mewar, my first answer will be Mewar is colour. There will be other answers, some of them more important, like our blind and indiscriminate bravery or valour. But that's not a spontaneous, instant reaction. When I close my eyes I see colours leaping at me. They skid and lurch and shove and push everything else out. Have you seen the reds and yellows and blues and greens in Mewar? There's the sun in them and a rawness that's like an open wound. I know that muted colours are a sign of sophistication. They are pleasing and beautiful, I won't deny that. But the daring and sheer nerve of the hues and colour combinations of Mewar is like a punch in the solar plexus. In the most ordinary and quotidian moments of life, my people rewrite the dynamics of colour every day. They are profligate and prodigal and yet so controlled, they re-invent colour every time they use it.
>
> Look at that women rubbing charcoal powder mixed with a bit of opium into her gums. I can't see her features but that kind of slow, suffused pleasure in your waking moments can only come from a border-line addiction that's been inherited over generations. Her red and black ghagra is topped by a banana skin yellow blouse and the phosphorescent green of a new mango leaf in spring. Her two companions at the well are lightning blue, pomegranate seed pink and eggplant purple. Who needs lassi when these colours can slap you

> awake first thing in the morning? The lord and master of the hut on the left is up and Mrs. Eggplant Purple is pouring water out for his bath.

Cuckold is told in the first person. It is because of this that the novel can take the full weight of two contrary and antithetical forces, the epic sweep of action and the introspective, reflective quality of the Maharaj Kumar's mind. But things are a little more complicated than that. Every once in a while, there's a switch to third-person narrative. Whatever his faults and flaws, the Maharaj Kumar, like Babur, is a person of not mere honesty but integrity. He does not gloss over his failings. But there is an open wound at the core of his personality and the narrative, which he is not able to touch upon or talk about. There is no psychoanalyst around who can make him lie on the couch and slowly tease the truth and the trauma out. Paradoxically, then, this private pain can only be dealt with in the third person. At least that is the rationale. Anyone who reads the book closely will see through it and perhaps even notice that I deliberately use and derive pleasure from the conventions of the 'suspension of disbelief' and am not looking for perfect logic.

The third-person memory in *Cuckold* is located in two entities. The first is the singer Sajani Bai, who as the 'remembrancer of Chittor', reflects the need to keep alive memories, whether happy, hurtful or sad, to confront them and to learn from them as it is about the peculiar fate of the central character in my novel, the Cuckold himself.

The second is the river Gambhiree.

> Mangal caught up with me in a minute; and the two of us rode out of the fort.
>
> The Ganga may be a holier river, it certainly is mightier but it is not my river. The Gambhiree is my mother and my memory. As she is Chittor's mother and memory. They

bathed me with her waters when I was born and, God willing, they will wash me with her before placing me on the pyre. She is privy to all my doings, my innermost thoughts and the dilemma that wracks my soul. She is not judgemental and she has no answers. Her role is to witness all but she may not interfere. Perhaps she has opinions even strong views, but she holds her tongue forever. Where do songs go when you cease to hear them? Where does the turbulence of the air disappear after thousands of birds flap their wings homeward at eventide? Where are the cries of the Rajput women who spatter their red palm prints on the wall and leap into the flames of jauhar? Where is my childhood, my catapult, my broken slate, my first parrot, my youth and the first sin and all those that followed, where is my old age and the first time I saw the woman from Merta? Ask Gambhiree. She knows it all. We are all safe because Gambhiree will keep her secrets. She is, as her name suggests, deep and sombre and meditative.

There is a mist on the river. The air is stifling, the moon is marooned in dark, sinister clouds. I take off my clothes, say my prayer and slip into Gambhiree. The water is black and cold. I sink in it like a stone. I let go. I float up. The waters swish around me. The strands of my muscles uncoil and my thoughts unravel. Black oblivion runs through my veins. Beware the river tonight. The tall ebony grasses sway sinuously and ensnare my feet. They call to me to come and forget the world above. Yama is abroad on his buffalo tonight. The river is his sister Yami. She is the temptress Death. Who can say no to Yami? Even her brother lies with her.

Flimsy phantoms rise to meet me. The watery faces of my ancestors scream soundlessly, their fluid octopus hands stretch and coil around me. Bappa Rawal, Rana Hameer, Rani Padmini, Hatyara, they all have urgent business with me but I can no longer lip-read their cacophony of demands.

Perhaps if I sink deeper into the underworld, I'll be able to help them.

Somebody's pulling me up against my wishes. The gentleness of the undertow of the currents is deceptive. It's going to kill me softly, sucking me down a spiral vortex. I can hear Mangal calling my name now. I do not respond. The river is my quietus and I have no intention of surfacing again. Mangal's cries become more urgent and desperate. I wish he would leave me alone. He has spotted me and is forcing me up. It's raining heavily. The raindrops pinch the skin of the river in a million places. My skin smarts as they pierce it and go right through. I am awake. Mangal calls out my name as if I had died. The water laps gently over me. I am exorcised of my demons. The moon is out and Gambhiree is a slow silver enchantress.

The Trees: A Belated Love Story

We lived in Hindu Colony in what used to be the invisible border beyond which the suburbs of Bombay started. Looking back, I realize that it was predominantly Hindu but was certainly not a bastion of fanatics or fundamentalism. The colony was mainly a single road, a rather narrow and quiet one with tall shady trees on either side. If you moved eastwards after crossing a road that seemed as large as the basin of the Ganges or the Mississippi (no, I had not seen either of the rivers, which is what made them seem even more gigantic) you were in Parsi Colony. The roads here were wide and the trees enormous enough to deceive you into thinking that you were in the midst of woods. They bore inedible fruit with a hard white shell that looked like the bombs Spitfires spewed out in the Second World War movies. Armed with a short spike, they plunged down without warning, and if you were lucky missed your head and instead burst open as they hit the ground and splattered their brown entrails.

I'm unable to explain my total lack of curiosity about trees in those days but perhaps it is a disease that affects most urban dwellers in India. Almost all the trees remained nameless for me. There were two ramrod-straight trees with a dark grey-black matt complexion (akin to that of elephant hide) in our compound right in front of our door which no one felt the need to identify.

There was, however, one exception to my universal ignorance. It was a gnarled tree about two metres in height which bore tiny green fruit directly on its body and branches.

It was called *awala* in my mother tongue or *Phyllanthus emblica* if you wanted to get technical about it. One bite into the fruit and the nerve ends at the roots of your teeth would sizzle and jangle like a quake of 7.8 magnitude on the Richter scale, your whole body would go into shock and your brains seize altogether. There's no fruit as tart as an *awala* and as crammed with vitamin C.

I finished my schooling and went to Fergusson College in Pune, one of the oldest colleges in the country, to get my bachelor's degree. In the very first month, there was a cataclysmic event. The dam that supplied water to the city developed cracks due to floods and then burst open. The banks and extended environs of the Mula and Mutha rivers were totally flooded. The damage was extensive, the loss of livestock, grain and property monumental, and my college closed down immediately for a month. But there was something so bizarre and inexplicable that happened at that time that to this day I cannot make sense of it.

The premises of Fergusson College boasted one of the oldest botanical gardens in western India. It was a natural consequence of the fact that in those days Pune was in the heartland of an agricultural area. There were certainly some small delicate plants in the garden that would die without water, but the majority were huge, hardy, ancient trees with roots that went deep into the earth and would easily have survived the shortage of water for a year or two. But by the time the college reopened a month later, most of the large trees had been cut down. In a very real sense it was the precursor of the kind of mindless massacre of trees that would become common in India and which is very much in evidence today.

Thanks to that unforeseen disaster, I was forced to come back to Mumbai. To my astonishment, the two tall trees with the elephant hide in our compound had suddenly undergone a radical change. They had begun to bear fruit almost at eye level and all the way to the top. And now the trees had also acquired a name, jackfruit. The jackfruits found their way into my novel *Ravan and Eddie*. Ravan's mother Parvatibai takes him to the Byculla market, a place that arouses surreal fantasies in the child.

> Parvati took Ravan to the Byculla market a couple of times, but he hated it. Lorries were parked three deep and stretched to the edge of one's vision and beyond. Hundreds of bent men, parallel to the ground from the waist upwards, carried loads of vegetables that were bigger than those on the trucks. They wobbled and tottered and couldn't walk in a straight line…
>
> The vendors sat on raised platforms with stack upon stack of brinjals, cabbages, spinach, potatoes, onions, beans, pumpkins, melons, bananas, carrots, green beans and cucumbers on either side of them. But there was life under the platforms too, where the reserve stock was kept. Ravan was transfixed by a dwarf at eye level who was burrowing in a hole underneath. No, not a dwarf but a man on his haunches whose duck feet paddled him in and out of the dungeon. On the way out he brought forth an oversized, tumescent jackfruit in his hands. Ravan had never seen anything so large and malevolent. It was breathing, you could see its pregnant body breathe and swell up and deflate. The man on his haunches raised the living, deformed fruit and yelled, 'How many more?'…
>
> The vendor on the platform grabbed the fruit. It was so heavy he nearly fell over. 'Another fifty,' he shouted and stood up on a stool and balanced the jackfruit on a pile that seemed to reach the ceiling. They were all breathing, those jackfruits. The pile expanded, Ravan could hear them inhaling. Then slowly they shrank back. The stench of the ripened jackfruit was buzzing in his head. It made him feel faint. He didn't know what he hated more, their

stink or their yellow-green prickly texture. They were hard and misshapen and made of stone. Any moment now they were going to come crashing down and he would be buried under them. Parvati was going to look for him for days but wouldn't recognize him because his skin would become hard and yellow-green and spiky and his insides would be pale gold and smell sickeningly sweet.

Parvati cut him open with a butcher's knife. It was her favourite fruit. It reminded her of her childhood and her mother's home and her carefree days. The suppurating yellow smell made her sigh in ecstasy. She gouged out his soft, pale, voluptuous, gold fruit-flesh. She gorged herself to her eyes all day long and dug in for more. Then she vomited. She vomited for days and weeks and months till she became nothing but a transparent collapsible shell. She was pale and lay dying in her own filth. The men and women who were shopping crowded around her and looked down, way down into the well where she lay. It was her last breath but she was trying to say something. They couldn't understand what she was saying but Ravan understood her. 'More, Just a little more jackfruit.'

I was familiar with Pune since childhood. My youngest aunt and her family lived there. We used to visit them every once in a while. They had a dog called Tiger. I look back now and wonder if my theory of shifts in nomenclature or misnomers began to crystallize because of Tiger. What if we called a lioness, 'cow'? And a cigarette, 'gun'? And cats, 'crocodiles'? And boys, 'ceiling fans'? Would the nature of the world itself undergo radical changes? Do animals have names for us humans?

My aunt's husband who worked in a government ordnance factory was transferred to Chennai (Madras then) and my mother, brother and I moved into her home in Pune for two years where my father visited us once in three or four months. It was a lively place in the daytime but at night it got terribly desolate. It is inconceivable for anyone living in Pune today to imagine how lonely and dark the two roads adjoining our tenements were. Ghole Road had two or three 40-watt lights in its entire length, but it was Apte Road with its eerie quiet, with its grove of *amrai* or mango trees, which still evokes primeval fears in my mind. In a passage in *Ravan and Eddie,* Eddie's grandmother relates the rather rushed and unsuccessful courtship of her daughter by the Portuguese governor's ADC in Goa. She recalls a walk amongst the mango trees that I suspect I took from my own memories.

> It was a moonlit night. There was a restless wind blowing. The mango tree is a strange one. It hoards darkness. We walked together for a few minutes, then I fell back. Violet turned round and called to me, 'Mamma.' The two of them hardly spoke to each other. They became invisible when they entered the pools of bottle green. Then suddenly the light caught the starched white of his uniform and I could see them for a few minutes before they disappeared again. I walked to the beach in front of the house and sat on the sand. How far was it to Lisbon from here if I drew a straight line? I thought it would be rather nice to cross the seas and visit a new country to see my daughter.

Oddly enough, when I seem to write about trees in my novels, I go back mostly to my childhood memories of Pune. There was only one tree in the tenement compound. It was a parijat tree (*Nyctanthes arbor-tristis* or the night-flowering jasmine). It never grew to be high nor did it spread out its branches in dozens of directions. And yet the fecundity of this none-too-large parijat was astounding. Come morning, the earth around it would be strewn thick with a carpet of the most exquisite flowers. Six white petals on a reddish-saffron stalk, both so fragile that the slightest rough handling would bruise the flower and it would wilt.

The protagonist of my novel *Cuckold*, the Maharaj Kumar, takes a branch of a parijat from the Kumbhalgarh fortress and plants it in his palace compound. When it finally flowers, he pours the fresh buds on his unfaithful wife every morning while she's still asleep. A year or two later he comes back victorious from a campaign to find that there is an ominous change in the tree.

> My tree is dying. There are plenty of leaves yet on its branches and every morning there are still drifts of parijat blossoms on the dew-drenched ground. But I know that my friend has turned its back on me. I have no idea what unspoken covenant I have broken, what unwritten laws of nature I have transgressed or in what way I have disappointed my joyous companion of the mornings. Who knows what pain we cause our dearest ones? And yet I tell you, tree, however great the error of my ways, it cannot compare with the hurt you inflict when you shrink at the sight of me.
>
> I can see you shrivelling, the sap slowing down, the heart growing fainter. Even in terminal cases, the doctors have told me that if the will to live is strong, both the disease and death are kept in abeyance. Who or what killed your will?
>
> What is it tree? Speak to me, you were like a three-hundred-armed goddess and your bounty was as prodigal as a summer shower, day in and day out. I remember the leap of joy in your face and the goose pimples on your body the first morning after I returned from the Malwa campaign. A thousand parijats leapt down and covered me; not even the pet dogs I had when I was a child have missed me so and made me feel so welcome. And now, barely ten weeks later, you are willing to fold your three hundred hands, withdraw into your tight little cocoon and bid goodbye to the concourse of creation, birds and worms and bees which nested in your breast.

No fever, no bruises, no symptoms and yet I know that something happened, something terrible.

Can we talk this over? I guess not. You can't talk to someone's back, to someone who's stopped listening.

I've brought Befikir's manure and buried it under the topsoil. I turn the earth every two days. I water the ground myself. I have rushed back sometimes even during office hours like an anxious parent or lover. I have played you the flute for hours. I've hugged you tightly and said I'll not let you go. You were but a fledgeling when I brought you from Kumbhalgarh. I don't know whether you missed home; or the terrain and nourishment here are different from those where you were born. You almost died but you didn't give up. You were a tough fighter. Do you know how young you were when you started flowering? Queens and princes and the most beautiful odalisques would stand and gaze in wonder. I thought when I grow old, I would sit in your shade and let your flowers drizzle on me.

Has the thing I fear most happened? Is there death in my touch?

(There's a PS to the parijat episode. One of my earliest readers caught me with my pants down. He pointed out that I had got it wrong. The parijat grows from a seed and not from replanting a branch.)

A Highly Personal View of Trees or Perhaps Just Mumbo-Jumbo

When did I start noticing trees? When did I fall in love with the big trees like the tamarind and the raintree, the banyan, the peepul (the *Ficus religiosa*), the wild badam, the teak, the birches? I wonder whether as usual sex was the prime mover, at least at the start? There was a pink shower cassia or *Cassia bakeriana* in front of my second-floor room in Pune when

I lived as a paying guest on Apte Road. It was so seductive when it was flowering, it was nothing short of an erotic experience to look at it. Years later I discovered the tamarind tree in the Pune University premises. How could a tree as huge as a mature tamarind have leaves which are so delicate and dainty? Many Indians love flowering bushes and the straight Ashoka trees which serve as natural screens when you want privacy from your neighbour's bungalow and inquisitive eyes. But it is the big, shady trees which have been around for decades if not centuries which exercise a magical and obsessive hold on me.

It came as a shock to me when the late Arun Kolatkar, who was my partner in advertising and also one of the finest poets in the country, told me in the 1970s that the Western Ghats, some hundred kilometres from Mumbai, were densely forested till fairly recently. It came back to me then that in my childhood it was well known that tigers and panthers used to roam freely here. The trees have almost totally disappeared in the last couple of decades from the Western Ghats and so have the big cats.

Sometime in the 1970s, or perhaps it was the 1980s, the Mumbai municipality planted casuarina trees on the small stretch of Chowpatty beach in south Mumbai so that their roots would help retain the sand in place. The trees grew rapidly, and it was a pleasure to sit under them next to the sea, even when the tropical sun was heating up the earth like an oven. But within barely ten or twelve years, the casuarinas had been cut down because apparently the trees had become a pick-up point for the ladies of the night. There was never any question of putting up powerful lights to discourage the pimps taking over or getting a policeman or two to do the rounds at night. The preservation of the sands on the beach was totally forgotten and the trees hacked down. It was the classic Mumbai solution to problems. If the pavements are occupied by vendors, get rid of the pavements instead of getting rid of the illegal vendors.

Something has gone terribly wrong with the Indian mindset. As children we were taught that the kings and emperors of yore in India planted shady trees so that the denizens and pilgrims who traversed the land could rest in their shade. But unbridled and systematic deforestation has been the mark of post-Independence India. The timber merchants, the sandalwood and the timber mafia have consistently erased vast swathes of forests. All over the country the water table is hitting rock bottom, and the great rivers which are considered goddesses and worshipped have shrunk drastically. We are seeing droughts and floods that could turn out to be forerunners of what the climatologists have been warning us about for over two decades, a disaster of an order that is impossible to grasp. Perhaps this is what officials think of as modernization.

The sad truth is that only when the trees in my front yard, so to speak, that's the Chowpatty beach, were so mindlessly cut down did I sit up with a jolt. It was as if the powers that be had cut my own legs. But that too does not do justice to the way I have come to think of trees; as I said earlier, the big trees. I doubt if there is any other creature more giving and more generous than trees. We are in denial, not just India but in the world at large, of even the fundamental truths which science has taught us.

Let me repeat the clichés, because we insist on forgetting or ignoring them. Trees are literally the breath of life. They oxygenate the atmosphere by absorbing carbon dioxide. They bear flowers which the bees and butterflies cross-pollinate, and they bear marvellous fruit. They are home to billions of birds. Thanks to them the temperature can come down by as much as three degrees in the hottest of countries. They hold on tightly to the earth, thus reducing landslides and mud slides. They never malign, and they don't have a mean bone in them. They welcome you with not two open arms but a hundred and even a thousand.

And then there is the matter of aesthetics. Here is the Maharaj Kumar talking about the grass in the monsoons in Chittor in *Cuckold*.

> It had begun to drizzle. He loved Chittor in the rains. Everything, even the stones, was just a little out of focus. The Tower of fame and the Digambara temple were lost in low-flying clouds. He always thought of the grass in the monsoons as an actor waiting impatiently in the wings to make his appearance. A knock, a slight drizzle and entire armies of grass showed up overnight. Why does green mean so much and make such a difference to men and women? Why is it that no one sings of the dry brown of summer with the same joy and excitement? Is green the colour of life or is it the colour of madness? The green of grass is a possessive, greedy colour. It doesn't have an inch of space for anyone else. I want, I want, I want. It takes over and like the salesman at a cloth shop, unrolls yard after yard of grass till all the three square miles of Chittor are a waving field of green blades. Every now and then you come across a puddle of sky. Suddenly there's a chink in the heavens from which the light tumbles out. Somewhere in the distance, I'm sure, there will be a rainbow.

I have no proof, none whatsoever for what I am about to say, and you would be quite right to believe that I have lost it, that I am trying to pass off some hokum as mystical pantheism.

The very presence of trees disseminates the peace that transcends all understanding. Indeed, if there is divinity made visible, it is in the trees around us. For years the Prince Siddhartha searched for the secret of breaking out of the cycle of life and death. Only when he sat under a peepal tree did he find enlightenment and became the Buddha. Perhaps I am making causal connections which are merely speculative and nothing more. But trees have always had a sacred significance in Indian culture. For me there is no being more contemplative than an ancient tree and none other which can give the benediction of enlightenment.

The highest gesture of respect and reverence for an Indian is to touch the guru's feet. Even today a disciple of a great musician will bend down and pay homage by touching the master's feet in public. I have so far not been given to that kind of obeisance. But of late whenever I see a magnificent timeless tree, I want to go and touch its feet.

Cinema

The Film Critic and His 'Artiste'

DO YOU KNOW WHERE film critics go when they die? Where all critics go? To hell. Not the ordinary hell where most sinners are sent, but a special hell where filmmakers take vengeance on all those who mercilessly savaged their films.

But there's a fate worse than going to hell. It's reserved for film critics, opaque and insensitive and unseeing, who have no foresight and vision, who are so ossified and dogmatic, they have to condemn any genuine original spark; who fail to understand and appreciate something momentous happening in front of their eyes: a departure, a trendsetter, a great work of art that leaves its mark on the times and modifies and changes our world view. For such critics there is hell on earth. They become the laughing stock of the world. The readers they are supposed to lead, spit on them. And as every critic's nightmare overtakes them, they recede into a world larger than our cosmos, a land called oblivion. No greater punishment hath God for critics than that they be forgotten.

Remember what happened to those asses, those dumb buffoons, who couldn't see beyond their noses, the ones who thought T. S. Eliot's *The Wasteland* was a literary atrocity, a barren desert the sooner forgotten the better? Or the fools who thought Impressionism and Van Gogh and Lautrec and Degas were aberrations and heretics? What happened was simply this: the works of these artists outlasted the critics and will outlast most anything else if the nukes don't put paid to all of us.

Ah, the tragedy of critics, knowledge comes but wisdom never. I can see my fate, I have the power and the knowledge to change it and yet I persist in my fatal blindness, in my obdurate obtuseness. When the critics damned Eliot, there was at least the courage and solace and strength that comes from numbers. For after all, only Ezra Pound and a few others – you could count them on three fingers – saw the light. But I walk a lonely, lonely path. For almost all the other critics have been blessed, partaken of manna and seen the light while I continue not to see the error of my ways. The majority of our art filmmakers bore the pants off me. In my heart of hearts, I know that I am a tasteless philistine. I infinitely prefer the crassness of the Hindi commercial cinema to the pretensions of the art film. Portentousness is the one unforgiveable sin. Untouched by life, the stranglehold of our theoreticians who pretend to be filmmakers injects a deadly sterility to all that they touch. Their impulse and motivation are a thesis; the only way they know to translate that thesis into film is schematically. They decide beforehand upon the values and interpretations to be given to each element in their film as if it were a problem in algebra where X is equal to 2 and Y is equal to 7. They seem incapable of grasping the simple truth that no thesis, however urgent, lofty and important, is material for a film unless it's touched and illuminated by art. Great and good intentions do not a great film make.

One must take the consequence of one's actions and beliefs. If the fringe cinema in Hindi is doing pioneering and seminal work, if it's a full thirty or fifty years ahead of its time, if the new wave filmmakers are building a film aesthetic on the frontiers of cinema, and I am unfeeling and unseeing, then I deserve to be damned. There are advantages to being a voice in the wilderness, in being a minority of one or less. Even if one raves and rants, there's little risk of being heard, leave alone being taken seriously. One's effectiveness or nuisance value is not limited, it is happily non-existent.

My friend Iqbal Masud, one of the few film critics in India worth reading, has a genuine understanding and love of the film medium. He also has a perspective that encompasses other disciplines like sociology, politics and psychology. In our past few meetings, he has frequently called me an iconoclast.

I am unworthy of the title. My concerns, preoccupations and bees in the bonnet are orthodox and old-fashioned. They boil down to just one thing: the search for good cinema. Give me Olmi's *The Tree of Wooden Clogs*, Bondarchuk's *Steppe, Iphigenia* by the Greek director whose name escapes me; give me Fellini's *Amarcord*, Adoor Gopalakrishnan's *Mukhamukham,* or Ray's *Pather Panchali* and I'll have been effectively shut up. Cross my heart, you won't hear from me again. Instead, one gets that hollow rattle called *Paris Texas*, or Bertolucci's abysmal *Luna* which was belatedly shown last year at Delhi or the primitive, simplistic and facile *Chokh.*

Instead one gets the Hindi art filmmaker-critic combine in India. Both parties are repeatedly and tirelessly pleased to find that they are intellectual and capable of generating and understanding refined, avant-garde cinema. It is the Indian critic – and he is the one who systematically killed the simple, straightforward 'artist' and invented the 'artiste'. A small, marginal example of the filmmaker-critic axis but symptomatic and symbolic of the hypocrisy, the flatulence, and the smugness of our critical tradition.

There are not too many ways in which the Indian film critic can boost his self-importance. If he discovers an 'artiste', he may bask in the reflected glory of that discovery.

It's not after an encounter with the film itself, but only after an interview with the writer-director that he detects hidden depths and profound symbolism. Having detected an original thinker, he proceeds to be his interpreter and exigesist, and in the process pats his own back.

If he can put the whole thing in high-sounding gobbledegook jargon, he establishes a niche for himself as a celluloid intellectual and a film theoretician.

It is the critic's business to interpret, explain and illuminate; make interdisciplinary and intercultural connections, show the relationship between life and art, detect trends while they are nascent. It is also his duty to excoriate the pretenders, not to suffer fools and frauds, to clarify the issues involved, and to give readers an outsiders' inside view of the art form. And moreover, to push filmmakers themselves to greater self-examination and rigour.

Bollywood and Me: The Family Connection

THE MYTHICAL LAND CALLED Bollywood is in the city of Bombay or Mumbai as it's called today, though try as you might to locate it, it won't show up in any Google map. Bollywood, however, was not even a term used in the days when I was a child. (We'll need a Dr Samuel Johnson or the Oxford dictionary to trace its very first appearance and how the term gained currency.) One thing though is certain. My relationship with Hindi films and the film industry by whatever name you call it, has remained a schizophrenic one. Schizophrenic not in the technical psychological sense but in so far as it is imbued with a split or divided consciousness, and is uneasy, ambivalent and contradictory. There are times when I am forced to admit that I'm in denial.

My parents almost never saw a Hindi film, at least not from as far back a time that my memory extends. We only saw Hollywood or British films or on the rare occasion when an Italian or Japanese classic like *Bicycle Thief* or *Rashomon* made it to Bombay. If you happen to take a peek at an MRI of my brain or an electroencephalogram as an earlier brain-mapping was called, you would see that instead of trillions of brain cells and neurons, there was only white bread pulp there, all of it emanating from Hollywood. Indeed if you trace my lineage, I have to confess that it is the worst. I am at heart, soul, body and flesh, the purest of that tribe called the philistines. Even as a child, the one thing that I hankered after was Hollywood movies like *Quo Vadis*, *Robin Hood*, *Magnificent Obsession*, *Samson and Delilah*. I think you've got the picture.

And yet my connection to the never-never land of Bollywood goes back to my childhood. My aunt, Leela Atya, as in my father's sister, was for a brief time a superstar of the Indian screen. She had been first a stage actress and then had graduated to films. I think by the time I was born she had had four silver jubilees to her name. She was something of an accidental maverick, a pathbreaker and a pioneer. She was married when fairly young, not an arranged marriage but what is still known on the subcontinent as a love marriage. My father used to speak glowingly of her husband as a quiet but unmistakable intellectual giant. I used to think that this was little more than the rose-tinted awe felt by a man who had not had a chance to finish his secondary schooling for a brother-in-law who very likely had earned his master's or whatever abroad. But some time long after my father was dead, a highly respected and extremely difficult to please Marathi playwright told me that he had read a rare copy of my aunt's husband's autobiography, and the man was nothing less than a genius.

Perhaps he was. But if he was, then he must have been a rather lazy genius. He and my aunt had four children, three boys and a girl. The boys looked like the cliché of Greek heroes from the Iliad or the Odyssey (that we carry in our minds) and like them all three of them had tragic fates. The daughter was luckier, she died soon after she was born. My uncle had in the meantime become involved with one of the great Marxists of the time called M. N. Roy who was on the most wanted list of the British and had gone underground in my uncle's place. I forget whether M. N. Roy was caught or got away, but my uncle who I never saw, lost interest in working for a living, and Leela Atya went back to studies to support the family.

In the early days of Indian cinema, actresses in the celluloid world belonged to a rather dubious background. They came either from an Anglo-Indian family or from the nautch-cum-singing-girl tradition. I remember Leela Atya's photograph in a university gown in our album (one of many others) holding her BA certificate in her hands. It was not merely unusual but almost unheard of for an educated woman from a respectable family to join the stage or films. Mother of four and a film heroine to boot, not even the only two other educated actresses at the time, Devika Rani or Duga Khote, could beat that combination.

Look at the films of an earlier day, for example, the very first significant effort in celluloid to deal with the subject of untouchability, Devika Rani's *Achut Kanya* or the entire oeuvre of the matinee idol and great singing star, K. L. Saigal, their acting style and speech delivery make one wonder whether they're just slow-witted or are they addressing an audience which they believe is brain-damaged. This is an artificial style that is alien to indigenous speech patterns and can put one off no end. What makes it even more difficult to explain is that Hollywood exerted such a strong influence on Hindi films, and the reigning style of Hollywood was naturalism. Think of any number of B-grade noir films or the quick-fire delivery of James Cagney or the coquetry of Vivien Leigh as Scarlett in the opening sequences, and the difference is glaring. If the Hindi film had deliberately chosen to go its own way in making every kind of movie, whether it was a social drama, a tragedy, a patriotic paean, comedy or a thriller, into a musical, had it also set out deliberately to evolve an artificial and stilted delivery in the same vein as the Japanese had developed the Noh or Kabuki tradition? I doubt it but I am not an authority on the history of Indian cinema. And oddly not too many historians or theorists of cinema dwell on this aspect.

How did my aunt address this issue? I'm afraid I never got a chance to see a single movie where she was the heroine. But if one is to believe critics and the actor, Ashok Kumar, with whom she made all four of her hits, she was one of the first to move away from both the bombastic delivery of the then theatre actors as well as the quasi hashish-induced variety of leaden and ponderous style of speech which was the hallmark of the other films. It was the 1980s or perhaps even later that Ashok Kumar, who had one of the longest careers at the top in Hindi films, said that my aunt had taught him one of the most important lessons in acting. Like most actors, he recalled, he too mistook acting to be an exercise in narcissism. All he was interested in was his own lines and his shots until Leela pointed out that much of acting was first about listening to the others in a shot or scene and only secondly about responding. If you were genuinely listening, then your face and body language became a mirror of your mind (and reflected what was going on in it).

I did see her on the stage once, though it was long after she had been downgraded to the status of a character actress. She had translated *The Sacred Flame*, a play of Somerset Maugham and acted in it along with her second son, and she was, to say the least, good; very good as a matter of fact. At no point did she mouth her lines as if she had memorized them. Instead the situation, the character and the dilemma the character was faced with at a particular moment of crisis dictated her response.

There was no Atya or aunt attached to Leela's screen name, but she was not exactly what one would imagine an actress to look like today. Forget oomph, she seemed to lack the kind of striking presence or in-your-face (aura/flash) magnetism one associates with a star. In the couple of brief excerpts I have seen from her films, she almost invariably wore two plaits. Was this to make her look younger or was it the fashion of the day? Whatever the reason, there was no doubt about it, she exerted a compelling charisma (attraction) over her fans, and they numbered in the hundreds of thousands. The premieres of her movies in Lahore in what is today Pakistan, Bombay or any place else were major events and she was mobbed wherever she went. I remember the ambivalent attitude of my closest friend's mother while I was in school. It was only years later that I learnt why she was hostile to me. Her late husband had known my aunt and had had a major crush on her.

The woman who was an actress and was known as Leela was a misty presence on the distant edges of my consciousness in childhood. We were the poor relatives though neither she nor my other paternal kinsfolk ever treated us as such. She was an exotic creature who would drive up once in a while in her black Citroën, park the car on the road and walk up to our tiny home. We lived in perhaps the most genteel area of Bombay in those days and hardly anybody was uncouth enough to let their curiosity get the better of them, and yet there was no mistaking the repressed excitement in our own buildings and those neighbouring ours. Once in a rare while my parents, my brother and I would go to her house in Mahim. It was a one-storeyed building in a leafy grove which gave no inkling of how sprawling it was. Atya stayed on the first floor. I look back in time and find it difficult to believe that the floor of a house in Bombay was made of wooden parquet. There was a fridge in the house and God knows how many bedrooms, though I myself never had an occasion to check them out.

My father's brother too made a brief appearance in films. Strangely enough I did go with my parents to see one of the movies where he had a bit role. Perhaps it was the only film he ever acted in. Was he any good? Who knows? I have no memory of him on the screen. As I sit here on a sunny evening in an apartment in Zurich, I realize that my memory is playing tricks on me. I am not as innocent as I make myself out to be. I was visiting my eldest aunt, Akka Atya who lived in Secunderabad in the state of Andhra Pradesh. Her husband had been the manager of two theatres near the racecourse, the Dreamland and Tivoli. Perhaps that's how she got addicted to films. All her children too were connected with Hindi cinema in one way or the other, the eldest appearing in the credits of Raj Kapoor's hit film *Awara* as a publicity agent. Now my aunt had become a widow and took in almost every movie running in town. She took me to see a weepy called *Dillagi* with Suraiya and the actor Shyam who died while shooting another film called *Mela*. I am not quite sure if he fell off a horse while shooting or the animal kicked him. What I do remember is that I was so bored and restless watching *Dillagi* I set a record of sorts. I forced my poor aunt who was in the throes of the tragic fate of the two star-crossed lovers to take me to the toilet nine times. I think there was still half an hour before *Dillagi* came to an unhappy end but my aunt got fed up and marched me home. I stayed with her for two or three more months, but she had learnt her lesson. She did not take me for another Hindi film.

My relationship with Bollywood remains troubled and strained to this day. But the operative word is ambivalent. For even as I am repelled by Hindi cinema, I am simultaneously intensely drawn to it because of the music. The music was entirely an overheard phenomenon since we had neither a radio, not even a single band medium wave one nor a record player. Not many of our neighbours did either. We were still a comparatively civilized city and did not believe in sharing our radio transmissions gratis with the rest of the subcontinent. So it's a bit of a mystery how and where I got to listen to film songs and become a compulsive 24/7 music afficionado. Perhaps part of the answer lies in the fact that I was lucky to be born in what was surely the golden age of melody in Hindi cinema. But there is a much larger question that remains unanswered. Silent films in France, America, England, India as well as everywhere else in the world were accompanied by a live musical score. Cinema took a giant technological step forward when it incorporated a soundtrack with dialogue and music into the 36 mm film itself. But why and how Indian cinema chose to have songs in every movie barring the rare exception will always be a matter of speculation and theorizing about the *nautanki* or folk theatre of song and dance traditions migrating to the new medium.

In 1991 I was invited to attend a seminar on what has turned into a major sub-discipline of sociology called public culture. Discourse in most educational fields, starting with politics, literature, social theory, gender studies at that time, was rife with technical jargon and obfuscation borrowed from a degraded understanding of Derrida and deconstruction and political correctness. During a discussion on Indian cinema, I put both my feet into my mouth when I ventured to ask why Indian cinema, but particularly Hindi cinema, despite our deep roots in mythology, mesmerizing oral storytelling traditions and the remarkable legacy of epics like the Ramayana and the Mahabharata, failed so miserably in telling stories when it came to the cinema. There was a hushed silence and the Indian scholars along with the rest of the august academicians blushed at my embarrassing naivety and shushed me as quickly as possible. I was told that I was not only completely off the mark but exhibiting colonial attitudes and prejudices.

I must confess that unfortunately there's not been much improvement in my condition, and I have not learnt my lesson. I'm still asking the same questions. There is, however, a curious paradox. While Hindi film stories and screenplays, barring honourable exceptions, can defy logic, and the direction and acting can fluctuate between shabby and abysmal, the songs and the lyrics were frequently memorable and many a time evinced a touch of genius. And let's not forget, an average Hindi film had anywhere between ten and fourteen songs in those days. And if they were any good, and most of them were shockingly and consistently good, they gave music for five to ten films per year. That's anywhere between sixty to a hundred songs, if not more, a year. How many western pop song composers, I wonder, can work under so much pressure? And yet keep pushing the bar in terms of innovation and quality?

By definition the film or pop song is ephemeral, momentary and evanescent. And hence rarely taken seriously. But think about it, there are few phenomena that are as inclusive as film or the pop songs. They are the great equalizers. They create that wonderful space where the rich and the poor, the cognoscenti and the philistines, the caste Hindus and the outcastes can all drink at the same fountain. Music is not only intangible in its essence and effects but the pleasure it gives can never be measured. What we tend to forget or dismiss is that the quantum of joy that film music gives rises exponentially by the sheer fact of the numbers to whom it appeals. We need to ask ourselves whether there is an elitist and insidious superiority in our cut-and-dried notion that classical music, whether north Indian, western, or any other variety is better? They are two separate entities setting out to do very different kinds of things, and we are blessed if we can partake of and delight in both of them.

Star Power

EIGHTY-FIVE PER CENT of students in the last year of school or college in Indian cities want to be movie stars. In towns and villages the number is higher. There's only one sure way of getting into the movies. No, it's not the casting couch, stupid. All you need is a superstar for a father or mother. Raj, Randhir and Rishi Kapoor, Sharmila Tagore, Vinod Khanna, Anil Kapoor, Shotgun Sinha, Sunil Dutt, Tanuja, Dharmendra, Amitabh Bachchan were all stars and so are their children. Now if you didn't choose your parents carefully, the only other alternative is to become a model or Miss India and hope and pray you will step out from the catwalk and walk straight on to the silver screen. Aishwarya Rai, Sushmita Sen, Priyanka Chopra, Lara Dutta, Bipasha Basu and many others, they all took this route to stardom. (Imagine what would happen to the subcontinent, if all 85 per cent had their way. There would be nobody in the audience in the cinema halls. And hardly any business managers, doctors, chartered accountants, engineers or IT specialists.)

Forget becoming stars, the fact is not even 0.005 per cent of the aspiring actors will end up being extras. Okay, I doctored those numbers but they are close, very close to the actual figures. The hold the film medium has on Indians is nothing short of astounding. It's not only that educated young women from all classes of society aspire to stardom, it's embarrassing how hard and shamelessly many parents will try to promote their children's film careers. Talk about volte-faces and sea changes in societal mores and values. It was inconceivable around the 1920s and 1930s for Indian women from middle-class families to enter the film industry. As for the rich, they would have preferred honour killings to seeing their daughters or *bahus* in the movies. Our children's and grandchildren's entire spectrum of general knowledge revolves almost entirely around the lives of film stars and films. And yet you will come up with an absolute blank when the subject is the early years of cinema in India.

In recent years there has been a steady stream of books by foreign and local scholars as well as dilettantes who write hagiographic coffee-table books about matinee idols from the 1950s and the 1970s. Raj Kapoor has always been celebrated as the 'great showman', and the new books have continued in the same old almost reverential tone. If possible they are even more politically correct and will praise the RK banner's social commitment instead of critically probing the RK oeuvre. Dilip Kumar and Amitabh Bachchan have also come in for similar genuflecting treatment. So it's a salutary change to find that Oxford University Press is bringing out a series on South Asian Cinema. Neepa Majumdar's book *Wanted Cultured Ladies Only! Female Stardom and Cinema in India 1930-1950s* is a scholarly study of a crucial and formative period in our film history. As such, it raises high expectations, especially since its range, its academic approach, its seriousness of purpose, its tone and language and its scholarship will no doubt set the bar for the books that will follow in the series and the general run of books on Indian cinema in the future.

WCLO may claim to be about cinema in India but it deals mostly with Hindi cinema. It's perhaps the world's worst kept secret that Bollywood survives on its parasitical connection with Hollywood. Things are changing substantially for the better on the fringes of Bollywood but mainstream Hindi cinema faces the West and prays five times a day for inspiration to that sign on the hillside in Los Angeles. But it was the same from the very beginning. The title of the introduction to Majumdar's book is 'Translocating Hollywood Stardom in India'. And that's exactly what the book proceeds to show us in chapter after chapter. However, the process is not as simple as a duplication or a cloning. Translocation also means transforming and putting an Indian spin on it.

The backdrop to cinema in the decades following the 1930s was the national freedom struggle and the notion of what constituted Indian womanhood. Women may have performed a very public role and stood shoulder to shoulder with men in resisting British rule but there was no confusion about or question of crossing the *Lakshman Rekha*: the stage and the cinema were a no-no. Full stop. That posed an almost irresolvable dilemma for the art form. In the good old days men acted the roles of women on the stage but that was a trifle difficult in cinema with the camera doing close-ups, and besides, the times were a-changing. The only way out seemed to be to recruit women from a different class. Curiously or perhaps with an elegant and quintessential Indian form of logic, cinema itself took an equivocal stance in its depiction of women.

In the 1920s and even the 1930s, female actresses were recruited from amongst nautch or singing girls. They performed a central role in entertaining the masses but there was a stigma to their names, and they could never be acceptable in so-called 'decent' society. Then came the crop of Anglo-Indian actresses. As with the earlier female protagonists, the sterling contribution of Anglo-Indian women too is almost forgotten. Perhaps this is because many Anglo-Indians left the country once the British departed, and also because in the post-Independence phase they seemed to occupy a no man's land in our perception and imagination.

Since we do not have a national academy of cinema (there are small mercies, you will admit) or major privately funded institutions like the National Centre for the Performing Arts in the country for cinema, it is doubtful if, however late in the day, we'll honour wonderful actresses like Ruby Myers aka Sulochana and Mary Ann Evans who came to be known as Fearless Nadia, the stunt queen, or those who came before them. It's unfortunate that Majumdar does not tell us whether these Anglo-Indian actresses knew Hindi or had to learn it. If it was the latter, did they speak with an accent? Again, while the author quotes from J. B. H. Wadia's *Those Were the Days*, the remarkable transition in their lives does not seem to interest her. They are not mere milestones and signifiers in the evolution of the concept of a star, they are women who dared to cross from anonymity to a profession that was considered taboo. They are rebels, daredevils in real life, and their stories, however briefly told, would have made the book lively and told us what made them take the risk and change their lives.

Durga Khote, one of the first actresses to come from a cultured, educated background also gets lopsided treatment. We are not told what was considered a cultured or educated family. What did Khote study? Did she come from a middle-class family or was it a notch above? We are told that she was married and then divorced before she got into films. Did she choose to go into films? Or did she, like Leela Chitnis who had to support three children, have little choice but to look for any employment she could get? And why films? If she was educated, could she not have got a job in another profession? Was it that she felt acting was her calling? Did it give her a sense of empowerment?

Neepa Majumdar puts forward a convincing analysis of the sleight of hand and the underlying conflicting standards involved in an episode in Raj Kapoor's *Jagte Raho* (directed by Shambhu Mitra), and which would occur repeatedly in films like *Aadmi* or *Amar Jyoti*, where the heroines assert their independence and yet in the end relinquish everything they have stood for and follow the paradigm of the model Hindu woman.

Film journals and even film production companies bemoaned at that time that the country did not have female stars as Hollywood had. Ironically this was due to the fact that journalists in the early 1930s refused to write about the private lives of the women who acted in films in those days. The times have indeed changed. Today, the relationship between stars and gossip columnists and film magazines is symbiotic. Stars may complain about their privacy not being respected but they can hardly think of a worse fate than being ignored.

Majumdar's book ranges over a wide variety of subjects. There's even a chapter called 'The Embodied Voice' which deals with playback singing, especially the aura associated with Lata Mangeshkar and, to a lesser degree, with her sibling, Asha Bhosle. There is a substantial section devoted to double roles and their significance for the stars themselves and the way the audience perceived them. Her chapter called 'Real and Imagined Stars' is particularly noteworthy for clearly exposing the hypocrisy and double standards at work in the Indian response to women in films.

But there is a problem at the heart of the book. It is almost a study in split personalities. There seem to be two Neepa Majumdars. One who sets out to be as opaque as possible. She seems to hail from the late 1970s, 1980s and 1990s when the mark of scholarship was to obfuscate with inaccessible jargon. It's as if she's hell-bent on being as intractable and tortuous as possible. But if she is difficult and unreadable at such times, you should read many of the other theorists she quotes. They are many, and they mutilate, mangle and desecrate the language in the name of scholarship. Let me for a minute give them the benefit of the doubt. If what they are writing is so philosophically complex and abstruse that they had to perforce cull it from the fringes and margins of language, then perhaps one could have made concessions. But it's nothing of the kind. Many a time it's nothing more than self-aggrandizing abracadabra.

The curious thing is that every now and then Majumdar will, without notice, lapse into normal English. You can actually understand what she is saying. She comes to grips with the dilemmas posed by a profession that suffered from the double talk of a society that could not square its prurience with its genteel pretensions, and in the bargain the reader too feels that he's getting a grip on the subject. Then ten or twenty pages later, he's at sea all over again. My copy of the book is strewn with abbreviations. GHUs (God Help Us) and ETGLCHUs (Even the Good Lord Can't Help Us.)

Cinema is a very recent art form, one that is a mass art form. But cinema, good and bad, is an amazingly juicy subject. Why study the subject if the intention is to squeeze every last drop of the juice and fun out and make it dry, arid and insufferably boring in the name of a lofty calling called high theory? The best theorists shed light and bring insights to their subjects and they are like viruses, they infect you with their passion, their excitement, their doubts, and they push the envelope. Will someone get them to engage with Indian cinema? Please?

The Other Bollywood

IT IS MY HALF-SERIOUS, half-jocular thesis that the Indian brain's relationship with the moving image is unique. I suspect that there is a very different electro-chemical reaction in the synapses when Indians watch cinema and TV.

Indian films, critics like to proclaim, are nothing but escapist fare, an escape from reality. They are so wrong. It is the preferred reality; it is so much more real than the banality of daily life. Films heighten everything; they heighten emotion, everything happens at crisis pitch, the fate of the protagonists hangs precariously between life and death. Truly, you live larger than life in cinema.

A B-grade actor became the President of the United States. But that's not a patch on what Indian actors become for their fans. Nowhere else in the world are actors deified. In Calcutta there's a temple dedicated to the super-survivor, Hindi film superstar Amitabh Bachchan. The phenomenon is even more pronounced in south India. Rajkumar, Rajnikant, NTR (N. T. Ramarao, actor, producer, director who became chief minister of Andhra Pradesh), are all worshipped and have stupendous followings. But the supreme example of the deification of actors is the late MGR (R for Ramachandran). Fat, flabby and way past his prime, he was as close to divinity as a resident of this planet can get. Then in 1977, they elected him chief minister of Tamil Nadu. When this darling of the millions suffered from renal failure, his devotees rushed to offer him their own organs, and when he died a few years later, some of them proceeded to commit suicide because the very idea of living without their idol was unthinkable.

Not only does our cinema turn stars into gods, it is powerful enough to create new gods and goddesses. Santoshi Maa is perhaps the first goddess mothered by cinema. Now she, along with the rest of the Hindu pantheon, smiles benignly at her millions of devotees from shrines, temples, posters and calendars.

A Change in Perspective

Even a diehard cynic will admit that there has been a sea change in the western response to Bollywood movies since the 1990s. It is ironic that despite all talk of literary and aesthetic independence, it is economics and market forces which colour, dominate, and even determine our artistic tastes. For decades after India won independence, the subcontinent was considered a basket case, way beyond salvaging. Poverty, starvation, famines, malnutrition, floods, rampant and endemic corruption .... the imagery of despair and hopelessness never changed. And intimately connected with it, as if it was a reflection of the mess the country was in, was another lost cause in western eyes: that bizarre animal called the Indian film.

Who would want to watch three-hour-long Hindi films that seemed to go on for an interminable thirty? They were just a hotch-potch, a potpourri, an inedible mishmash. Comedy, melodrama, high tragedy, social themes, coincidences galore, tear-jerkers, song and dance numbers, archetypal motifs like friendship, betrayal and, of course, love stories unlimited, they were all rolled into one and the same movie.

Come the 1990s, India began to fervently embrace liberal policies, and opened its doors to foreign industry and business. As the new millennium stepped in, multinational corporations perceived that the country had a 200-million-strong middle class and what a bonanza and market opportunity it was. Overnight we became 'India Shining', an economy poised for a vertical take-off. And lo and behold, Bollywood was in. It was exotic, it had pizzazz and it rocked. Hindi movies were no longer infra dig. Quite the contrary. The Swiss, the Germans, the French and the Brits now discovered that kitsch was indeed endearing, the over-the-top sentimentality heart-warming, and the dance numbers with seventy chorus girls, fun. In Germany alone, there were over forty Shah Rukh Khan fan clubs. Cinestar and other movie multiplexes in Europe were now exhibiting Hindi films regularly. Times had indeed changed.

Had the Hindi film undergone a radical change? Or was it the West which had altered its standards? Certainly recent Bollywood films had a polish and technical slickness that was lacking earlier. Bollywood stars had become slim, svelte, very sexy and had a pan-universal appeal. The number of extras for the dance sequences had jumped from ten to seventy or a hundred, and a whole new genre of Bollywood dancing was now the rage. But at heart the Hindi movie was still the same, shamelessly plagiarizing from Hollywood, a *bhel* and a *khichri* of every conceivable genre and a monument to excess. But with one small but significant new wrinkle. The independent or 'indie' spirit exemplified by the Sundance festival was finding an echo in Bollywood.

The Art Cinema Movement

In the 1960s and 1970s there was a movement amongst some film directors to make cinema more meaningful. It was the start of what came to be known as parallel or art cinema. This was indeed a laudable enterprise, especially since many of these directors had strong Marxist leanings and one would have expected them to address and inspire both

India's vast working-class people and village populations. But unfortunately, many of these directors made such inaccessible films that they almost completely failed to draw large audiences, and the whole parallel cinema movement did not really challenge Bollywood products. However, a few directors like Shyam Benegal and Govind Nihalani explored the middle ground between the two schools with films like *Ankur*, *Nishant* and *Aakrosh*.

The Other Bollywood

Since the beginning of the new century, a new generation of directors is making its presence felt. They are savvy and know how to exploit audience segments, benefiting from the economics of multiplexes. This is where 'the other Bollywood' was born and has the potential to make a big difference. These filmmakers work within the Bollywood ambience, use mainstream actors, they have no qualms about using Bollywood conventions like songs and dances, and yet manage to create a separate space for themselves and be true to their vision.

Two outstanding films from 'the other Bollywood' which you are going to watch in this festival are both by the same director, Vishal Bharadwaj. He started out as a music director in slightly offbeat Hindi films and then, without giving up his musical career, moved to screenplay writing in collaboration with others and began to direct subjects of his choice. These films will prove my thesis that it is possible to make really good cinema in the commercial format. Both *Maqbool* and *Omkara* are loosely adapted from the Shakespeare classics *Macbeth* and *Othello*. I use the word adapted advisedly. Bharadwaj is not in awe of Shakespeare. He's obviously intrigued by the bard's work, but he does not need to follow it sedulously or slavishly. He's fascinated by the central or core idea, and from there on, he's his own man.

The best homage he can pay Shakespeare is to appropriate his work and treat it as his own without compromising its integrity.

When a novel is adapted to the film medium, the audience is constantly comparing the one with the other. If possible, forget the original work for the time being. Take these two movies at face value, and evaluate them as independent works. Only then will you do justice to both, the original plays and the new versions. And each will enrich the other.

I could go on and on. And ruin the movies for you. Let's talk after the two shows, not before.

Ladies and gentlemen, welcome to 'the other Bollywood'.

Film Reviews

Conan's Hedonistic Ode to the Body: *Conan the Destroyer*

Do the aficionados of *Star Wars* follow the adventures of Indiana Jones? Do the devotees of these two pay obeisance to Conan? Or are these three watertight camps and does each camp, convinced of its superiority, sneer at the others? Is there a correlation between the fantasies that children choose and what they become as adults? Do the Star Wars kids become Republicans and the Indiana Jones ones Democrats? Do the fairy tale followers of Walt Disney and Snow White end up voting against abortion, and does the Conan crowd support the Contras cause?

There are a couple of PhD theses here, maybe many more. Have Stanford, Yale and Harvard gone to work on them yet? The mythical figures mentioned here are by and large irrelevant in our context. The English-speaking, English movie-going audience is a marginal phenomenon in India. But the same kind of research needs to be done in our country. We make so much of our children, at least of male children, and yet we are so utterly indifferent to what they read or watch.

Was it the cardboard-cut-out culture of *Chandamama* that made us choose MGR and NTR to rule our lives and shape our destinies? What really is the effect of eight hours of TV or video daily on our children's brains?

This prelude, meditation, or plain shooting off at a tangent, is nothing short of an insult to *Conan the Destroyer*, visiting at the New Excelsior this week. Because Conan is fun, pure and simple, wholesome or unwholesome be damned. Richard Fleischer, the director, is having a ball, and if you'll stop pretending to be a serious, rational being and just let yourself go, you too might end up having a lark.

One of the most memorable images of cinema, one is told repeatedly, is the extreme close-up of the face of that unbelievable caricature of the Method school of acting, Marlon Brando, in *Apocalypse Now*. Well, Brando can go mumble himself into oblivion, now that Arnold Schwarzenegger's here. That first frame where the camera hangs on tightly to Arnold/Conan's torso is surely one of the great campy moments in cinema. All you can do is shake your head in awe and disbelief because, God almighty, this guy can't be for real. Someone at the press show had the gall to ask about Schwarzenegger's acting talent. Give me a break, brother. What we have here is genius in the flesh. Every rippling, bulging, straining, bursting sinew is a memento to Arnold's dedication. Is this musculature or is it enough steel to build New York City and Tokyo together? If every single popping vein in Arnold which is tauter and stouter than the cables which hold up the Golden Gate isn't a hymn to the man's acting ability, then we are not talking the same language. As one of Arnold's bodybuilding colleagues said, 'For the next thousand years, no one will look like him ... he has a combination of bone structure, muscles, body tone, muscle separation and harmony that is unique.'

One last image before we get on with Conan. We are in a five-star hotel in Mexico within motoring distance from Churubusco, one of the biggest film studios in the world. Arnold and his colleagues have had a gruelling day at the shoot and are back at their hotel. Guess what they are all about to do for relaxation? They are all going to the specially set up gymnasium fully equipped with every kind of weight and pulley machine, dumb-bells and barbells. There's Arnold, five times Mr Universe and seven times Mr Olympia, pumping iron into that neck of his which is broader than the Himalayas, and into the thighs which could feed the whole of India for a couple of years if we turned cannibals. If cinema is a visual medium, Arnold is certainly its greatest symbol.

With *Conan the Destroyer*, the saga of the Sumerian thief, wanderer, slayer with gigantic melancholies and gigantic girth continues. A wicked queen enlists Conan's help to go on an expedition with her virgin niece and her chief of guards, Bombaata, to secure a great mythical diamond and a horn, so that the marble statue of the God of Dreams (and evil and destruction) can be brought back to life. In return for this favour, she promises to bring the woman Conan loves back to life.

Even as they are about to start, the wicked queen instructs Bombaata to kill Conan as soon as the mission is successful. Strange and wondrous adventures befall Conan and the band in their search for the jewel and the horn. Conan saves a magician and an Amazonian, Zula, from death, and the two become his loyal followers. Conan knows that brawn alone will not help him on this mission. What he is up against this time is a wizard. How he defeats the man-beast who is even stronger than himself (can such a thing be possible?) and who is utterly immune to swords and other such instruments, in the mirrored chamber, is perhaps even more thrilling than the multiple mirror scene in *Enter the Dragon*.

The next stop is for the horn. En route, the virgin princess develops a crush on Conan. There is also a hilarious scene where Conan's companion, the petty thief, tries to make out with the Amazonian. It's touch and go for a while in the underground temple which houses the horn. The might of one magician is pitted against the magician Conan has saved.

But that's not the end of the adventure. Because the queen is bent upon sacrificing her niece.

Hold on to your seats. Conan won't disappoint your children or you.

One Hell of a Watchable Film: *Shakti*

It is difficult if not impossible for the critic of commercial Hindi films to take himself seriously. He hacks away with a pen or and typewriter for a machete. Week in and week out. Year in and year out he hits out, lashes and flails at the commercial cinema. What he sees must corrupt the substance of his soul. His brains must go soft, turn green and rot. You can't parody Hindi film, because consciously or unconsciously they've been parodying themselves since time began. The only way a critic can retain his sanity is by being smart-assed. Since the films he watches repeat themselves endlessly, he follows suit. Soon, without knowing it, he is parodying the parody of a parody.

The world becomes polarized. Black and white. The critic conditions himself. He feels guilty about panning everything in sight. There is a side of his vocabulary and his nature that needs to be asserted. If he is to feel constructive, he must encourage good cinema. So he begins to believe that the very act of making a different kind of film, the kind that downgrades communication and the audience and has the dubious label 'experimental films' or 'parallel cinema', makes it worthwhile.

Stick to the evidence, within the film, not the intention, not the stereotypes, not the labels like 'commercial' and 'experimental', and a critic may yet make an honest man of himself.

Shakti is really one of the biggest events in the history of Hindi cinema. Dilip Kumar and Amitabh Bachchan together for the first time. Clash of the titans, the ultimate confrontation, the glib phrases are already on the tip of my tongue. The story writers are Salim-Javed, the director is Ramesh Sippy, the three guys who put together the box-office phenomenon *Sholay* and the damp squib *Shaan*, right? The scenario, as you can see, is already explosively loaded. And the story is about a police officer and his son. Spare me, I want to scream. What we have here is a rehash of *Ganga Jamuna* and *Deewar*, *Farz aur Kanoon* and a hundred other Hindi films. Wise guy, why don't I write the review before seeing the film.

Let me not pull any punches any more. *Shakti* is one hell of a watchable film. You'll seize upon all the faults when you see it. They are many. But glory be, this is a nice tight film even if it's more than three hours long. There is something about competence, about doing a thing well that is gratifying. It's the kind of pleasure and satisfaction you get from watching a master carpenter making a table or a traditional craftsman knocking a brass plate into an exquisite frieze.

Shakti is a craftsman's film. Make no mistake, 'craftsman' is no pejorative or second-class term. One good craftsman is better than ten phoney 'artistes' with an e between the t and the s.

The first honours go to Salim-Javed. They take a hackneyed formula and turn it inside out so that every time you expect the plot to take a predictable turn, it does something different and goes its own way. In retaliation for the capture of one of his men, the villain JK kidnaps police inspector Ashvin Kumar's son Vijay. The child is brought up by JK as a crook-cum-smuggler. Son and father play chor-police till the climactic discovery scene when they recognize each other. After killing off hordes of villains, son goes to jail, is given reprieve, father and son and respective families live happily ever after.

Wrong. What happens is quite different. Vijay escapes after he has heard his father say to JK on the phone: 'You can damn well do anything you want, kill him you hear, kill him. It makes no difference to me. I'm not handing over your man to you.' It is the beginning of the son's alienation from his father. A permanent wedge is placed between them. They are set on a collision course. It is to the great credit of Salim-Javed that they never waver. The father (Dilip Kumar) is undemonstrative, and the son (Amitabh Bachchan) is a lonely, introverted brooding young man. Torn between the two is the mother.

At every critical turn in his life, instead of his father, Vijay finds a police officer. He rescues lovely Smita Patil from four young goondas on a lonely local train late at night. The next day he's charged with beating up four innocent men. The father allows the law to take its course.

Vijay gets a job in a hotel. His father wants him to leave it because the hotel is owned by a well-known smuggler. The son points out that every profession including the policeman's has its share of crooks. The father is infuriated.

When Vijay is jailed for a rigged murder, it is his smuggler patron who puts up the bail and not his father. This is the parting of ways. Vijay consciously (no tricks of fate, for once) opts for a life of crime.

At the very beginning of the film, you know that Amitabh is going to die. It's a matter of waiting and finding out how he dies ...

He dies a lonely, isolated, inaccessible man. He dies true to character. True to his character in the movie and not to the persona he has created over God knows how many Hindi films.

He is lost and bewildered. He cannot understand the nature of his relationship and bondage to his father. All his thinking life he has kept himself aloof and distant. He hates his father because, according to his lights, his father has betrayed him. Shot by his father, he wonders in the moment of death, why he still loves and respects his father. 'Because

I love you too,' his father answers. That would have been a nice, moving answer.

But Salim-Javed, like the two heroes and the director in this film, are out of character. There are no sudden revelations and instant changes of heart. This is the best thing about *Shakti*. People within the framework of the film do not move in and out of character. They are not puppets. They follow the logic of their personalities.

'Then why didn't you ever say so?' Vijay asks his father. The question is left unanswered because Vijay dies. It's also unanswered because there are no answers. We become the victims, the film seems to suggest, of the roles we play in our lives. What makes Ashvin unapproachable and rigid is not just honour and duty, but also an excessive regard for what people say. The policeman's reputation is more important to him than his son.

There is no space to go into the film's shortcomings. They are shoddy failings because they were unnecessary and easily avoidable. I am not talking about Amitabh and Dilip taking on ten to fifteen thugs single-handed. That's a rhetorical convention of the Hindi film like the song numbers. The villains are the weakest. They are neither devious nor resourceful. Salim-Javed are far too slick not to know that mafia bosses operate much more subtly, intelligently and with almost foolproof alibis.

Never mind. Within the commercial set-up, they have taken enormous risks. Critical acclaim notwithstanding, very likely they'll have to pay a heavy price at the box office.

What an intelligent director of genre films Ramesh Sippy can be. Except the slack beginning and that silly epilogue, he keeps things moving at such a fine pace, he never gives you a minute to dolly around or get bored. He has a gut feeling for tension and his touch is sure and clean. What is amazing are the performances he has elicited from Dilip Kumar and Amitabh Bachchan. Sippy has his temperamental male prima donnas under superb control. And how they benefit from it.

It's a pleasure to watch the two actors without their mannerisms. Dilip Kumar is restrained. Caught on the horns of a dilemma, between his duty as a police officer and as a father, he asks his wife, 'What went wrong? Where did we fail?' Here is this fat, podgy man with platform heels who looks ridiculous in the early youthful scenes and then grows and grows to his full stature.

Amitabh Bachchan was never so good. (I went to pan and stayed on to praise.) It's a laconic, strong performance in low-key. He does not falter or slip into the maudlin. He is an angry young man but the fire's frozen.

Shame on RD [Burman] for the songs. But the background music with the first few notes of Bach's 'Toccata and Fugue' is excellent because it's unobtrusive.

More power to *Shakti*.

Past the Gates of Hell: *Nosferatu*

If one is to do justice to Werner Herzog's *Nosferatu*, one would have to take the entire day off, maybe the night too, camp out in a mini-theatre and watch all the versions of the story, from Murnau's original 1922 *Nosferatu* to the Christopher Lee series of mainstream horror-movie *Draculas* to Polanski's whimsical treatment in *The Fearless Vampire Killers*.

Every age feels compelled to define its beliefs and failings and to take its bearings by harking back to archetypal themes as portrayed in, say, *Antigone*, *Becket* or the *Mahabharata*. Because, like it or not, each individual must confront the issues that bedevil the heroes and heroines of these tales. It is, however, more difficult and intriguing to understand why each generation of filmmakers is drawn to the vampire.

The question takes on serious undertones when an exciting and intellectually serious filmmaker like Herzog is bitten by the infamous nocturnal count.

Surely if Herzog committed himself to a subject that has already been worked upon time and again, the reward would be in the mutations, because it is in these that one would find the key to any new interpretation of a familiar theme.

Unfortunately, while some of the images from the film, and the memorable performance of Klaus Kinski (who plays Dracula) linger, there's no telling why Herzog bothered to make a new *Nosferatu.*

There is one clue to the director's motivation, but while it is valid in its own right, it is inadequate. Herzog 'saw' *Nosferatu* first, he perceived it as retinal sensations, as bleak and arresting tableaux. Film may be a visual medium but to function only at the formal visual level (as so many of our serious/parallel filmmakers' work does) is to grossly underutilize its possibilities.

Paradoxically, because *Nosferatu* is visually such a mesmerizing film, the lack of any vision at its core is felt even more. Why is it that Herzog won't dig deeper, take more trouble to enrich the content and context when the opportunity presents itself? Why is he happy to scratch the surface (and the film is all surface and not even skin-deep, at that) and let go?

He gets little or no mileage from the gypsies, the last supper, from the horses, the invasion of the rats, the plague or from the characters.

Apart from the count, no one is given definition, and to that extent the count, too, is a loser because there's very little by way of contrasts, even of the subtle variety.

Taking the mood from Beardsley's illustration, Herzog has deliberately chosen the pallor of death as the colour of his film. But oddly enough, Isabelle Adjani has more colour in her face after she has sacrificed herself for her husband than in the initial sequences where her make-up is the same phantomime-white as Count Dracula's.

Perhaps the only significant contribution that Herzog makes to the Dracula demonology is the negative one: there is no horror in the film. There are moments when it seems to be lurking around the corner, but even in the scene where Bruno Ganz rushes to the subterranean vaults to uncover Dracula in his coffin, there is no cause for nervous titters.

A horror movie which eschews the claptrap of horror is fine, but there is no sense of evil either – only talk of it.

Nevertheless, do go and see *Nosferatu*. There are some marvellous things in it, like the hallucinatory intercuts of a bat in eerie slow-motion flight, and the ghostly 'Ancient Mariner' ship with its coffins as it proceeds towards the centre of the town.

There's the exquisite and utterly unobtrusive music. And then there is Klaus Kinski. His performance is part of Herzog's visual style – but what a performance! Frail, waif-like, malingeringly weak, there is something vulnerably childlike about him as he drinks at Isabelle Adjani's jugular.

No other Dracula has been so cadaverous, so past the gates of hell, and yet as human. Death has wasted him, and his bloody thirst has made him servile.

There is a sequence at the dining table when Bruno Ganz cuts the inside of his left thumb with a knife. Kinski's eyes pick up a murky light, his whole body is transformed with anticipation as the cut reddens. For a moment his table manners help him to control himself, then with sudden and swift rapaciousness, he stalks the terrified Ganz and with something akin to an orgasm sucks at the bleeding wound.

See it, but book beforehand. It was houseful on opening night. What's happening to Bombay? At this rate, even a Fellini or a Scola may have a chance here.

The Brutalization of Indian Cinema in *Dacait*

The shape the Hindi film of the 1980s – and of the 1970s – has taken, is to a considerable extent the result of the direction it was given first by screenplay team Salim-Javed and later by Javed alone, thanks to the sheer quantum of his output. It will pay to examine Javed's latest opus *Dacait* closely because though time alone will tell whether it is a box office success, *Dacait* is the apotheosis of the Javed method.

A study of his modus operandi will help us understand the hiatus between Javed's (and the Hindi film's) high intentions and slick but obvious manipulation, its bogus sentiments, its oversimplification and its crass commercialism.

I had been informed that the press show of *Dacait* was at 6.00 p.m. I was there on the dot. The movie was already on; they had preponed the show. Was it Aristotle who said that every story or drama must have a beginning, a middle and an end, but that if you wanted to hold the audience's interest, start in the middle? Without setting out to do so, I was testing the validity of the maxim. It works. At least in this one instance it did. I was willingly drawn into the maws of the big screen. There was a compelling quality to the narrative. Frame by tight frame, it grabbed you at the gut level and pinned you down.

In the intermission I asked that wise old colleague of mine Iqbal Masud about the part I had missed. 'Does it matter?' countered he, 'it will all turn out the same as always.' I found his answer unduly cynical at that time. But Masud saheb was right. And wrong. Absence from Hindi films had not made my heart grow fonder but it had certainly made it more naïve. Despite the authentic touches of the first half, the film pans out as all Indian dacoit films do. But *Dacait* is also a more deadly and deadening manifestation of the Hindi film bug than the ordinary variety.

Though the credit for this must be shared by the director Rahul Rawail and screenplay writer Javed, it is my guess that the lion's share must go to the latter. Javed is not just one of our most talented and prolific screenplay writers, he is also one of the Hindi film's most careful plotters. It is the care with which he advances his plot, the attention he pays to detail that make his products so much more dangerous. I used the word 'deadening' earlier advisedly. Because that is an important component of Javed's method. For the detailed, advanced publicity build-up anesthetizes the audience to the exploitation, the blatant and self-righteous violence and the glib and mendacious sociological conclusions.

Javed's theme has never varied. It is vengeance or *badla*. An ordinary but honest and upright man is wronged by colleagues, society or the zamindars. He does not go to the police or the courts of law (in the course of the screenplay it is suggested that it is futile to go to either) but takes the law into his own hands and wreaks havoc and carnage till a primitive and simplistic justice is done and the audience is sated with violence. A Javed script never leaves us with a sense of tragedy or the tragic waste of lives, nor does it offer us the benefits of the cleansing act of catharsis. Instead it batters our sensibility till it loses track of the fact that by the end of the film the hero or protagonist is no better than the criminals who victimized him.

As a matter of fact, what is truly horrifying and repugnant is that instead of decrying and condemning the new criminals, the audience ends up rooting for them.

This is not really Javed's unique gift to Indian cinema and the Indian public. You can track it back to *Butch Cassidy and the Sundance Kid* and *Bonnie and Clyde* in America, or *The Brutalization of Franz Blum* in Germany. The thrust or impetus is to humanize criminals. William Goldman makes Butch Cassidy and the Sundance Kid loveable and fun-loving, and the raindrops keep falling on your head till you are numb in the brains and want to join those two and their lady love. Arthur Penn shoots *Bonnie and Clyde* with such style and colour that you grieve for that much-misunderstood couple killed in an endless hail of slow-motion fire.

The real culprit of course is that school of sociology which went overboard and thought that once a causal connection was established between a man's deprived childhood and later criminal behaviour, his actions could be explained or worse, justified.

While theories about whether there is such a category as 'criminal types' are still being debated among sociologists and psychologists, there's no denying the need to see their problems in human terms rather than abstract moral ones. The truth is that while the attempt to understand criminal behaviour is necessary and laudable, if one hopes to change society and the circumstances that lead to criminality, it can never justify such behaviour nor does it exonerate us from judging criminal acts.

Let us, however, be clear about one thing – Goldman wrote *Butch Cassidy and the Sundance Kid* as a lark; it was not meant to be taken seriously. Arthur Penn was attempting to move away radically from the former B-grade stereotype gangster movie. It is set in the Great Depression of the 1930s. The great American values like money and success have crumbled along with American society, and the only larger-than-life figures are gangsters like Al Capone and his ilk. Bonnie and Clyde are small-time crooks who suddenly find themselves in the glare of publicity and try to live up to their new media image. At no point is Penn promoting a thesis or claiming validity for his protagonists. Javed, on the other hand, is a rank, albeit skilled, exploiter.

He has worked the same vein time and again till he's refined it to the level of an equation in pure maths. While the masala gets more and more elaborate and polished, so does the sophistry of his argument – that violence can be justified.

The Further Reaches of Romantic Love: *The Story of Adele H*

There's only one satisfactory way of reviewing the film at the Strand this week. It consists of two words and a full stop repeated thrice. See it. See it. See it.

It would have been easier to deal with *The Story of Adele H* had it been a great film instead of being an anomalous one. To do it justice would require space, time and research, extensive interviews and retrospectives of director Truffaut's and cinematographer Nestor Almendros' work.

Perhaps the closest one can come to suggesting the quality of the film is to deliberately reduce the plot (whatever little there is of it) to banalities, to the vocabulary of popular romances. Because that alone would help focus attention on the fact that *Adele H* is special in the telling of the story, rather than on the story per se.

In the days when he was still directing. Alexander Korda was forever making films about 'the private life of' Don Juan or someone or the other. Whatever the merits of the films, the pulling power of the prefix was irrefutable. There's a nice, prurient soft-core sound to it.

As voyeurs who need our daily fix of *Stardust, Society* and film gossip, we love to look through the keyhole and watch what we like to imagine are the concupiscent thoughts and deeds of famous personalities.

Without attaching Korda's famous prefix, Francois Truffaut has made a movie on the ultimate private life – the world of a woman diarist who wrote in code. It is Adele H's story, H for Hugo. It is the true story of Adele's unrequited love. Beware. Beware of Adele's private life.

Lieutenant Pinson of the British Army has had a brief affair with Adele and forgotten all about it. Adele, on the other hand, can remember nothing else. Against her parents' wishes, she travels alone from Guernsey in the Channel Islands to Halifax in Nova Scotia where Pinson's battalion has been posted.

Adele worships the man she loves. Does that sound trite enough? Good. At least we are close to the central problem – and achievement of the film. Someone who could have been the heroine of a true confessions magazine becomes a tragic and harrowing figure. Adele H literally worships Pinson. She lights candles in front of his photograph in an enclosed niche in her room.

The protagonist of Sartre's *In Camera* says, 'Hell is other people.' Truffaut seems to disagree. Hell, he suggests, is oneself.

If you are besotted by a single idea, you may end up as a visionary, a great villain, a revolutionary or, as in the case of Adele H, a madwoman. Frenetic, febrile, overwrought and contrary, Adele is a compulsive diarist. The words flow faster and faster. While she stares at the camera, her voice hurtles past. She lies, she fantasizes, she deludes herself. Perhaps she cannot tell the difference.

As she descends into her private hell, she pursues and persecutes her beloved Pinson. She is generous, destructive and completely unpredictable. She offers the perennially out-of-pocket Pinson money, buys a whore's services for him, and is responsible for breaking his engagement with another woman. She calls it the religion of love.

If the callous and promiscuous Pinson suffers at her hands, there are no limits to what the high priestess of love herself suffers. To watch the unhinging of the tortured and tormented Adele is to gradually come apart.

Money is really the only reason for her contact with her family or the outside world. She emotionally blackmails her father to send it, and yet she is totally averse to making capital out of the greatest literary name of the times, her father's. The only member of her family she identifies with is her sister, whose death by drowning she re-enacts frequently in her dreams.

Pinson is all she lives for and yet there's a superbly unobtrusive ironic moment in her life when he too becomes extraneous to her. By internalizing him, she becomes sufficient into herself. When, as a married man, he follows her in the streets and alleys of Barbados, hopelessly wondering whether he can persuade her to leave him alone, she walks through him, unrecognizingly. The circle of Adele's isolation is complete.

The American Civil War, her father's triumphant return to France after years of self-imposed exile, her mother's death, the turbulent events of the world at large, have barely touched her in the past. Now the world has altogether ceased to exist for her.

In so short a review, there's no point writing the obligatory line about the film's cinematography. It's not stunning, it is not flashy. Except one shot of Pinson next to the window when he visits Adele at her landlady's, there's no attempt to be painterly. The photography is. Period. Which is why the evocation of the mood at every point in the movie is so subtle, so perfectly attuned.

The colours in Halifax, Nova Scotia, are russets, rusts and reds, the colours of the earth. Adele, even as she is drifting, is still one of us, of the earth. The light in Barbados, ah the light in Barbados! You can touch it – but by this time Adele is already insubstantial.

If anybody had doubts about Truffaut after seeing *The Man Who Loved Women*, it is time he or she made peace with him. The man who made *Jules et Jim* is alive and in good form, even as Adele mistakenly accosts him in the street; the only obvious bow to Hitchcock in the film. And Isabelle Adjani? There is no Adjani. There is only Adele.

Victor Hugo's last words before his death were, 'I see a black light.' Adele survived him by many, many years. What did she see when the privacy of her world was finally annihilated?

PART II

On Society and Politics

Bombay: A Hope and a Prayer

YOU ALWAYS HEAR THEM before you see them. Muted drums beating a tattoo with subterranean memories of Brazil. And the soft husky roll of the dried seeds and pebbles in maracas.

They have me fooled every time. I can see Ava Gardner in *Night of the Iguana*. Even going to seed, she is more ravishing than the latest Miss Universe seducing you with outstretched arms in a commercial for a deodorant. She has pouches under her eyes, but her voice is still capable of killing you softly. And all around her and over her, undulating, slithering, twisting and turning their tight asses, are the two-coloured gigolos, maracas in hand. In perpetual motion the sound of the maracas washes in and out of the soundtrack.

Now they turn the corner, the sound becomes stronger, and I see them in the flesh. The lame and the halt dragging the halt and the lame. A woman, her head covered with her saree pallu, sits in a wheeled cart two inches above the ground. There's no bridge to her flared nose. Her fingerless hands hold the handles of rusty cans and jerk them with remote-control rhythms. On her left stands a man in pyjama trousers and a paratrooper's camouflage jacket. Instead of teeth he has a cigarette tilted rakishly at the side of his mouth. The face is raw pink rubber. There's a gentle distortion of the features as in a papier-mâché mask. Slung around his neck on a tatty cord hangs a drum. Three half-fingers do the same thing that the muscular mascot in J. Arthur Rank films did: strike the gong. His index finger falls off. Now there are only two.

He transfers the stick to the right hand. It is covered in a bandage the colour and texture of the grated ice that the *golawala* in front of your school used to make for ten naye paise. The simile is apt. A little bit of flaming red sherbet from the brass-topped bottles is oozing out of the bandage.

There's a third man. No musician this, he must be the impresario. From the stub of his right wrist hangs a large, discoloured Amul baby-food can with a makeshift handle like the tube on a Geiger counter. He thrusts it at me. I suck in my belly and retreat. A red glow appears at his mouth as he sucks at his bidi. Both his feet must have been bandaged a few months ago. Now they blend nicely with his dark skin.

His left hand pulls the rope of the cart. The lady jerks and jolts. The trio moves on. The music is sinuous and mesmerizing. I hear the sound of coins being thrown into the tin. My ears are now sharp enough to make out a rupee coin from fifty paise. We don't accept anything below that.

They are all over Bombay now, the leper trios and quartets. I have occasionally even seen sextets crossing the road in single file. Like the eunuchs who accost you in the middle of the street as you come out of a Udipi restaurant, they too must move in groups.

Who organized the lepers of Bombay? Where is the lair of this door-to-door marketing genius? Who is the leper king, so much more powerful than the beer-bottle baron of Prohibition Bombay? As the apotheosis, the paradigm of his kind, is he without hands, face, limbs, stomach? Just all mouth? A piggy bank that swallows coins and notes.

Bombay, my fair and lovely. Wife, mistress, whore, tramp. One body on sale, 8 million pimps and madams hustling. And 300 more coming into the city daily. Your only hope and prayer, my love, is the leper king. Seek him out, my sweet. Maybe, just maybe, with a little luck and a friendly poke from the king, you too may catch the disease. And one day, one glorious Monday, the first of the seven original islands may fall off like the drummer's finger. On Tuesday at 11.45 a.m. when the sun rises at Trombay, the nerve endings for the whole of Chembur and its satellite suburbs may be hit by a grey breeze heavier than the simoom, and drop off silently into the Arabian Sea. Wednesday, a freak acid-rain blizzard will strike the city, and Malabar Hill, Kemps Corner, Victoria Terminus, Byculla and everything in between will sink like dead weight. On the fourth, Elphinstone Road to Virar will go under. At 4.30 p.m. sharp on the fifth day the siren for the second shift at the mills will go off and trigger the collapse of Lalbaug, Parel, Dadar, Ghatkopar, all the way to Thane. The dust will not have yet settled down when at the twilight hour Colaba, Cuffe Parade, Nariman Point, Mazgaon, Sewri and the remainder of Bombay will soundlessly slip out of sight into the Indian Ocean. (No more corrupt businessmen, dirty politicians, and an acquiescent population. No more pollution.)

Sabbath, the seventh day. The day of rest.

Bombay. Virgin once again. Only the mouth of the leper king still open.

Rejected by *Times of India*

*

TIMES OF INDIA BOMBAY
21/10/88

My dear Kiran,
I am enclosing your piece on ugly Bombay. It makes very uncomfortable reading and will not go at all with the rest of the stuff we have. I am feeling awful about not using it after hustling you to do it.

You might have heard that my first ever play 'Avinash' directed by Satyadev has had 8 shows. As usual there are areas of disagreement between him and me – two of them major – but his response to the play when I read it to him was dead on and I was very happy when he decided to do it.

About 85% people have liked the play. The remaining have felt either confused or indifferent or haven't liked it. I wish you could have seen it. I have a hunch about how you'd react to it. I'll give you the script to read one of these days – may I?

Take care,

Love,

Shanta

Bombay by BEST: The View from the Flying Upper Deck

We perceive and understand ourselves, our homes and our cities by the ways in which outsiders see us. This is all the more so, if, as Edward Said and his parroting acolytes on the subcontinent will tell you, the country has had the misfortune (and if I may interpolate, also on some occasions the good fortune) to have been a colony of some big power.

The iconic images of Mumbai for foreigners, and through their eyes for us inhabitants, are many: the local trains with thousands of commuters crammed in with a few dozen falling out every day; the chawls; the immersion of the clay images of Ganapati at Chowpati beach; the Dharavi slums; the Gateway of India; and the Hobson-Jobson mutation performed by the British on the Portuguese name for Mumbai which is even today common currency, Bombay.

For me, the most telling image of Mumbai is another gift from the British: the BEST bus service. The history of Mumbai (and perhaps it's tragic, dead-end future too) could be written by studying the growth of the BEST and its routes.

In the beginning was the BEST double-decker. There were no wide-bodied, aggressive, get the f--- out-of-my-way, single-decker buses in my childhood as there were no numbered buses then. Bombay–Mumbai was a comparatively humane place in the good old times because its scale was still human. The megalopolis and 'maximum city' had not yet arrived. You could encompass the whole of Mumbai in the twenty-six letters of the English alphabet by which BEST bus routes were named. Route 'A' plied between Colaba and Andheri via the Prince of Wales Museum, Victoria Terminus, Byculla, Dadar and Shivaji Park.

The only exception to the alphabetical buses was the 'A4Ltd'. She was the Flying Ranee, the Deccan Queen; express train; she skipped four or five stops at a time. And if you were sitting on the very front seat on the upper deck in front of the window, the wind whipped your hair and your eyes smarted and the world flew by, and you knew you were flying across Marine Drive and Vincent Road, which would become Dr Ambedkar Road, and the rest of the city.

Chinchpokli, Sandhurst Road, Marol, Danda, Breach Candy, Lalbaug, Kemp's Corner, Khotachi Wadi, Haji Ali, Chor Bazar, August Kranti Marg ... ah, the romance and call of the road. The Odyssey, the Mahabharat, the Nibelungenlied, Beowulf, they all happen here, and every name in Mumbai has its own epic.

To see an English movie at Metro or Rex, we caught a 'D' or 'N' from Dadar where we lived, which ran between Sion and Ballard Estate. And it was the same 'D' or 'N' we had to take if we wanted to visit our family physician whose clinic was near Opera House. Doctor Ranganekar was always late, and I would stand at the window of his rooms and look at the elaborate mechanical display on the main road in front of Swastik Cinema. One day I went into a panic at what I saw. A wooden cut-out of Rehana or maybe it was Nigar Sultana was about to jump off a cliff but just as she leapt, Raj Kapoor would rescue her time and again. But then about fifteen minutes later something went wrong. The cut-out of the lovely actress jumped, and Raj Kapoor, the horrid man, just stood and watched as she fell into the treacherous valley.

Nostalgia, as youngsters will quite rightly tell you, is nothing but fairy tales. The BEST fairy tale has another little wrinkle. People in Mumbai did quaint things like following a queue system. (Not always but most of the time.) No other city in India did that.

Some things change, others don't. People in the West talk of something bizarre called maps. Not just talk, they can actually read them. No wonder they conquered the world. You ask them simple directions to your cousin's place and they will tell you, 'Go seven blocks south, then turn east till you hit 32nd and Third and then take the exit north on Allyson.' Actually they can go on like this for an hour or so. I usually switch off at the first mention of south or north. I can find east and west ... but only in daytime. The east, after all, is where the sun rises and the west is opposite. How in God's name is one expected to find the north or south-west? But what is really inexcusable about Westerners is that not only can they read maps, they can actually find places through them. How else do you think Vasco de Gama found India? Or Columbus, America when he was looking for India? Think about it.

By and large, Indians have always had far more advanced ways of locating places. As a nation we live for and by the moving image, that is the cinema. All directions in India are through the medium of cinema houses. For instance, Victoria Terminus, sorry, Chhatrapati Shivaji Terminus, is opposite Capitol Cinema. But where is Capitol Cinema, stupid? The smart-arsed answer would be, opposite C S T, but I am a kindly man and don't take offence. I am patient with fools who don't know where Capitol Cinema is, for God's sake. Capitol is right next to the lane which houses New Empire and Sterling cinemas. Got it?

Some people use the stars as a compass, Indians use cinema theatres. And don't forget, if you still can't find a place, why, you dummy, all you've got to do is to ask someone. Three people might give you three different directions, sometimes as different as diagonally opposite ones, but what's the hurry? The earth is round, my friend. Whichever direction you take, you are bound to get there.

We are 18 million people going on, it would appear, to infinity. We are no longer human but mere numbers. No wonder the BEST had to switch from the alphabet to numbers. The last time I counted, there was a bus route 355 and that was merely in Worli or maybe in Bandra. Perhaps in Meera Road they already have four-digit routes like 1075, and five years down the road there will be Route 66,666.

The uses to which buses are put are also changing with time. Outsiders think we burn only our brides when we want more dowries. Not true. We burn buses too when we are agitating for more buses or better transportation; when we are feeling strongly about any damn thing like, a bomb blast, a fatwa or an 'unacceptable' movie. Or frankly when we have nothing better to do.

Climate Change: From Bombay with Smog

EVERY NOW AND THEN, the state government of Maharashtra declares that it would be a good idea to sell the last four or five substantial public open spaces like the racecourse, the Oval and others left in the city of Bombay (Mumbai) and develop them as real estate. It is an idea not even Joseph Heller or Kurt Vonnegut could have surpassed in their most manic satirical mode.

Bombay is my city. It is a fine case study of the head-in-the-sand syndrome, a city in denial. As with any metropolis, there are two Bombays: 'Bombay One' for the affluent, and the 'Other Bombay' for the poor. The 'Other' is of no consequence except during elections when political parties promise it the earth and the moon so long as they are voted to power.

As the purported powerhouse of the Indian economy, 'Bombay One' has bought wholesale into the current theology, self-delusion, or whatever you wish to call it, and embraced by the West, of India Shining, India Booming. The leading English newspaper in the country, indeed the media in general, have been claiming that in its sixtieth year of Independence, the subcontinent is not only poised for its great leap forward, (or is it on the brink of the abyss?) but that this is the year of India. Hallelujah, the golden age is upon us.

Here's how golden: this winter, the smog was not the usual annual grey curtain; it was a block of dirty concrete that started at times a couple of metres from where you stood and stretched 5 miles into the sea and all the way to the sky. The major part of the credit for this seasonal cement installation must surely go to the hundred thousand new cars that roll down the streets of Bombay every year, not to mention the near-doubling of air traffic and the industrial sprawl that has converted distant townships into the city's satellites. Lung diseases and infections have risen between 30 and 40 per cent. The good news continues: for the first time in the history of Greater Bombay, there will be no power for industry one full day every week in summer. The residents of Bombay city too will discover the joys of power cuts for the first time. Land prices in the last year alone have risen by 20 to 30 per cent. Add to that now we are assured that, thanks to climate change, very soon the ocean will start reclaiming vast tracts of the city.

It is by what an individual, city or country aspires to, that one can judge its mental health. 'Bombay One' seems to be a victim of schizophrenia and suffers from a fractured sense of reality. It now has a new role model: Shanghai. It wants to be Shanghai 2, a city whose very existence is unknown to the 'Other Bombay'.

Geographically, Greater Bombay is a tiny tadpole clinging to the western littoral of the subcontinent. Its land mass is 437.71 square kilometres. Estimates vary but Wikipedia takes an informed guess and puts its population at around 18 million. Shanghai's population is 16.41 million while its landmass is 6,340.5 square kilometres. Bombay is already considered one of the world's most polluted cities. In ten years, it will probably also become the most populated one.

There's good reason for 'Bombay One' to feel a disconnect between itself and the 'Other Bombay' so far. When there's an acute water shortage, 'Bombay One' will continue to buy its supply from tankers. When the power cuts become operative, it will buy power, whatever the cost. When the sea starts a massive land grab project, it will move into the sixty-storeyed high-rises that the government now permits.

But soon, sooner than later, even the rich and privileged will find that they too must face the day of reckoning. There's only one earth and only one atmosphere. Like it or not, Bombay One and the rest of indifferent India, the American neo-cons, and the Chinese, who don't subscribe even to the wan and emasculated Kyoto protocol, must breathe the same air as the Other Bombay. We can continue to blame the developed world, especially America, for its rapacity in consuming the earth's resources but it's a little late for finger-pointing.

Unfortunately, Scarlett O'Hara's favourite phrase in *Gone with the Wind*, 'I'll think about that tomorrow' will not rescue them. Because the earth has run out of tomorrows. Because for better or worse, we are in this together.

Last and final chance, my friends, it really is now or never.

Coaching Classes

A REVOLUTIONARY PROPOSAL TO DISPENSE with the national education system, save the country billions, cut down study time by half, and dramatically raise the quality of education

So you think it's impossible to get into a Bombay local train? Try getting your child admitted to the first grade of a school in the city, especially one where the medium of instruction is English. It would be foolish to hold out any hope but here are some of the options you have, all of them limited. Register your child in school the day you are born; donate a kidney, preferably both, to the principal of a school; part with a few hundred thousand (hurry though because the number of zeroes goes up every few weeks); at the very least get a letter from the chief minister of the state, or better still one from the new Mother India, Sonia Gandhi; start an international baccalaureate school of your own. But even then, there's no guarantee.

There is a clear vision and a strong education policy on the subcontinent. It's called politics, ideology and anything goes. Education has nothing to do with the awakening of the mind, a passion for learning, inspired teaching and, least of all, with the kind of questioning and curiosity that lead to the discovery of other worlds, those within oneself and without. (It was, after all, that same accursed inquisitiveness that got Adam and Eve thrown out of paradise.)

Too many students, too few schools, horribly underpaid, overworked and demoralized teachers. Apart from a few elite institutions, most urban schools work in shifts and each classroom has fifty to sixty students at the minimum. Willy-nilly they learn the secret of teaching: learning by rote or *ghokkampatti* as it's so vividly called in Marathi. Never, not even in jest, make the mistake of encouraging students to think for themselves.

God is not a lottery; he is a bookkeeper. If you've committed heinous crimes in your past lives, you will go to municipal schools or worse, to a school in a village in Uttar Pradesh where the teacher is absent nine months of the year, and the students have holidays in the remaining three. On the other hand, if you've walked the straight and narrow in your previous incarnations, you will go to the latest fad in the country, an air-conditioned IB school, and rule the world.

Even the rank outsider may have noticed by now that the education system in the country is in a perilous state. The heartening news is that it has been so for the last fifty years. The reason it still works is because there's a parallel institution simultaneously at work. It's called coaching classes. They are at every corner, lane, by-lane and dead end.

Everything in India comes in pairs. There's a parallel economy, purportedly much bigger and far more efficient than the official one; commercial cinema has its counterpart called parallel or art cinema; local constabularies are complemented and countered by parallel militias; both the Congress and Left parties split into two a long time ago and run on parallel lines. But there's a far more pervasive but underrated parallel industry that is really the bedrock of the entire Indian education system: coaching classes.

In the fifth lane off Sir Bhalchandra Road in Hindu Colony in Dadar, the last stop on Central Railway before the suburbs of Bombay began (in what was then considered Metropolitan Bombay), there lived an unrecognized national treasure and institution called Mr Chaphekar. He had spent his youthful years in Britain where he had hoped to start various ventures like colonizing a small patch of the colonial master's land by opening perhaps the very first Indian restaurant in London, or printing maths books in a unique, if not revolutionary, way: the pages would be glossy black while the text would be in white type. It's not clear what the fate of these daring schemes was. All we know is that he returned home after India won independence, never to go back. He then forayed into an altogether new field. Indeed he is considered one of the pioneers of an industry that today runs into billions of rupees: coaching classes.

Chaphekar wore an ankle-length dhoti, unlike Gandhiji's short one, a white shirt, black jacket and two-and-a-inch-thick glasses. In Bombay he taught dull, dazed and indifferent students algebra, geometry, trigonometry and English while he stuffed oodles of snuff into his nostrils and sneezed into his brown-stained kerchief. He never used physical chastisement, he had no need to, since he had a turn of phrase that was sharper than any rapier. It could cut, slice and lop your head off. When a student calculated that seven sixes are forty-three, he shook his head in despair and said, 'Aho tumhi keeti dhadadhadit khota bolta ho? How can you tell such blatant lies? Think – I realize that that's asking the impossible of you – and see if you can bring yourself to tell the truth.'

Those were innocent times. Parents sent their children to extra tuition classes because they were weak in a subject or two and needed a little guidance, especially as they approached the matriculation exam. Chaphekar was superb at maths and his English was impeccable, if just a touch old-fashioned. The classes were his only source of income, and though his son and nephews were dragooned into the teaching faculty, money was not the reason he was in it. It was a thankless job, and however sarcastic he got, one thing was certain – he loved teaching.

Over the years the notion of coaching classes has expanded beyond recognition as well as undergone a few changes. The age at which a child needs extra help has gone down steadily. Boys and girls from the 1st to the 10th standard all boost their daily dose of school with a supplementary education. Life, as we all know, is a series of tests, trials and tribulations. But there is only one ordeal by fire. It is the interview that an Indian child of five has to give when he is about to move from kindergarten or Montessori playschool to standard one. There are instances, rare as they may be, where the child has survived the occasion, but the parents certainly don't. Considering the stakes, even the most hard-hearted mother would not refuse to send her child for coaching for the life-and-death interview which will decide whether he or she will get admission to a good primary school.

Naturally (as is only fair) amongst the affluent, education and enlightenment begin earlier. Two and three-year-olds are now sent to bone up on the basic skills of life. What exactly is taught here is a bit of a mystery, but the word is that these children learn survival tactics like how to curtsy to Q E II on the off chance that she might take it into her head to drop in on them. Or how to enact a steamy love scene with Shah Rukh Khan or Brad Pitt while riding on a two-humped camel without outraging the modesty of the animal.

In your teenage years, there are classes to coach you in every subject in the arts, the social sciences and applied and pure sciences. You want to get into the incredibly competitive engineering or medical colleges; much sought-after establishments like the Indian Institute of Technology; the top-of-the-line Indian Foreign or Administrative Service; or appear for any exam that would make you eligible for colleges abroad, you make damn sure you go to a renowned coaching class. Which explains why it's crucial in India for children to choose their parents with great care. Otherwise you will end up having to take coaching classes in plumbing, TV repairs, driving taxis or buses. Or worse still, being trained to speak in bizarre versions of Texan or Oxbridge accents using pseudonyms like Cedric, Jeremiah, Tanglewest or Augustus, for call centre jobs.

Teenage girls, babes in cribs, women in the first blush of youth, married women and spinsters, great-grandmothers, housewives, doctors, lawyers, salesgirls, IT whiz-kids, beggars, investment bankers, vegetable vendors and fisherwomen, pilots and clerks ... every woman in the country, barring the occasional freak, aspires to be an actress in Bollywood movies. Now even a child will tell you that one important way to become a film star in this country is to become Miss India, Miss World, Miss Universe or at the very least Miss Most Ravishing Canines, Miss Oomphiest Little Toes, Miss Best Come-hither Eyebrows.

Beauty contests used to be such innocent affairs in the past. You looked good enough to eat and you got your crown. But things have got frightfully complex in the last decade or so. You must be coached to act like a lady James Bond and learn how to save the world, or at the very least your country, single-handedly against all odds. You need coaching so you can tell the judges, not to mention an audience of millions across the world, in a voice choking with emotion, what you would consider your topmost priority as prime minister of your country. Now there was this bewitching Indian woman, lithe and slender and svelte and unbearably beautiful, who was a dead-cert shoo-in for Miss World when she opened her mouth and uttered perhaps the most memorable line in the history of beauty contests. As PM of her country, she said silkily, her over-riding objective would be to build a sports stadium.

The would-be beauty queen may have fallen with the speed of Lucifer as God flung him down to hell, but her gaffe started something altogether unique: the world's first coaching classes for the post of PM.

A school-going child in India spends seven hours a day in class, an hour or two on homework and special projects, and anywhere from an hour to three on extra tuitions in coaching classes as he heads for the higher secondary exams. College life can be much easier, especially if you've mastered the art of being present in class while you are making pioneering forays in exploring hetero or homosexual physiognomy in a theatre nearby. But come what may, you don't miss your coaching classes in physics, economics, biology, English literature, statistics or whatever your subject. And as the crucial final exams approach, you go into overdrive, study late into the night but, most important, you take extra tuitions in more and more subjects and put your faith in the good Lord above and your coaching class below on earth.

Your parents may find themselves in debt, but it will be well worth it if your after-school classes can get you into that impossible 1 per cent bracket which ensures you an entry into any course in any institution you wish to join. Man, you are made for life, not just locally but anywhere in the world.

The trick, of course, is to know which coaching class will deliver the highest scores. Fortunately, the day after results of the major exams are posted, the classes with the heaviest firepower put out half and full-page ads in the newspapers with photographs of their students who figure amongst the top fifteen or thirty rankings. That should settle the issue unequivocally. After all, what better proof can you ask for than a glowing track record? But never underestimate the ingenuity of the Indian entrepreneur. Some of the biggest coaching establishments will co-opt students with retrospective effect. What that means in simple English is that these students have indeed done brilliantly but on their own steam and not under anybody's tutelage and have now been persuaded, naturally for a consideration, to lend their names and pictures.

But even the finest coaching institute will find it a trifle difficult to transform dross into genius. It is in this context that one discovers what true parental love is. What matter if their son or daughter is mediocre or a little limited. This is India, you can buy anything here. But give credit where it is due, to the students themselves. They know that there is a far more effective tool than coaching classes – copying. The plain and simple, nothing-clandestine-or-furtive-at-all kind of copying under the eyes of teachers and with their approval. Indeed it is one of the most revered institutions in the educational system on the subcontinent. Recently when some deluded idealist in Uttar Pradesh decided to put an end to this revered practice, the students taught him a lesson that he will not forget. They set the examination hall on fire.

Will the Government of India and especially its education ministry finally see sense and come to its senses? Schools and colleges are redundant and a waste of students' time and a colossal and appalling burden on the exchequer. Do away with duplication and leave education to coaching classes. They do a far better job anyway.

Looking for Gulbadan's Kite

I NEVER MET ANY of my grandparents. So I ask myself, how did my paternal grandfather Balwant Nagarkar, a man who died a good thirty years before I was born, influence my life so considerably, and turn my face in the direction of the conscious and unconscious choices I would have to make for the protagonists and characters of my novels?

Yet what I know about him is precious little. He came from an orthodox Chitpavan Brahmin family from Ahmednagar. The word is that he was attached to a temple as a child to train to become a priest. He was a 'madhukari', a boy who ate at certain fixed houses, a different one for every day of the week. The next thing you know about him is that he has joined Wilson College in Bombay. How? Did he have a rich patron? Did he come under the influence of some British missionary? Your guess is as good as mine. There is also some talk that he may have been asked to leave Wilson College for some paper he wrote on Christ.

The year is 1893. My grandfather goes to Chicago for the Conference of World Religions along with Swami Vivekanand. Vivekanand represents the Hindu faith, my grandfather but a minor branch of it: the Brahmo Samaj, which harked back to the monotheism of the Upanishads. From all accounts it appears that Vivekanand was the star of the day. My grandfather didn't make it that big, but he was invited once again to another Conference of World Religions in 1903.

Questions: What made him change his faith? What motivated him? Why would he give up the certainty and security of the Hindu faith, and the livelihood from a highly respected Brahmin priesthood? Why did he risk the appalling prospect of being kicked out of his community and being persistently shunned? Why did he choose to risk ostracism by crossing the shores of India not once but twice? But he hadn't had his fill of rebellion. After his first (or maybe it was his second) wife died, he married again, this time outside his community. He married a Jew.

He had nine children with her. My father was the eldest and it was natural that he should give up his education before his matriculation and take up a job. He joined the Railways as a clerk.

I was four years old when, without realizing it, I felt the consequences of my grandfather's actions and choices. One of my father's childhood acquaintances had moved to Hindu Colony in Bombay where we lived. She had four daughters, the youngest of whom, Mita, was my age. My parents would invite Mita to come to our flat to play with me. Every time she left, the parents of my closest friend who happened to live opposite would tease me about being Krishna and ask me how my 'gopis' were doing. It was thanks to them that I thought I was doing something that was not the done thing.

Somewhere it began to register in my mind that our family was different. We were Hindu but different from other Hindus. They worshipped the images of many gods. We had no images and we believed in only one God. What did I make of this? I'm not quite sure. All I can say with any certainty is that I began to dread going to temples, and to feel uncomfortable with the whole pantheon of three or four-headed gods and goddesses with eight and sixteen arms. Instead of temples, we went to the Prathana Samaj, the Maharashtrian version of the Brahmo Samaj, to listen to a sermon interspersed with 'abhangs' and 'dohas'. It would only occur to me later on that the Brahmos were as much influenced by the Protestant forms of worship that had come with British missionaries as by the Upanishads.

After four years at a Marathi school, I was sent to an English-medium school run by priests. I spent six years at Don Bosco, yet during all that time I did not learn the school prayer that we were supposed to recite every day. For some reason I can't explain, I mumbled some gibberish without intending any disrespect, and got away with it.

After school and then college, I found that I had begun to distance myself from both the monotheism of the Brahmos and the gods and goddesses of my Maharashtrian friends. I was well on the way to closing the doors on all religion and had begun to dislike organized religion with a passion.

And yet my novels and plays are the site of an almost obsessive concern with religion as they are of every kind of inter-, infra- and counter-cultural conflict. Shri Krishna is at the heart of my play *Bedtime Story*. He appears in *Ravan and Eddie*, and is the kabab-me-haddi between Meerabai and the Maharaj Kumar in *Cuckold*. *Seven Sixes Are Forty-Three* does not stray much outside the Hindu fold but it explores the cross-currents and conflicts within Hinduism itself. *Ravan and Eddie* is the story of two religions, two cultures running parallel but almost never meeting, seen through the eyes of two children, one a Hindu, the other a Catholic. *God's Little Soldier* is a journey through both Islamic and Christian extremism.

Sometimes I think my grandfather has put a curse upon me: I cannot believe and yet I cannot leave well enough alone. I keep trying to exorcise him, and yet I am not sure if, along with him, my muse too will vanish. Who asked him to be a maverick and break out of the happy certitudes of the Brahmin priestly class? Why could he not have continued to toll the bells of his temple in Ahmednagar clangorously so that I would neither hear nor have to confront the terrible dilemmas of our self-righteous violence, of Ram and Rahim, the touchables and untouchables, of Osama bin Laden and of Bush, of the terror of 9/11 and the tragic trajectory of the conflict between India and Pakistan, India and Palestine?

When will I find Gulbadan's kite?

Twenty-five years ago, maybe it was thirty, I came across a biography of the Emperor Babur's daughter, Gulbadan. I learnt that she used to fly a kite with her brother Humayun. It was such an insignificant detail, but I sat there with a sense of utter wonderment and joy.

I felt that I was holding the string of the kite that Gulbadan flew and it stretched all the way to the Prophet Mohammad, who surely flew kites, and to Christ and to Prince Siddhartha who would become the Buddha. Gods come and go, for they too are subject to change. Great upheavals knocked out the matriarchal hierarchies of the Greek pantheon and replaced them with a patriarchal order. The Earth mothers in India made way for Varun, and then Varun was replaced by Indra. Yet who really remembers and worships this one-time top honcho today? Easy come, easy go.

The only constant we can hold on to for dear life is Gulbadan's kite. It is our only hope. It's as if the future of mankind and this poor benighted planet of ours depends on it. So long as we are aware that all the 4 or 5 billion of the earth's denizens are flying that same kite, what matters what religion we practise or to what caste or country we belong?

Ghar (Home)

I'M NOT VERY FOND of people who preach. I prefer to tell stories. I'm about to tell you a story whose end I don't know. Perhaps you will be the real-life heroes and heroines who will make sure that the end of this story is a happy one.

Now suppose, just suppose that I enter your home at night and slip pesticides in the water system, leave the gas cylinder tap open, cut down the beautiful trees in your garden, put poison in your food, lock the garage door while I leave the engine running so that all the exhaust fumes engulf the drawing room, kitchen and bedrooms and you cannot breathe. Then I catch hold of your Alsatian and while you are sleeping slit his neck. Next I walk over to the fish tank with seventeen different types of species in it and empty it and watch the fish die on the floor. But then I run out of luck and your father catches me by the throat and asks me, 'Tere baap ka ghar hai kya ke tum mere ghar ko barbaad kar rahe ho?' He then proceeds to call the police and has me thrown out of the house and into prison.

At this point it would make sense to look at the concept of 'ghar'. Your father can throw me out because he owns the house or at least rents it. Trespassing, as you know, is a criminal offence in law. In America, your father would be within his legal rights if he decided to pull out a gun and shoot me dead. But all of us also live in a much larger 'ghar' or home. I am of course talking about our planet, the earth. In the context of the larger home, if your father had asked me, 'Yeh tere baap ka ghar hai kya?' My answer would have been: 'Sirf mere baap ka nahi, hum sabke nana-nani, dada-dadi, aur unke baapzaadon ke baap ka bhi ghar hai.' Indeed, the earth is home to billions of human beings and beasts and birds and fish, insects, and weevils and worms. Unfortunately, when some industries – or rich vandals – pollute and abuse this large home of ours, we cannot throw them off the planet.

For decades now, my generation and the one after that have been single-mindedly destroying this beautiful and bountiful home of ours. The greater responsibility for bringing this blight upon our planet rests with the rich, highly industrialized, developed nations far more than the underdeveloped ones. The Holocaust or the murder of the Jews, Gypsies, the Poles and the handicapped by Hitler's regime is one of the darkest chapters in mankind's history, and yet even that cannot compare to what we have done and are doing to the earth. We have wiped out thousands of species of animals, birds, fish, trees, plants, and continue to do so merrily. All the scientific evidence points to a time in the near future when millions of human lives will be at risk. The world will be divided between those countries with swathes of land that have droughts and famines and those which have disappeared under water; those countries which have water and those which don't; those which have enough crops and food and those which don't.

Climate scientists have been warning us for several decades now that if we do not take immediate and drastic measures to control consumption and the use of fossil fuels, the temperature of the earth will rise by three to four degrees centigrade. We are already seeing the effects of this deadly climate change, but we are all in denial. Hurricane Katrina and hurricane Sandy, the super-typhoon called Haiyan in the Philippines, the dreadful storms that hit the Orissa and Andhra Pradesh coastline are mere curtain-raisers of what is to come.

Sadly, we in India too are trying to be like the rich countries. We want Porsches, Rolls-Royces and SUVs. We have all turned into highly talented liars and double-talkers. The recent presidents of the United States and most leaders of the other developed countries give urgent and moving speeches about global warming and its deadly effects but do almost nothing to really cut down on consumption, carbon emissions and pollution. The strategy they adopt is the old Lucknowi one. Everyone is super-polite and says 'pehle aap' 'pehle aap'. Add to that, there are scientists and economists paid by the mega oil-producing companies like Exxon, Shell, Chevron, Gazprom and others to denounce and deny the reality of climate change. Think about it, ninety giant international corporations are responsible for 63 per cent of the pollution in the world. One of them is the Coal Authority of India.

Even as we are gathered here, the ice caps in the Arctic and Antarctic are melting at an alarming rate, the ozone hole in the environment may already be well beyond repair. Low-lying areas in many South Asian countries like Bangladesh, parts of our own country and Sri Lanka, as well as in the UK and various other parts of the world, are likely to go under water in the not-too-distant future.

Few words in recent time have been as overused, misused and abused as 'globalization'. Its thrust is always trade, and it is the purported panacea for all our ills. Hardly anyone, however, talks about the globalization of individual responsibility. The earth is indeed a global village: so interdependent are ecosystems and individual actions and decisions, that what each one of us does or does not do affects the whole planet. The plastic bags, air conditioners, detergents, the genetically modified crops, the fertilizers and pesticides our farmers are forced to use, the plane rides we take, our heedless consumption, the deliberate and conscious decisions our leaders and the last two generations took, all evidence to the contrary, have been systematically destroying our environment. They all come with a price tag, one that all of us are already paying for, very dearly.

When it comes to taking the difficult but absolutely urgent steps to stop and reverse the climate crisis, world leaders find a hundred excuses to not keep their promises and to disown responsibility. The question is, why are they lying? It is as if they are all pretending that they live on some other planet. If the leaders of a country are wilfully blind and refuse to see the writing on the wall; if they will not take difficult decisions and firm action, then mankind is in very serious trouble.

The worst offender is the USA. It refused to ratify even that token gesture called the Kyoto Climate Change Protocol. The middle class, the affluent and the intelligentsia in China and India too must now share the blame for not taking measures to preserve their forest cover, water tables and the environment or to curb their recent insatiable need to consume. The villain, we are told, is selfishness and unrestrained self-interest. I find that view difficult to buy. If we were really selfish, we would desist even today. We would alter our profligate ways and put the brakes on our consumption, because if we don't, the consequences will be unthinkable.

Since time immemorial there has been an unspoken covenant between the previous generation and the next. Parents all over the world have always considered it their duty to preserve and protect their precious assets and resources for their children. Your parents too will have told you time and again that you are the future, that everything they have worked for and saved, the family business, all the compromises they have made, all the palms they have greased, all the wealth, property and jewellery they have accumulated, is for you. But what's the point of inheriting all that money and property if the earth as we know it does not survive? So, you see, no generation has ever been betrayed the way you have been by us older, supposedly wiser, people. There is, however, no point indulging in the blame game. It's too late. This is our last chance, and we need to act, and act promptly and responsibly.

Fortunately, the polluting industries and disinformation agents are so wrong. The cost of harnessing alternative energy on a global scale, they claim, will ruin the economy. That's good scaremongering but false. GDP growth, most economists are agreed, will be lowered by maybe one-tenth of a percentage point over the next twenty years, but alternate energy is getting cheaper and cheaper, and the sector will employ millions. The problem, as you can see, is still tractable. It is eminently possible to save the planet, and all its various life forms including mankind, if we set our minds to it. It's going to be a long, long haul. It will demand serious changes in our lifestyles. And serious sacrifices. What exactly does that mean? I can only think of a few rather simplistic examples. We'll have to do a bit of backtracking. In European countries like the Netherlands, the bicycle is the preferred mode of local transportation. Far wider, in-depth and urgent emphasis will have to be placed on expanding public transport systems like the metro, trams and buses, while simultaneously making them much more energy-efficient. For long distances, unless it's desperately urgent, trains could be the primary choice. But let's be honest: things are rarely that urgent or desperate. Many of the climate scientists only travel by train. It took two of them eleven days to travel from London to China. They said it was very comfortable and they worked hard during the train ride. As to obsessive consumption, it is about time we stopped being so criminally wasteful.

But that is just the beginning. What is needed is fresh ideas and new strategies for clean and safe sources of renewable energy instead of knee-jerk reactions like:

'Nuclear energy is our only hope'. The Fukushima disaster in Japan which continues to pose terrible health hazards should be an unforgettable lesson to all of us. As we all now know, that bogus concept of carbon trading has been a complete failure. Instead, we will have to devise highly innovative technologies to clean up the carbon levels in the air, oceans and lakes; we will need to heal and restore the delicate balance in the atmosphere and in the forest cover. But the most fundamental change we must seek is in our attitude to the earth. We can no longer take it for granted. We need to earn our place in it by respecting its integrity and organic inter-relationships.

I am sure there's hardly a single student in this gathering who does not watch Superman or Superwoman, Spiderman, Catwoman, Batman, Iron Man. They all tell the same story. The hero or heroine single-handedly saves a city, the earth or civilization. In real life, unfortunately, there are no supermen or superwomen who will take it upon themselves to save our planet. Our only hope is young people like you. Will you worship money and unhindered consumption? Will you buy three Lamborghinis and two Alfa Romeos like the young Chinese entrepreneurs, or acquire a 40-million-dollar luxury yacht as David Beckham is supposed to have done? Or will you be the heroes and heroines who will do something exceptional for mankind? Will you think creatively and come up with winning solutions? Solutions that will turn the tide and save our planet?

At the UN Climate Change Conference in Warsaw, Poland this year (2013), the executive director of the Philippines Climate Change Commission, Mary Ann Lucille Sering delivered one of the gravest indictments against the rich nations of the world: 'Every time we attend this conference, I am beginning to feel that we are negotiating on who is to live and who is to die.'

What exactly did she mean by that statement? What she was referring to is something that we all know in our hearts: barring exceptions, the rich don't give a damn about the poor. The only difference was that she was talking about the consequences of the insatiable greed and self-centred view of the rich nations which will result in the deaths of millions of poor people. The urgent question is, what choices will you make? First as school-going teenagers, and then as young responsible adults? Will you be totally absorbed in your own aggrandizement and your pursuit of wealth at any cost, and ignore the poor? Or will you remember that the earth belongs as much to the underprivileged as it does to you? Will you recall that the well off do most of the damage but those who are less fortunate than them pay the terrible price for it? Will you have the never-say-give-up patience and the perseverance and the sheer grit and imagination to fight and win the earth back for mankind? All I can say is that if you do, you will save the earth, our home, our ghar.

Gore Vidal

AMONGST MY VARIOUS CLAIMS to fame, here are the three most important. One, in the early 1970s, I have ridden twice or thrice on the same elevator as Ratan Tata, never mind that he was not head of the Tata empire at that time. Number two, Salman Rushdie said hello to me in a totally unplanned appearance at a literary seminar at Cambridge. The third is the story that I knew Gore Vidal personally and was on first name terms with him. Ah, these apocryphal stories, if only there was some truth to them.

But to get back to Gore Vidal. If you were to read all the obits, I doubt whether there's a single one that doesn't mention that he was acerbic, cantankerous, argumentative and cold-hearted. While I don't doubt that he was a difficult man, I was lucky. He was kind and generous to me. *Cuckold* was about to be published when my then agent asked if I knew any major international authors who would write a blurb for my new book, and I had to shamefacedly confess that I didn't know anyone but the one person whose critical oeuvre I respected most amongst contemporary writers was Gore Vidal. My agent was a large woman with a heart and a sense of what's-to-lose that was just as big. Write a letter to Mr Vidal, she emailed me, and I will have it sent to his publishers. I was absolutely certain (and simultaneously hoped that Gore Vidal would prove me dead wrong) that this was an absurd idea, but I did write to him and got a handwritten reply asking me to send the book to him. When he had finished reading it, he sent me a blurb and told me that he would write to his editor about *Cuckold* but warned me not raise my hopes, for the one skill that most publishers lacked, he told me, was a sense of literature; they would publish only that which their tiny minds could grasp as a marketable quantity. He was right. No publisher in the US or UK bought *Cuckold*.

I don't recall when or how I began to read Gore Vidal. I could be wrong, but I suspect, as so often happens, it was nothing but an accident: a happy one in this case. It is difficult to grasp how many different things Vidal could manage with such ease. But before I come to the one reason why he should be at the very centre of any canon that deals with 20th-century American literature and political thought, let me first very briefly get rid of all the scandalous stuff.

Vidal was as much a generator of gossip and intense controversy as he was the subject of it. He had a lethal turn of phrase and he used it against all the people he liked to provoke. In a debate with William Buckley, the founder of the conservative *National Review*, he called his antagonist a crypto-Nazi, and Buckley returned the favour by calling him a queer. He and the Hemingway-obsessed macho Norman Mailer always tended to see the other as the competition and their scraps were legendary. After one such run-in, Vidal was headbutted by the shorter but pugilistic Mailer.

Vidal was good-looking in the quintessentially 1950s Hollywood tradition and was a major presence there for a few decades. His homosexual bias was never in doubt, and, like many other young men of his ilk, he was in extreme sexual overdrive, but even in this area he was unpredictable, for he seemed to have gone to bed with women as well. His relationship with other famous homosexual authors was almost always uneasy, if not downright bitchy. His recollection of Tennessee Williams' meeting with John F. Kennedy is a classic example. President Kennedy was leading the way to the White House when Williams commented on the President's delectable arse. According to Vidal, he related the remark to the President, and when the author of *Suddenly Last Summer* asked what Kennedy had to say, Vidal reported that the President was excited.

It's uncanny how often Vidal's barbs hit the nail on the head. When Truman Capote died, Vidal wrote that 'Death was his best career move'. In perhaps one of the strangest and ironic turns in literary history, Capote was unable to write a single novel after his path-breaking and superlatively successful *In Cold Blood.*

In his autobiography *Palimpsest*, Vidal confessed that the only person whom he loved, Jimmy Trimble III, had died in the Second World War, and since then, he declared, his heart had remained frozen. Vidal lived in Italy and in the States and had a lifelong partner with whom, he claimed, he had never had a sexual relationship.

All these and many other trivial footnotes and shenanigans that tell-all biographies will no doubt endlessly recycle, are best buried with the physical remains of Vidal, and we can now turn to the prolific, exacting and extraordinarily erudite novelist that Gore Vidal was. As an essayist, he was in a class by himself. There's no one who could touch him when he was in perfect form, and he almost always was. Besides, it's truly mind-boggling how often his insights and observations were dead on. The depth and range of his interests and knowledge did not turn him into a recondite writer. On the contrary, he was an impeccable stylist who wrote transparent prose, often laced with biting, red hot chilli sauce.

Vidal fought in the Second World War and was a precocious nineteen when he published his first novel *Williwaw* in 1946. Along with his compatriot and later rival, Norman Mailer's *The Naked and the Dead*, these were the two most influential literary war novels of the times. Vidal's next novel died a quick death, and the third one, *The City and the Pillar*, which dealt with homosexuality, got him into serious trouble. It appears after that book, even the *New York*

Times kept him out of its pages for many years. By today's standards *The City and the Pillar* must appear rather tame and bland but that is the kind of misplaced anachronistic reading which makes many a critic and reader feel superior.

It looked like the end of the road for Vidal but his writing took a different turn then, and he wrote his first historical novel, which in a fundamental sense, would represent the author's highly distinctive and uncompromising take on life, philosophy and politics. The novel was called *Julian* and dealt with the remarkable life of the apostate Roman emperor who wished to revert to the older pagan gods instead of being in thrall to the Christian faith.

In all, Vidal would write twenty-five novels, many of them chronicling the decline of social values in American society. His favourite weapons in this genre were corrosive humour and merciless satire. The satirical take-off on transsexuals in the novel *Myra Breckenridge* was turned into a film with Mae West making a comeback in a not insignificant role. But it is the three historical novels, *Burr*, *Lincoln* and *Empire*, about America's early years, that will surely leave their imprint for generations to come. They are formidable in their epic sweep, interpretation and their ability to make us rethink the founding myths of that continent and the great men who participated in its momentous rise to power. Vidal proposes that the issue of the abolition of slavery was an afterthought for Lincoln. If the Civil War had been won earlier, slavery may have dragged on for God knows how much longer. As always, Vidal carries his learning and historical insights lightly without ever simplifying them. It's not merely that he's a compelling storyteller, he has that rare ability to allow us to see the philosophical underpinnings of history: how ideology and 'isms' get reflected, deflected, distorted and corrupted in the evolution of democratic processes.

The words 'a renaissance man' are constantly misused and trivialized in our times. But they describe the full spectrum of Vidal's multifaceted personality. In the lean years after *The City and the Pillar,* Vidal became a highly successful screenplay writer and script doctor. He wrote hugely popular plays, two of which (*The Best Man* and *Visit to a Small Planet*) were big hits on Broadway and on the silver screen. He worked with Christopher Fry on revising the script of *Ben Hur* but neither were given credit for their contribution. He got his name removed as one of the scriptwriters of the film *Caligula* since he believed that the script had been butchered by the director and the main actor, Malcolm McDowell.

That brings us to Vidal's incomparable and monumental contribution to the essay form. There seems to be hardly any subject that he does not deal with. Literature, of course, is one of his main topics. His analyses of the semiotic and deconstructionist discourses is a superb lesson in how to write with great clarity about highly complex disciplines, and yet make it clear that the author does not take too kindly to all the convoluted thinking and the obfuscating jargon that often conceal vast tracts of bogus intellectualism and posturing.

Another distinct area of Vidal's interests is the hypocrisy and opaqueness that prevailed, and perhaps still does, in the public libraries in many states in America. They had banned children's books like the Tarzan and the Oz series, and Vidal took on the challenge of exposing their petty minds and the way they could affect future generations of readers. One other related area for which we all owe a huge debt to Vidal is reviving interest in authors who have gone out of fashion and been forgotten. For instance, Somerset Maugham has indeed fallen upon hard times. It's infra-dig to read him today, but Vidal took the trouble to re-examine the man's entire body of work. He can be scathing but he also rediscovers much that is valuable in *Of Human Bondage* and *The Moon and Sixpence*. This was something he did time and again with different authors who had fallen by the wayside of time.

And yet his most memorable contribution will remain, I suspect, his steady, unflinching vision of American politics and policies under both Republicans and Democrats. Not once in all his years of writing, no, not once, did he lose sight of the nation's rapacious and grand imperial ambitions. The current United States had been a colony of a tiny nation called England but since the time it won its independence, for all its lofty talk of democratic ideals, and its frequent retreat into isolationism, the imperial project always crept back to the centre stage. Phrase it any way you want, superpower games, overarching mendacity, lighting the torch of freedom, protecting its interests, double-and-triple speak, capitalism, free market policies ... everything boiled down to the grabbing of power, territory, influence, resources, monopolizing commerce through trade agreements, the corporate takeover of politics and the machinery of the state, everything was grist to American greed and self-interest. Not that the USSR or Russia in the last decade or two has been any different, except they don't pretend to be holier than everybody else and full of self-righteousness.

Time and again Vidal exposed the sheer hypocrisy of American leaders of every hue. There was just an unbridgeable infinity of difference between what their words claimed and what their actions spoke. Vast tracts of Mexico were swallowed; the Philippines were turned into a colony. They are still pretending to take democracy to different parts of the world while continually aiming to corner markets and resources. Iraq, Afghanistan, Vietnam, Panama, they really believe they are the good guys. Vidal never bought into any of this high-minded hokum but kept puncturing and exposing the hollowness of every American doctrine. Nixon, Reagan, George W. Bush, Clinton and then Obama, nobody but nobody was spared. It was not a monotonous, repetitious harangue. Vidal watched, he observed, he kept accounts of the terrible wrongs done to different countries, of the chicanery, the political murders, the stage-managed coup d'états, and he spoke out without fear and without thought of consequences.

He was supremely witty, entertaining, humorous, satirical, abrasive, irreverent and unputdownable. And he was most of the time very wise and prescient. Ah, my friends, read and reread Vidal. His novels, plays, and the essays. Many of the issues he deals with will have died but not his insights. If anyone wishes to learn about the state of the world, be advised, keep Vidal always by your bedside. He is the voice of sheer sanity, and he is wise to the ways of the world and he will catch you too when your ethics become shaky and you take the high moral ground.

You may not like all the novels, you may differ and dispute angrily with him, but you will always find him hugely readable, exuberant, egregiously right in his analyses, delightful and sharp as a razor cutting into your jugular. If you feel acute discomfiture, it is because he so often challenges your most dearly held beliefs.

Thank you, thank you, thank you, Gore Vidal.

(This short essay does not pretend to do justice to Vidal's work. It is nothing but a jhalak, a mere glancing look at his multifarious writings. It has been written from my memories of reading his books and without being able to consult the books themselves and without the benefit of the internet. I trust both he and the reader will forgive errors, if any.)

How Did We Lose Tomorrow?

(*While there are hundreds of people and organizations of conscience and commitment in India who do excellent work for the environment, unfortunately they are hugely outnumbered and it is a moot point whether they will be able to turn the tide.*)

AT THAT ANNUAL TEN-RING circus called Davos, the BBC tried to pin down the then Indian commerce minister, Anand Sharma in an interview. As we all know by now there is only one question that the West – not to mention Indians themselves – have to ask when it comes to the economy: India's doing well in terms of industrial development and GDP growth. But not as well as China. Why are you lagging behind?

Anand Sharma bravely jumped to the country's defence, reeled off facts and figures and outlined the steps the subcontinent was taking to catch up with China. Along with much of the world, we too now have only one role model, China. Again, like much of the world, we have terribly ambivalent feelings towards this burgeoning superpower: envy and fear. We would give an arm and a leg to be in the economic shoes of the Chinese. But we also live in the shadow of this minatory neighbour to the north. Since China refuses to honour our border with it, we fear that it will attack us again as it did in 1962.

The question is why would we want to emulate China in the first place, and why would we want to forsake the incredible gift that the Constitution of the country has given to the Indian people. We are a democracy, albeit like all democracies, not flawless. We go to the polls at least once in five years. Barring the very occasional violence, the elections are free and fair. China, on the contrary, is quite simply a totalitarian country and the elections there are a travesty of democratic institutions.

But the minister, not to mention the country, tends to ignore the most outstanding experiment and event in our history. I am adverting to Mahatma Gandhi and the extraordinary nature of the Indian freedom struggle. Even India's enemies will grant that we won independence in a manner unknown till that time. It was an absurd confrontation: the might of the largest empire in the world and one frail man's notion that the power of righteousness and the force of truth expressed through an altogether new and, at that time, risible weapon called non-violence could bring the empire to its knees.

It is almost incomprehensible how Gandhi was able to inspire the most extraordinary and motley band of young intellectuals, lawyers, professionals and scions of landed gentry like Jawaharlal Nehru, Vallabhbhai Patel and Mohammed Ali Jinnah, to name just a few, to follow him and his principles, to become the leaders of an independent India. But even more astonishingly, it will always be a mystery how this not very prepossessing man could galvanize and make the greater part of the populace of the subcontinent embrace the doctrine of *ahimsa* or non-violence and active resistance through non-cooperation movements, like crippling the colonizer's economy by refusing to buy goods made in his country, and through peaceful civil disobedience.

India became independent on the 15th of August 1947. No other nation has won freedom the way we did. That exceptional legacy should have been at the very centre of the nation's consciousness and our thinking and actions.

It should have coloured every aspect of our life without indulging in hero worship or turning it into a bogus master narrative. Our heritage should have taught us that GDP is not the only measure of a country's success, and there are far more important goals than being a superpower. For instance, the eradication of poverty, malnutrition, killer diseases like malaria, TB and AIDS, and the caste system; the urgency of saving farmers who are forced to commit suicide by the hundreds of thousands because of appalling debts; the need for education for the entire population of the country.

When and why did we lose sight of Gandhiji's vision and these noble objectives? Ironically the Father of the Nation began to seem irrelevant not too long after winning Independence. The idealism of those years went down the drain and the rot set in almost immediately. The bureaucracy and politicians discovered red tape, the Licence Raj was created and the country plunged with unnerving celerity into pervasive and institutionalized corruption. Graft, bribery, venality, extortion, profiteering, the black market and the parallel economy became not only universal but a fact of life that was taken for granted on the subcontinent. The police, the poor, the middle class, the rich and the super-rich, even parts of the judiciary caught the virus.

How did this shift from a belief in high ideals to a 'me-me-me' culture come about? How did we become so insatiably grasping? There are doubtless many explanations for this, but one of the main reasons was that as a people, we lost tomorrow. (Look around today and it's evident that the whole world seems to be suffering from this condition.)

In the 1950s Oscar Lewis studied the poor in various countries and published his remarkable theory of the Culture of Poverty. The poor, he told us, must perforce live in the present. Thanks to their impecunious circumstances, they can only understand the here and now. They do not know when and where their next meal is going to come from or if there is going to be a next meal. In this sense they are like children and have no notion of 'deferred pleasure'. If they get a roti, they'll eat it instantly. And if there's a religious feast and they get a free, eat-as-much-as-you-can meal, they will grab half a dozen rotis, mutton kebabs, two plates of biryani, three types of dessert and anything else they can lay their hands on, and try to polish it off right then and there. Let alone a refrigerator, very likely, they do not have a vessel in which to store the food. Hence they must make the most of what they get now and not trust the future.

We must live in strange and topsy-turvy times, for what we see is that the rich and the super-rich too no longer have a sense of 'deferred pleasure'. Somewhere in their heart of hearts, they no longer believe in tomorrow. What exactly do we mean by 'tomorrow'? Tomorrow is the future, the one we wish to leave for our children. The import and implications of the future are that we do not seek instant gratification but are willing to invest in today so that our children can benefit tomorrow. So what is it that I am trying to suggest: That the middle class and the rich no longer wish to leave their fortunes and their businesses to their children? Quite the contrary. The parents work just as hard, if not harder, they cheat, take and give bribes under the table, stash their black money in Swiss banks, and of course, as with previous generations, bequeath it to their children. But it was also customary in the past to leave behind something less tangible: a sense of right and wrong with a strong preference for the former. Unfortunately, more often than not the moral compass is rarely passed on to the next generation now. The notion of setting a good example is not just passé but scoffed at.

One of the most stubborn myths that mankind clings to is that the engine of human motivation is self-interest. If only this were so, the earth would not be on the brink of the worst crisis it has faced in the history of mankind. But as the

Copenhagen Climate Change Conference of 2009 proved, we are in denial and clutch at straws to disprove climate science. Till at least the 1960s, there was a universal belief that we are part of society and we do best when we share goals and our interests are interdependent. This has been replaced to a large measure not just in India, but across the world by a rampant individualism and a bizarre underlying assumption that our families, tribes or countries live in a vacuum or perhaps on a different planet.

Let's take the example of the two most developed cities in India. Currently Mumbai has a population of 18 million. In less than ten years this thin strip of land will become the most populated city in the world. As always, planning in Bombay, not to mention the country as a whole, caters to the demands of sixty years ago instead of sixty years ahead. Water, power, roads, the total infrastructure in this megacity might perhaps work if two-thirds of the population moved to Australia or the moon. The year 2009 was one of the worst years for the subcontinent. Thanks to a shortfall of 50–60 per cent in the 2009 monsoons, water shortages this year (2010) are so severe that apart from the poor who have always suffered silently, the middle classes in the suburbs have blocked roads and staged violent demonstrations. Sixty-four years after Independence we still blame the monsoons and not the utter lack of any major initiatives, will or vision for water management. Forget irrigation schemes, even mandatory water harvesting is missing. (There's a booming private water supply business in the city for those who can afford it. Water tankers ply back and forth 24x7. Guess where they get their water from? Even *Catch-22* could not better this one. From the main water pipes, with the indifference or connivance of the municipal authorities.) And yet over a year ago, the state government in its wisdom gave permission to construct sixty-storeyed buildings within the city limits. It is merely a matter of time before the water wars in Mumbai start.

The traditional source of water for both the poor and the rich in Delhi was the river Jamuna. But the river has been polluted and neglected to the point that in many places it is nothing but a dirty, clogged runnel. For decades the affluent used to resolve the problem by boring wells and tapping groundwater. The other Delhi, the Delhi of the poor, had no option but to drink and wash in the dirty puddles of the Jamuna. After all, 'that is not a need which cannot be satisfied.' Now the water table has sunk farther and will soon disappear altogether. The obvious solution was to clean up the river so that both the rich and the poor would have access to water round the year. But the Delhi authorities solved the problem in their own inimitable way. They piped in the water from the Tehri dam over 200 kilometres away and spent far more than it would have cost to clean up the river. And of course the poor are once again left high and dry since only those in the city proper and with taps can have piped water.

If that's the case with Delhi and Bombay, imagine what it's like in the rest of the country. The sad truth is that, like it or not, the rich must make do with the same city in which the poor live. And if one were to frame the problem on a macro or global level, then with the same planet. If that mechanism called self-interest had really worked, the entire populace of Delhi and Mumbai would have risen up and forced the government to take drastic measures to make the cities viable.

The fact is we have failed our children miserably. You can leave them all the money in the world, and yet they will have no option but to breathe the same abysmally polluted air and get gridlocked for hours in traffic. They might not suffer the same power shortages since they can afford generators, but one of these days the groundwater will run out, and at some point, because of mankind's perverse denial of appalling climate changes, the Himalayan snow cap will melt away and the rivers will run dry. Without water there will be little farming and less food. Without water, energy, food and a strong customer base, it will be difficult to sustain business and industry.

The fruits of our indifference will be visited upon our children. Sow the wind and reap the whirlwind. When life becomes untenable, the people will rise, a revolution will take place and the rich will be the first victims. This is no Marxist fantasy. As the film director, Sudhir Mishra, said ironically, 'It will be coming soon to a city near you.'

One of these days, hopefully before it's too late, we must decide whether this is the kind of tomorrow we wish to leave our children.

Never Again – For Whom?

In 2008 when I had finished giving the last of a series of lectures for the Poetikdozentur at the University of Tuebingen, I was asked to suggest a subject for an essay competition. I had recently read Mahmood Mamdani's *Good Muslim, Bad Muslim*, and a remark from the Israeli vice chancellor of the Budapest-based Central European University whom he mentions had got stuck in my mind: 'Never again, yes. But for whom?' he asked. Indeed, my feeling was that the future of mankind would depend on how we and generations to come interpreted those words. Never again for one's own people or for all people? That was it. I was convinced that I had got an extremely relevant but at the same time, an utterly non-controversial subject for the essay competition.

If I had ever prided myself as an occasional writer of fiction who knew something about human nature, I was about to discover how mistaken I was. A woman who had just heard the announcement and had, as a matter of fact, attended all three of my talks, came over to the table where I was signing copies of my books and told me that I was a rabid anti-Semitic. I thought I hadn't heard right and said, 'I beg your pardon?' She looked at me distastefully and said, 'It's obvious, you hate Jews.' 'I would appreciate it if you waited just a few minutes,' I told her. 'We could then sit down and talk this over.' 'What for?' she sniggered, 'I already know where you stand.'

It is a sign of our intolerant fundamentalist times that we now feel free to level any charges against anyone and do not feel the need to substantiate them. Rush Limbaugh and Fox News spread the most egregious lies and scurrilous canards without fear of libel or slander. On the other hand, as we have recently witnessed after the elections in innumerable other so-called democracies, dissenters are not only marginalized but at times severely persecuted. The notion that the essence of a lively democracy is to encompass contrary opinions is not only under serious threat but seems to be viewed as highly suspect and dangerous. The maths is simple: if you are critical of your own country, people or religion, you are a traitor. Since I feel rather strongly about the pervasive and institutionalized corruption in my country and the fate of my poor benighted and beleaguered city of Bombay and am shameless enough to voice these concerns in public both at home and abroad, I must surely qualify as a latter-day Judas.

Speaking after 9/11 to announce the 'war on terror', George W. Bush may have given new currency to the polarizing phrase, 'You are either with us or against us,' but the idea has been around, I suspect, since tribal times. Our ancients had grasped one of the most sophisticated principles of group dynamics: introduce a series of initiation rites and rituals, formulate strict rules, and excommunicate anyone who transgresses them, so that the members of the community believe that they belong to a select body. Every religion promotes and perpetrates the concept of the chosen as an exclusive club with specific commandments and privileges. Heaven is only for those who have followed the rules and paid their dues. Hopefully there are different plots reserved up there for different faiths. Otherwise there is likely to be serious trouble in paradise, what with Christians, Jews, Muslims and Hindus and other denominations claiming that theirs is the only one true heaven. As to the atheists and agnostics, whether they believe in heaven or not, they will be packed off to hell anyway.

The genesis of the phrase 'never again', as we all know, is of course rooted in the Holocaust. A small-time corporal rose to be the Fuehrer of his country, promulgated something monstrous called 'The Final Solution' and almost wiped out the entire race of Jews in Europe. There comes a time in the history of certain countries when its people say enough is enough. This was such a time for the Jews. They had been persecuted for centuries. 'Never again' would not merely be their prime survival strategy but also an assertion of their new pride and spirit of independence, and the fact that they would not permit any power on earth to abuse and ill-treat them in any fashion.

One of the tragic offshoots of the genocide, however, was the transference of the concept of exclusivity, of the idea of a privileged community, to a rather unusual context. Some people began to treat the Holocaust as some kind of monopoly on suffering. There is no denying that the 'final solution' wiped out 6 million Jews. The number of Polish people, gypsies, homosexuals, and mentally ill who were murdered and annihilated, either in concentration camps or in the gas chambers, was far lower. But the tragedy of any genocide is not in the arithmetic of numbers but in the suffering and loss of each individual life. It lies in the realization that human beings can be appallingly inhuman; that they can treat others in the most horrendous and barbarous ways; that without any provocation they will wilfully and consciously set out to annihilate others of their own species. Few things can bind human beings tighter and closer than shared calamities. And yet it would appear that when it came time to build memorials to the Holocaust, the survivors introduced a class and a caste system; a fully functioning apartheid between the millions of Jews who died and the others who lost their lives.

Indeed, we have learnt nothing from John Donne's noble and moving words some four centuries ago: 'No man is an island entire of itself: every man is a piece of the continent, a part of the main. If a clod be washed away by the sea, Europe is the less, as well as if a promontory were, as well as a manor of thy friend's or thine own were. Any man's death diminishes me, because I am involved in mankind; and therefore never send to know for whom the bell tolls; it tolls for thee.'

World leaders, politicians, economists and other thinkers talk endlessly of the importance of globalization, but it is our tribal instincts and mores which really dictate human behaviour. Deep down, our world view even today remains 'it's us against them'. With many honourable exceptions, Americans continue to be inward-looking and uninterested in the world outside. By and large, so long as Americans can look after their own interests, they don't care what happens to the rest of the world. The Chinese will disregard the most glaring genocides and human rights abuses in Africa and elsewhere so long as they can continue to search for oil and protect and preserve their own self-interests. Quietly but steadily, they continue to broaden their spheres of influence and aim to be the other, or preferably, the only economic and military superpower in the world. As to Indians, sometimes it seems the world begins and ends with Pakistan for them. We'll sacrifice any remaining vestige of morality to hang on to Kashmir, whatever the human cost, and that too not because we care about what happens to the Kashmiris but for some primitive notion of pride and honour. The Kashmiris are under no illusion about Pakistan. They know well that the mother country alienated its own other half till there was a civil war that led to the founding of a new nation called Bangladesh. Pakistan's most powerful weapon against the direst economic adversity and internal problems, including talibanization, is to inflame troubles in Kashmir and mastermind terrorist attacks in India. It is no different in Russia, Iran or any other country in the world. Naturally, beyond paying lip service to lofty platitudes, who has the time to give a thought to the rest of mankind and to the planet?

No century in the earth's history has betrayed its young as the 20th. 'Never again' has become a pet catchword. We invoke it to decry injustices. We promise that we will never again permit another Rwanda, or Srebrenica, and yet Zimbabwe, Myanmar and God alone knows how many other countries continue to persecute and torture their own. We cannot prevent famines, droughts, floods but we make empty promises about not allowing the victims of these monumental calamities to suffer starvation and acute deprivation. But the poor keep dying, and frankly, we tell ourselves that there's only so much we can do and then just throw up our hands. And all the things that should never happen, happen over and over again because our promises and our words have ceased to have any meaning.

Our own legacy to our children is mostly a shameful one. The earth's very survival hangs in the balance. The end of the Cold War has exacerbated local conflicts to the point that the whole world is teetering on the brink of a great conflagration. It seems impossible for us to talk to each other to resolve our problems. More often than not, when we wish to sort out our grievances or the wrongs done to us, we take it as read that the only dialogue and communication possible is violence. Our greatest gift to future generations is terrorist and suicide attacks and a climate of utter uncertainty.

'Never again' was the only response possible after the trauma of the Holocaust. But nearly sixty-five years have gone by, and it is high time we re-examine the relevance and scope of those words. The Israeli vice chancellor, whose name we do not know, may have grasped something which might yet save mankind and our birthplace called earth. 'Never again' for whom, our own people? Or all people?

Our only hope lies in moving away from the self-centredness of a clique mentality to an all-encompassing inclusiveness. Perhaps we can finally begin to understand that our salvation is in understanding and acting upon the knowledge that we are in this together and we have no option but to reach out. That 'never again' makes sense only when it is made to work for all the peoples of the world.

Any takers?

On Memory

THIS SHORT PAPER ATTEMPTS to touch upon three of the uses to which memory has been put in recent times. The three may not be integrally linked but they all deal with ideas about mass annihilation and large-scale suffering. The topics are: the Holocaust, the Communist mind games in Russia, and memory as autobiography and history.

I'm going to start off with a quote about memory from *Cuckold*.

Sajani Bai is singing at a concert celebrating Mewar's victory over Mahmud Khalji of Malwa. She chooses to sing a song about Dhola-Maru, a song that she had sung many years ago on another happy occasion which went sour when Prince Bahadur of Gujarat murdered the protagonist's (called Maharaj Kumar) cousin.

> 'Does not our song give you pleasure, Maharaj Kumar?'
>
> 'It does, madam, it does, but I cannot deny that it awakens painful memories.'
>
> 'And you fear that some terrible catastrophe will follow as on the previous occasion? But there is no cause and effect operative here, Sire. If we consign a song to amnesia because of the burden of our own memories, then it is possible that an entire people will push a dastardly act or even the life of one of their own into the black hole of oblivion merely to seek forgetfulness and absolution.'
>
> 'Do you really think one can wipe out a people and events that easily?'

'We rework our own memories and re-invent ourselves to suit our tastes and predilections every day. Who is to notice a hiatus in history a few centuries down the road?'

'Why is it so important,' Father spoke almost inaudibly, 'to remember, Sajani Bai?'

'Because otherwise our lives would be lies, and we may never tell our children to speak the truth again.'

'Will you be the remembrancer of Chittor, Sajani Bai?'

'I would be honoured, Your Majesty.'

'Then the truth will never be in jeopardy, at least not in Mewar.'

The truth. Now that is a subject which has been debated and written about since as far back as memory can reach and we are none the wiser for it. However honest one may be, the truth is always in jeopardy.

The Memory Sweepstakes

Memory or remembering is like courage or grammar. It is an essential virtue but nonetheless a secondary one. Its value lies in the use you make of it. The West, particularly the Jews, quite rightly stress that the world not forget the Holocaust, lest it occur again. Yet neither that experience, nor remembering it, has brought understanding, empathy or compassion to many Jews. Successive governments in Israel have ghettoized Palestinians, made them second-class citizens, and deprived them of work and basic freedoms.

It could be argued that the central and seminal experience that came out of the British departure from India was not our first taste of freedom, but the effects of partition. Our political, social, communal and cultural perceptions, not to mention our sports too, have been coloured by the madness that overtook us in 1947 and still visits us every few years. Hindus remember how Muslims killed lakhs of Hindus during Partition, and Muslims keep alive the memory of how hundreds of thousands of their kin were murdered, maimed and raped by Hindus, and thus both sides ensure that their children too will continue a communal vendetta.

Remembering, it is obvious, is not enough.

The Chorus in my play *Bedtime Story* is a nasty piece of work. He is a self-confessed Nazi and is obsessed with the theme of responsibility.

> Some time ago I went to see 'The Diary of Anne Frank'. What a play. I am sure you've seen it too. How I wept. I identified with Anne so completely, she and I became one. What courage that girl had, what faith in humanity. When I came out, my heart was deeply stirred, my spirit soared. I felt uplifted as I had felt years ago, listening to the Fuhrer's speeches against the Jews and crying out Heil Hitler! ... Oh, it was wonderful to be alive then, with all that power and blond camaraderie singing around you ...
>
> What a play. Everybody can identify with Anne Frank. How upright and comfortable it makes us feel. But if all of us are Anne Frank, then maybe there never were any Nazis. Maybe they were just a figment of our imagination.

The Nazis, we need to remind ourselves, were no freaks, nor can the movement be dismissed as a Germanic aberration. They were ordinary human beings like you and me. We need to understand and admit that we too are capable of behaving exactly like that. We prove that time and again, most recently in the 1992 post-Babri Masjid massacres in Mumbai and elsewhere. The Hutus and Tutsis proved it in Rwanda, and so did the Bosnian Serbs in Srebrenica.

In a 1997 issue of the *Guardian Weekly*, Anthony Julius wrote a a review-cum-brief article on Anne Michaels' novel about the Holocaust called *Fugitive Pieces* which won that year's Guardian Fiction Award. Striking a pontifical note,

Julius, who was also a judge for that award, wrote: '[The novel] quails before the subject of our times, which is the Holocaust.' Let's ignore the pompousness of the man and examine the phrase '*the* subject of our time' (emphasis mine). The Holocaust was certainly one of the worst disasters visited by man upon man. So were Hiroshima and Nagasaki. So was Cambodia. One can go on for at least a couple of pages. But are we to now have contests about the scale and degree of tragedy, and award, along the lines of Miss Universe, a trophy and title like the World's Most Worthy Calamity? Why is only one tragic memory singled out as 'the subject'? Tragedy, however large, is most devastating at an individual level. The constant death threat on Rushdie is as tragic as the burning of a bride, a blinding in Bhagalpur, or a lynching. Primo Levi's experience of concentration camps, and later his suicide, are as horrific and wasteful as a terrorist act. It is the horror, the terrible horror, of man's inhumanity to man, and the appalling suffering of the victims that is soul-wrenching and devastating, not the colour or race of the victim. Prioritizing the importance of certain memories is the first step towards rewriting and inventing memory.

Airbrushing Memory

The airbrushing phenomenon found its finest practitioner in Stalin. Perhaps someone greater may appear but till then Stalin is the high-water mark. The most poignant and memorable portrayal of the airbrushing technique occurs in Milan Kundera's *The Book of Laughter and Forgetting*. Kundera's prose has a lightness that makes it all the more lethal.

> In February 1948, Communist leader Klement Gottwald stepped out on the balcony of a baroque palace in Prague to address the hundreds of thousands of his fellow citizens

> packed into Old Town Square. It was a crucial moment in Czech history – a fateful moment of the kind that occurs once or twice in a millennium.
>
> Gottwald was flanked by his comrades, with [foreign minister Vladimir] Clementis standing next to him. There were snow flurries, it was cold, and Gottwald was bare-headed. The solicitous Clementis took off his own fur cap and set it on Gottwald's head.
>
> The Party propaganda section put on hundreds of thousands of copies of a photograph of that balcony ... where the history of Communist Czechoslovakia was born. Every child knew the photograph from posters, schoolbooks, and museums.
>
> Four years later Clementis was charged with treason and hanged. The propaganda section immediately airbrushed him out of history and, obviously, out of all the photographs as well. Ever since, Gottwald has stood on that balcony alone. Where Clementis once stood, there is only bare palace wall. All that remains of Clementis is the cap on Gottwald's head.

It was Stalin who had helped orchestrate the show trials and executions in Czechoslovakia. We've known for some decades now about the Soviet leader's talent for deleting, diluting and fixing memory. But it is only now, with the publication of David King's *The Commissar Vanishes: the Falsification of Photographs and Art in Stalin's Russia*, that we are beginning to grasp the enormity and implications of his obsession. Nothing less than reinventing history could assuage the man's megalomaniac insecurity, and so he had to cast himself as the god of memory, or rather of revised memory.

In a photograph taken in the Red Square on 7th November 1919, Lenin, Trotsky and a commissar, Artashes Khalator, along with many others, are celebrating the second anniversary of the Russian Revolution. In the airbrushed incarnation of the same photograph released in 1967, Trotsky and Khalator have vanished. The mother of airbrushing is purportedly that dubious and highly variable quantity called political necessity. It is political necessity which dictates whether history needs to be corrected, cleaned up, revised or newly fabricated from scratch. If in the process 10 or 30 million die in the Gulag, it is of little consequence.

The question is what is the practice and the protocol when the same necessity rehabilitates someone who had not been bumped off, or had not succumbed to the rigours of Siberia but is still surviving out there in the cold? China could have thrown light on this subject, especially since Deng Xiao Ping made it back from the wilderness of the Cultural Revolution to the premiership of the country. But China has been given 'most favoured nation' status by that most favoured of all nations, the USA, for a decade now, and it doesn't suit US economic interests to probe such matters too deeply. Besides, China's airbrushing activities are very much under wraps since, unlike post-Stalinist Russia, the Communist regime in China is still all-powerful and pervasive.

But, as recent history has taught us, it would be a grievous error to think that totalitarian regimes alone have a copyright on the subversion and re-creation of memory. While there's little awareness in Kundera's writing of how America too marginalizes its own dissenters and rewrites the histories of other nations like Vietnam, Cambodia and Chile, to name only a few, he unconsciously encapsulates the American paradox when he is in reality talking about his own country, Czechoslovakia. 'True,' he writes in *The Book of Laughter and Forgetting*, 'the Constitution guaranteed freedom of speech but the law punished any act that could be construed as undermining the state. Who could tell when the state would start screaming that this or that word was undermining it?'

The USA screamed for years in the McCarthy era when the senator worked up hysteria across the country and went on a national Red hunt. In the Land of the Free, how could there have been a government body called the Committee for Un-American Activities which hounded thousands of innocent people, deprived them of jobs and airbrushed them right out of America? Who is to decide what is American and what is un-American? If the Politburo in the USSR indulged in naked aggression and repression, America too often does the same, albeit on a much smaller scale within the country. The only difference is that the latter does it in the name of freedom. Henry Luce, the magazine mogul, is just one example of how American media tampers with and distorts history. Luce rewrote and often entirely fabricated the dispatches of his own correspondents like Theodore White. Almost single-handedly, *Time* Magazine with its paranoid propaganda propped up Chiang Kai-Shek's repressive and faltering regime and created the climate for the American government to finance the Generalissimo. Disinformation is not an American invention, but the US is just as adept at it as are the leaders of any number of countries.

And what about us? We can never see our heroes whole for fear of discovering that they have feet of clay. In the bargain, we never permit ourselves to discover their greatness either. If a scholar speculates about the disastrous consequences of Subhash Chandra Bose's ethically misplaced overtures to Germany had Hitler won, the scholar is likely to run into serious trouble. What would happen if Shivaji caught my fancy and I attempted to write a novel about him that was not entirely adulatory? We know of at least two scholars who lost their jobs because of their views on the Maratha hero. Our culture has withstood a thousand years of upheavals, cataclysms and foreign invasions. Yet it is only in the last thirty or forty years that we have become fearful that any criticism or openness will destroy our gods, our heroes and our culture. We feel continually threatened and embattled.

We perceive danger from all quarters: the enemy within (read the Muslim community; or if you happen to be a Muslim, the Hindus); the Foreign Hand; and God knows what else. Our preferred mode of defending ourselves is censorship, legal and extra-legal. Stanley Wolpert's *The Crisis of India, Nine Hours to Rama, The Satanic Verses,* Scorsese's film *The Last Temptation of Christ* ... all banned because we no longer have faith in the sturdiness of our institutions. Add to that, the fundamentalist parties are busy doctoring our history and reinventing it just as successfully as the other airbrushing artists in the world.

Memory as Autobiography

Since my late teens one of the questions that I have asked repeatedly is 'What happened on the night of 15th August 1947? How come we lost our idealism and became corrupt overnight?' Of course I am exaggerating. But there is no denying that we went into galloping decline and moved from high-minded selflessness and sacrifice to the single-minded pursuit of Mammon. There has been the occasional generic answer: the ideals of any revolution dissipate the moment it achieves its goals. All Third-World countries evince the same trends. Self-denial and the energies directed against the common enemy bind people into a closely knit team. When the colonizer/common enemy leaves, the glue comes unstuck and it's each man for himself.

Granted, but that's theory and abstractions. What were the precise stages and stations of the fall of our leaders and fathers? How did we deteriorate and abandon our values? How come even our self-interest could not see beyond its nose. There's almost no way of knowing since we do not have a tradition of autobiography which is the most obvious keeper of a people's memories. Some of our fiction dealt with the trauma of Partition but hardly ever touched upon our moral degeneration with imagination and insight. (*Midnight's Children*, incidentally, arrived in 1982.)

In the late 1960s and 1970s, Dalit writing in Marathi made its appearance. Dalits possessed almost nothing but memories. Memories of centuries of injustice, physical hardship and ill-treatment, often bordering on unspeakable cruelty. A lot of their work was autobiographical. It was the story of various marginalized castes, or rather 'outcastes'; of Mahars, Maangs, Mochis, Paradhis; of cobblers, petty thieves, night-soil carriers. Of people who lived on the edge, literally outside the village boundaries. They wrote about extreme poverty and persecution, hunger and humiliation, and unimaginable physical and psychological abuse and violence which we 'caste Hindus' visited upon them. They wrote without embellishment and their prose could singe with its rage and raw power.

But literature cannot survive on memories and autobiography alone, however shattering, tough and unadorned the writing may be. Memories and memoirs can be urgent, immediate and intense. But the alchemy of imagination liberates an author from a literal truth and a constricting adherence to memory and fact. Fictional truth has a different kind of searing impact, for it captures not the letter but the spirit of an experience. Its indictment, symbols and insights are elliptical and hence far more disturbing. As with all great fiction, long after you've finished a book it keeps ticking and detonating inside you.

Oddly enough, it was middle-class Maharashtrian women, mostly married to celebrity writers, actors, directors, who also explored the autobiographical form. These were traditional women for whom the husband should have been lord and master. On 'Wat-Savitri' day, they should have prayed that they would get the same husband in the next seven lives. Instead, on the tide of feminism, these women writers began to tell it like it was. They exposed the pettiness, the egotism, the hypocrisy, the foulness and the double standards of their famous husbands and of men in general. The most notable of these were Sunita Deshpande's *Ahe Manohar Tari* (1990), Kamal Padhye's *Bandh Anubandh* (1993), Shantabai Kambli's *Majhya Jalmachi Chitterkatha* (1983). These memoirs too performed a long-overdue task. They began to right the balance between the much-written-about story of men and the untold story of women. The best of them, like the most famous autobiography in Marathi, Laxmibai Tilak's *Smrutichitre* (published in four parts, 1934–37) went way beyond that and drew a sharp, witty and nuanced picture of their societies. They delivered a double whammy: they helped us understand their own lives and they led us to understand ourselves. They were marked by a rare sanity, wisdom and compassion. Some other women authors often seem to write to settle scores and get even: perhaps a necessary and worthy objective but a limited one.

There's a conundrum here: there are Dalits all over India. Why did Dalits in Maharashtra alone find such a powerful voice? I can only hazard a few inadequate guesses. Dr Ambedkar set a powerful example in this state: he proved that, given half a chance and education, there was no end to how far an 'Untouchable' may go. He was entrusted to help evolve and draft the most powerful document in the land: the Constitution of India.

Another reason may be the power of the city of Mumbai. In spite of the outbreaks of riots and communal violence, Mumbai permits anonymity. The metropolis is under far too much pressure and is far too self-absorbed to have the time or the inclination to bother too much with anyone's caste.

Memories, Memorials and Monuments

(That sub-head is a lift from at least a half dozen post-Modernists.)

Both memory and its public manifestation, the collective memory called history, are under attack today. Many people including some leading educationists see the study of history as irrelevant for our times. Since there is such a premium on technology, the applied sciences and subjects like commerce and business management which translate into jobs and higher salaries, the time spent on history in schools, these people feel, could be better spent on more materially beneficial subjects like information technology.

The past, others argue, can also become a quagmire of nostalgia and a bank of terminal fantasies for a bankrupt people. There is no gainsaying that if we stand perpetually facing the past, we'll atrophy rapidly and die. But there is no future without the past, nor can we negotiate the present without it. If the first principle is to 'Know Thyself', how can we gain this knowledge without memory or history? It would be impossible to understand our institutions, Hindu Law and the Shariat, our gods, castes and outcastes, our hatreds and our persecutions, military strategies, our feelings, repressions, our diseases, our architecture and our cultural treasures, our arts, our languages, and our political systems without understanding how we came to be the way we are.

If a people wish to be a dynamic polity, the first prerequisite is to confront our collective memory, all the high points along with the skeletons in our history closets; our betrayals and our defeats, our colonial past and our lame and halting post-colonial progress towards the fiftieth anniversary of our Independence. As always, there will never be one view of history. Let us confront and live with them all – the Marxist, the subaltern, the classical or religious or any other view of history.

It is but natural that for the past two decades anthropologists, literary critics, historians and philosophers who deal with the Third World have been mainly preoccupied with colonialism and post-colonialism. Edward Said, Homi Bhabha, to name just a couple, along with earlier thinkers and theoreticians like Gramsci, have not only defined the parameters and terms of the enquiry but brought about a sea change in our understanding of how it suited our colonial masters to see, talk and write about us, but also about how our own perceptions of ourselves, our role in life, our politics and our destinies were drastically altered by this view.

One of their major projects is to look at memory and to ask how we should deal with our past. The implications and ramifications of this investigation are many but there is one particular strand which has been the subject of much debate in India and which concerns all citizens. A recent exhibition called 'Dominion and Power' at the Piramal Gallery in Mumbai displayed photographs of the various visits the kings and queens of England paid India after 1857. From this and from many other sources, it is clear that the British in their role as colonizers and masters wished to engrave upon the native mind that we were the conquered and subject peoples; that Queen Victoria, Edward VII, George V, Edward VIII and George VI were the long-distance empress and emperors of India, and that their culture, mores, art, industry and religion were infinitely superior to ours. They continued to do this in a sustained fashion through varied means lest we heathens with our innocent and devious minds forgot our fallen status and place in life. (Nothing new about this: the Lodis, the Slave Dynasty, the Mughals, the Mewaris, the Vijayanagaris, the Cholas, and Hitler did it to impress their own people as well as conquered races.)

What better way to glorify your rule and to keep your subjugated people in a state of awe than to erect monumental buildings that will last a thousand years, perhaps longer. That was certainly the avowed purpose and intent of the Empire when it commissioned Edwin Lutyens and Herbert Baker to conceive the imperial capital of India. The architects of New Delhi certainly went over the top and overboard. But that was the idea. You can't blame the two men and the Empire for doing precisely what they set out to do: make a hybrid, tumescent and rhetorical imperial statement in perpetuity. The colonial buildings in Bombay too are evidence of the same impulse: glorify the Empire and subdue the natives.

The question then is: Why should we preserve these colonial memories and monuments and thus glorify once again a highly exploitative regime? Why should we spend new money highlighting this legacy? We must re-examine our history and decide what parts we should remember and emphasize, and what we need to ignore.

I am not quite clear about what these critics want to do with colonial monuments. Should we exercise benign neglect towards them and allow them to fall into a state of disrepair? Or should we break down CST, or VT as the Central Railway Terminus in Mumbai was formerly called, and the other colonial buildings on Ballard Estate, Dadabhai Naoroji Road and elsewhere? On the contrary, we need to confront our history, not to sweep bits and pieces of it under the carpet or, worse still, doctor it. Let me emphasize that Said and the others do not set out to do this. Historians will always have a viewpoint, ideology or a bias, be it classical, Marxist, subaltern, or whatever. They will highlight a few things, ignore some things, and downplay others. But it is an entirely different project when fundamentalists go about doctoring our history and reinventing it, just as the Committee for Un-American Activities and the Communists who airbrushed photographs and memory did. Because people in a democracy must have free access to all varieties of histories for them to understand the different forces and ideas that went into the making of India, its neighbours and all the countries of the world.

Prohibition's Dead. Long Live Prohibition

THERE ARE FEW DIARISTS as ruthlessly honest as Babur, the founder of the Mughal Empire. In the *Baburnama*, as his diaries came to be known, he tells us how often he had vowed to give up wine and alcohol and just as often broken the vow. But on the eve of the crucial battle of Khanua in March 1527, which would alter the fate of Hindustan for centuries to come, his troops panicked and were on the verge of going back to Kabul. They had heard tales of the foolhardy but unstoppable bravery of the Rajput warriors, and now, faced with the prospect of fighting the largest Rajput army ever assembled under the formidable leadership of Rana Sangram, the King of Mewar, decided that fleeing was the better part of valour.

That night Babur gathered his most trusted nobles and deputies in his tent, forswore liquor along with all of them, and then to stress that neither he nor they could go back on the new resolve, smashed all the gold and silver goblets. This time he kept his vow. However, the succeeding rulers of the mighty Mughal dynasty were hardly averse to drink. Some of them like Humayun and especially Jehangir were, as a matter of fact, major imbibers and were given to other addictions as well. However, Aurangzeb, not the last, but certainly the last of the great Mughal emperors, was a teetotaller.

It's almost unthinkable to take the name of Aurangzeb in the same breath as that of Mahatma Gandhi but the two did have at least one thing in common. Like Aurangzeb, Gandhi too did not touch alcohol. Perhaps the similarity didn't end there. Given half a chance, both of them would have enforced prohibition on their countrymen.

The new theology of free markets, unbridled capitalism, and rampant consumerism has not only conspired to make the Father of the Nation irrelevant but also to insinuate that Gandhi was some kind of a crank and his theories about agriculture, the economy, the environment, were just so much poppycock. The most risible of the bees hovering over his bald head, according to this all-pervasive faith, is supposed to be prohibition.

Gandhi had certainly mooted the idea of prohibition many a time. His reasons were not only obvious but sound. Every scientific study had shown that drinking was a serious killer of people, especially the young. Too many poor families found themselves sinking into ever greater poverty because the man of the house was addicted to alcohol. The worst victims were the womenfolk. The men lost their jobs, and the burden of supporting the family and the addiction of the husband fell upon the wives. And almost always, alcoholism exacerbated the pervasive domestic violence.

But there was another shrewd tactical reason why Gandhi had promoted prohibition. He had started the Civil Disobedience movement because he sensed that the Achilles' heel of the British was the economy. What better way to hurt the government than to boycott all British goods including the consumption of foreign liquor?

When India won independence, there was no longer any need for civil disobedience. But Gandhiji's lifelong concern for the effects of alcohol on the poor was so strong that Article 47 of the Directive Principles of the Constitution which was proclaimed in December 1948 just two months after the Mahatma's murder, recommended that the consumption of alcohol be prohibited. Directive Principles can just as easily be seen as so much hokum and hot air as being the finest aspirations of a nation. They are not obligatory, but the Bombay Presidency, which at that time included both Maharashtra and Gujarat, was amongst the first states to pass the Prohibition of Alcohol Act in 1949.

The reason Bombay took the lead was because it had two chief ministers, Balasaheb Kher and Morarji Desai, who were committed disciples of Gandhi. Desai was an inflexible martinet and the butt of innumerable jokes since he was a proponent of urine therapy. Piss was often referred to as Morarji bhai's scotch.

Gandhiji had been aware of the failure of prohibition in the United States but he attributed it to a lack of the moral tradition and abstemiousness which he felt India had in plenty. But prohibition turned out to be the mother of hypocrisy, mendacity and the Licence Raj in Bombay and wherever else it was introduced. It was a deadly bone of corruption on which the Indian bureaucracy, the police and the politicians cut their teeth. The measures taken to enforce prohibition were often droll and absurd, like the police check post at Mahim close to St Michael's Church where all road-transport vehicles, private or public, had to stop for scrutiny while just a few hundred metres away you could carry any contraband with impunity on the local trains. Speakeasies, or Auntie's joints as they were called in Bombay, proliferated across the city to cater to the enormous demand.*

The tragicomedy called prohibition has been running almost as long as Agatha Christie's *The Mousetrap*. At the height of prohibition, you could wangle a permit 'for preservation and maintenance of health'; this despite all medical evidence to the contrary. But there's no denying that all parties involved benefited from the transaction: the doctor who wrote the recommendation, the said party who was suffering from alcohol deprivation cloaked as a heart

---

* The novel *The Extras* recreates this era vividly.

condition, the clerk who issued the permit for services rendered, and last but most importantly, the government which collected the fees. Needless to say, at least half of Bombay would have liked to plead acute health problems, all of them curable with vast infusions of liquor.

As is often the case, it was economics that induced a modicum of realism into the picture. Bombay collects the highest taxes in the country, and yet the city has been in the red so long that the Maharashtra state itself is considered by many a failed state. The solution has been a classic Indian one. The charade and the chicanery of the law continue on paper. You are still officially required to get a permit for reasons of health if you wish to buy beer, wine or the hard stuff, but anybody above eighteen can walk into a liquor store and ask for whatever he wants as long as he can pay the price. The reason should be self-evident. Alcohol is nothing less than a mint. The revenues accruing from its sale have risen to the point where the customer ends up paying far more in taxes than for the liquor.

American media and Hollywood transformed Al Capone and other Mafia hoods who made their names and their enormous fortunes in the Prohibition era into mythological figures. The fascination with gangsters, their Cosa Nostra connections, the feuds between the different ruling families in the mob, their deep links with the political apparatus and the unions in America would continue to mesmerize directors like Coppola and Scorsese and enthral audiences across the world. Prohibition would certainly be a gold mine for the Indian mafia too. But luckily in India, the prohibition saga remained what it really was: a squalid, seedy and sleazy business.

All that, however, has changed. Both the Indian media and Bollywood have discovered that crime not only pays handsomely but that covering it also yields a bonanza since the public never tires of the romanticization of godfathers and their nefarious activities.

As with so many other nations which have attempted to impose prohibition, the experiment has proven to be a sordid chapter in the history of independent India. It continues to be so in Gandhiji's own state of Gujarat. Nothing makes as much money in Gujarat as banned alcohol. At the peak of prohibition in Bombay, foreigners could get drinks in five-star hotels by merely showing their passports. Ahmedabad, the capital of Gujarat, has gone one better. Even as foreigners, and that includes visiting Indian NRIs, alight from their planes, they can get a licence at the airport itself.

It is intriguing and simultaneously futile to speculate how the Mahatma would have reacted once he realized what an unmitigated disaster prohibition had proved to be despite its noble aims. Prohibition has subverted and sabotaged the very principles which were the foundations of his philosophy and code of conduct, and which had steered the country to a unique freedom struggle. Truth, honesty and integrity had been the first casualties and victims of prohibition. The rot, sadly has spread from the highest echelons in the government to the rank and file.

Would Gandhi have changed his mind now that it has been proven beyond any doubt that prohibition does not do away with or even control drinking? On the contrary, it has increased the consumption of alcohol and endangered the lives of the poor because every now and then it is laced with turpentine or something even more deadly. Gandhi, unlike his disciples, was a pragmatist and flexible enough to adjust his strategies to political reality without compromising his fundamental beliefs. But he was also a hardcore idealist and could be unreasonable and obdurate. The truth is, we'll never know, and all our conjectures will be just that, academic speculation.

Staying Indian

HOW TO BE AN Indian and stay that way, etc., etc., etc. ... I thought that this is the kind of vacuous but dangerous question which is raised only at lit fests and other rare occasions.

I most definitely do not want to be an Indian – unless you nuance what you mean by Indian. I don't want to sing 'Saare Jahan Se Achhah and I certainly do not want to sing the Stars and Stripes', or any of the other gung-ho patriotic national anthems that have bred so much hatred and violence. Americans profess to love their country. So do Iranians and North Koreans, the Russians and the Chinese, the French, the Rwandans, the Sudanese, the Brits, not to mention the Iraqis, even under Saddam Hussein, or our own countrymen – and look where it's got us. The end of the Cold War was supposed to signal not only the end of history but also wars, genocides, massacres and holocausts. But the exact opposite has been the case.

If being an Indian means turning a blind eye to the massacre of Sikhs after Prime Minister Indira Gandhi's assassination or the 2002 Gujarat riots, then I want no part of being an Indian. If being a follower of the remarkable Chhatrapati Shivaji Maharaj means breaking into the Bhandarkar Oriental Research Institute in Pune and burning 2,000-year-old manuscripts; if being a pillar of Hinduism means we deny our Islamic heritage and take the law in our own hands to riot, terrorize innocents, and burn public property; if being an Indian means we don't give a damn about the suicides of cotton farmers or the silent death called malnutrition that affects hundreds of thousands of our children, then I want no part of it.

If being an Indian means we cannot tolerate free and open discussions about even the most sensitive subjects without taking recourse to violence; if being an Indian means we have the right to torture and burn our women, our Dalits, the deprived and the downtrodden; if being an Indian means passing the legacy of endemic corruption to our children; if being an Indian means throwing the scraps called quotas at all those whom we have brutalized for centuries in the hope of getting their votes instead of spending the money on giving them the very best education from kindergarten onwards; if being an Indian means nothing but the rapacious pursuit of money, more and more conspicuous consumption, more cars and more and more luxury goods, without a thought for our earth, and the environment; if being an Indian means we are incapable of making sacrifices for our children and leaving a viable tomorrow and munificent planet for them, then why, in God's name, would I want to be an Indian?

On the other hand, if by remaining an Indian, you mean going the Kabir way and not caring whether one's god is called Ram or Rahim, Jesus or Jehovah, then yes, and yes again, I want to stay an Indian. If by Indian, you mean we get Gandhiji out of the attic and the neem leaves and naphthalene balls, not as we do twice a year to pay him lip service but instead give him a good, permanent airing and live his ideals of non-violence and tolerance, I am with you all the way. If by being an Indian, you mean appropriating the founding fathers of America and their principles, if by Indian you want me and everybody else in the world to practise the two great attributes of Allah, mercy and compassion, then certainly call me an Indian. If by Indian, you will bring out the child Jesus in each one of us, Jesus who loved the wretched of the earth more than anybody else, then count me in and hold me to my word. If by Indian you want a billion-and-odd of us on the subcontinent to exercise restraint in consumption and in generating carbon dioxide and all the other harmful gasses instead of waiting for others to take the first step, let's get off our butts and prove what good Indians we are.

Sometimes greed is indeed a good and godly thing. Tolstoy, Dostoevsky, Beethoven, Rumi, Thoreau, Balanchine, the Beatles, Satyajit Ray, Leonardo da Vinci, Shakespeare, Balzac, Kalidas, Einstein, Baba Amte, Mohammed Yunus, the Buddha, Camus, I don't give a damn which nationality they belong to. I just want them. I want them for all of mankind. If that's what globalization means, I can't have enough of it. Unlike money and the universal finite pie which we all want to grab for ourselves, there's more than enough for all of us. Actually, here's the best part: as my mother used to say about *vidya* or knowledge, the more you share it, the more it grows.

The Fine Art of Intolerance

LET ME BEGIN AT the wrong end. Let me start with what should be footnotes. Romain Gary once said that there is only one thing worse than intolerance. It is the intolerance of intolerance.

I hope to briefly explore the role of legal and extra-legal censorship and then move on to the insidious and dangerous ways in which both these controlling mechanisms have enlarged their scope and reach to unexpected areas and the danger they pose to our constitutionally given fundamental rights and freedoms. (Fortunately we Indians don't think we have any duties either towards our Constitution or towards our fellow men and women. Duties like paying taxes, eschewing bribes and corruption, fair-mindedness or looking after the fundamental rights of others, especially the poor.) While the thrust of this paper is severely anti-censorship, let me state in the clearest terms possible that I support censorship when it comes to issues like child pornography. Secondly, I'm not sure whether books, pamphlets or films that provoke hate and violence against a community should be banned or negotiated through argument and debate.

The Genesis of Censorship

There are no historical records about how exactly censorship evolved but here's one of the more plausible theories. The impulse behind censorship in primitive times when tribal societies were homogeneous, and even today, was normative. The elders had a vision of how members of the tribe should conduct themselves; what they should do and not do; what they could say or not say; what would bring honour to the group and what would bring dishonour. In a real sense censorship could have served as the basis of the concept of codified law itself; the Ten Commandments, like the laws of Hammurabi and the edicts of Ashoka can be seen as but logical extensions of censorship.

Things have changed a little since those innocent days. Since there are many more groupings, religions, factions, denominations, political ideologies, caste and class interests, special interest cliques, we now have multiple and often conflicting visions of an ideal society, especially in those countries which claim to be secular. And even more important, they are in constant competition. Whether we like it or not, the normative high ground has given way to one-upmanship, keeping up with the Joneses and a flexing of muscle that is nothing but a power kick.

In a country like India there are currently two kinds of censorship: legal and extra-legal. The first might come across as unreasonable but it has the full weight of the law and the state behind it. Extra-legal censorship occurs when a group of people decide to take the law in their own hands and ban a book or prevent a performance of a play, a concert or an exhibition of paintings.

Political parties may start with high ideals and their manifestos may outline lofty mission statements but as we all know, in a country like India, come election time, there is only one overarching consideration: the vote bank. *The Satanic Verses* was a victim of the misconceived idea of appeasing the vote bank. A member of Parliament, Syed Shahabuddin needed a cause for his flagging political fortunes and *The Satanic Verses* came in handy. A few people died during the protests that followed and Prime Minister Rajiv Gandhi banned its import. It is doubtful if anyone in Parliament had read the novel but that should not come as a surprise. It is one of the preconditions of censorship that the offending text is mostly unread when it is banned. What happened next is well known. Grand Ayatollah Khomeini, the Supreme Leader and both the political and religious head of Iran, issued a fatwa asking the Faithful to kill Salman Rushdie.

It augurs badly for a nation and its people that while the courts will make sure that a legal ban is respected, they will not defend the right of freedom of speech and expression when the only ban that is operative is an extra-legal one and is enforced through the intimidating tactics of a section of the public, usually backed by some political party.

Take just one case, a particularly harmless one. The movie version of the Dan Brown book, *The Da Vinci Code* was seen several times by members of the Indian central censor board and later by the minister of information. Nothing offensive was found in the film, but to be on the safe side, the film distributors were asked to attach a disclaimer both before the film started and immediately after the end, that the story was pure fiction and did not lay claim to any sort of veracity. Yet even though the central censor board had okayed it, it was reported in the press that eight states refused permission to show it. The courts did not feel the need to mandate that since the film had a censorship certificate, no one but no one could prevent it being shown.

When the courts do not take a stand on such issues, the glib defence put forward is that they cannot be expected to rush in every time the mob decides to dictate matters. The fact is, just a few cases of a strong response from the courts ordering the governments of individual states to do their duty, if necessary by calling in the police, will ensure that political parties and the populace learn to respect the rights of the 'other'. It will work even better if the same courts mandate that any guilty party which tries to threaten a performance or an exhibition of art through extra-legal means will be fined so exorbitantly for wasting the court's time that it would serve as a serious deterrent.

An All-pervasive Culture of Appeasement

Politicians of every hue, aided and abetted by the denizens of our country, have grasped what an enormous political cache extra-legal censorship is. A few decades into Independence, we began to realize the political potential in becoming highly oversensitive people with extra-thin skins. Everybody is on the lookout for slights, innuendoes, real or imagined slurs, and everybody takes offence whether or not there is a suggestion of something untoward or deeply hurtful in his or her select field or group. The police, doctors, lawyers, the engineers, teachers, armed forces, members of every sub-sect of every religion, not to mention our esteemed politicians, become apoplectic at any suspicion of criticism. (Obviously all talk of the monumental scams covered daily in our media are *maya* or sheer fiction.) Their response follows a familiar path: immediate, vociferous protests, often followed by violence.

National and regional political parties have exploited and honed the business of intolerance into a fine art. With the latter, the platform changes every few years and so does their choice of villain. Sometimes it's jobs for locals; the toll tax on highways; at other times it's the local language and signboards which are not in the regional lingo. At times it's a book which may portray the party in a not too favourable light. Or they might go after Bangladeshis or Biharis. What is reliable is the quality of the reaction. It is utterly disproportionate, even on the rare occasion when there might be a genuine grievance. Violence, of course, is the most common response. Blackening a teacher's face, destroying the rarest of ancient manuscripts or cricket trophies is par for the course. But the repertoire does not end there. *Rasta rokos* and bandhs are just a few other variations on demagoguery and mob rule.

The national parties work at a different level. They have grasped that their most potent weapon is God and what passes for the honour of God. In the name of religion they practise the most malevolent and explosive violence. Thousands are killed, entire neighbourhoods are burnt down, and the residents of the 'other' community forced to flee for their lives. The bloodbaths of the Partition, the demolition of the Babri Masjid, the 1993 Bombay bomb blasts, the Gujarat massacres of 2002, you can put every one of them down in the debit and credit account of God as interpreted by the religious zealots of every hue with the connivance, if not outright provocation, of the political leadership of the state.

Choking Creativity and Original Thinking

The effects of censorship, both state-sponsored and that practised by political parties and religious institutions, has far graver consequences than the banning of a book, a performance of *The Last Temptation of Christ* or the persecution of an artist like Hussain till he is forced to flee to a foreign country. Artists and authors are often asked if the mere presence of censorship leads to self-censorship. This is such an asinine question, it doesn't merit an answer. Of course it does, even when artists might claim the contrary. Censorship quite simply closes door after door; though many of the subjects would never have posed a threat to society. Who in India, for instance, would hazard to write a robust, critical (and that word doesn't mean dig-out-the-dirt on someone), balanced and fearless book on Chhatrapati Shivaji Maharaj or Subhash Chandra Bose when the majority of critics themselves prefer to stay within the ambit of hagiography?

But there is a new wrinkle to the notion of competitive censorship. We have now entered the age of altering and revising history. A few years after we gained independence, *Shankar's Weekly* had highlighted the slow, deliberative pace at which the Indian Constitution was being written with a cartoon depicting the prime mover of the document, Dr Ambedkar, sitting on a snail and the then Prime Minister, Jawaharlal Nehru, goading the snail to go faster. More than sixty years later some members of Parliament objected to its being reproduced in an NCERT school textbook. The reason for this belated censorship? It hurt the sentiments of the Dalits to see their leader being made fun of. The irony is that while both Ambedkar and Nehru were conversant with the idiom of the cartoon medium and its enormous potential for bringing sanity and a sense of perspective to political life, their followers were immune to its charms and vital commentary. In truth they are a sad lot who can only exercise power and feel important by making an issue of total non-issues. Mrs Sonia Gandhi was only too happy to accommodate the protesters in the hope that when it came to the crunch, they would stand by her party. But there's a larger issue here. Instead of addressing the enormous problems which confront the polity, these gentlemen wish to whitewash and tamper with history.

There is a rather convenient belief that censorship is operative primarily in matters of literature, painting, theatre, cinema, in short, art. The general view is that art is nothing but 'time pass', as the lovely Indian phrase tells us, and so it doesn't matter if art gets a rotten deal. After all, it's science which will save mankind by inventing new technologies for food production and inventing new drugs to cure diseases and extend life, and so it must remain unfettered. But there is a bit of self-deception here, if not a singular ignorance of the history of science. Copernicus was fortunate that he died soon after he published his book *On the Revolution of the*

Heavenly Bodies, but Galileo was not so lucky. His *Dialogue Concerning The Two Chief World Systems* earned the wrath of Pope Urban VIII and was not only banned, but he had to face the Inquisition and recant while also being forced to live under house arrest till he died. The history of science is often a history of persistent ignorance and persecution. Darwinism is still under severe attack in the United States from the believers in Creationism. Our own country is a fine example of superstition, astrology, ignorance, witchcraft, numerology, vastushastra, black magic, babas and swamis triumphing over the scientific temper and method. Our political leaders, starting from the late Indira Gandhi, are more often than not under the thrall of tantrics and other religious gurus.

A free, uninhibited and open atmosphere is the oxygen that allows scientists, mathematicians, architects and those from other disciplines, not to mention the arts and the humanities, to think without walls, taboos and claustrophobia; and to dare to take risks and venture into unknown and unexplored territories.

But that too does not reveal the wily but palpable far-reaching effects of an atmosphere of Big Brother looking over your shoulder every minute. Light and openness are scotched out and an atmosphere of suspicion and fear reigns. Much worse, the horizon shrinks at an alarming rate and all your values get skewed. Your air supply starts to dwindle. Creative minds in the sciences as well as in the humanities and the arts can breathe, thrive and contribute to their disciplines only when there are no barriers to knowledge and ideas.

The New Avatars of Censorship ... The Gag Order on Whistle-blowers

What we are witnessing today is that both legal and extra-legal censorship are steadily enlarging their scope and reach, and criminalizing the very people who, at grievous risk to themselves, stand up and raise their voices against corruption and the flagrant abuse and disregard of the Constitution and the fundamental rights of the people.

I am referring to the international tribe of whistle-blowers: Bradley Manning who leaked hundreds of thousands of damning classified American state documents to the Wikileaks founder, Julian Assange; and Edward Snowden who leaked the National Security Agency's (NSA) clandestine work in America which revealed that it was snooping on millions of its own citizens, not to mention billions of others across the world, including the prime ministers of European countries like Germany, France, and even America's closest ally, Israel. We in India too should have got extremely worked up about Uncle Sam spying on us. But neither the government nor Indians at large seemed to be at all exercised by the fact that the United States was spying on our state secrets or by the blatant intrusions on Indian citizens' privacy. Who knows, considering our obsession with all things American, we might even have been proud to be of interest to the NSA.

I guess most of you were not even born when Daniel Ellsberg's revelation of the Pentagon Papers ultimately brought down President Nixon. And let's not forget our own heroic whistle-blowers like Ashok Khemka against whom several cases have been registered; Manjunath Shanmugam and Satyendranath Dubey, both of whom were murdered; and many others who endeavoured to be loyal to the Constitution and the Indian polity but were severely punished. As you can see, the whistle-blower is a very rare but universal phenomenon. Almost always she or he is much reviled by those whose corruption and wrongdoing are exposed, and believe it or not, often by Presidents and Prime Ministers who should be honouring them.

The Soldier's Dilemma

Let's look at the dilemma posed by the phenomenon of the whistle-blower for a minute. It is akin to the quandary that a soldier faces when he disobeys his bosses for what he believes to be his ethical duty. Since ancient times, soldiers are required to follow orders without questioning their superiors or the consequences of the orders. Now here's the problem. German soldiers, just like the Allied forces, had to take the oath of loyalty during the Second World War. When on Hitler's orders, the officers in charge of concentration and death camps killed millions, the Nuremberg trial judges were appalled. Why hadn't they disobeyed orders which resulted in the Holocaust? Thus a soldier will, on occasion, find himself in dire trouble if he disobeys his commander, and perhaps even worse trouble if he obeys him. Either way the soldier finds himself in a terrible no-win situation.

Take the case of Jeffrey Wigand, the scientist who was working for one of the five or six tobacco companies that control the global cigarette business. In 1993 he was thrown out of his job and his life threatened because he revealed that his company was using a tobacco additive that posed a potential health risk, and thus broke the confidentiality clause he had signed at his company. He was seen by many as a turncoat who ratted on the very firm which had allowed him to live a plush lifestyle. But the fact was his conscience wouldn't allow him to let smokers suffer terrible damage, and hence he spoke up even when it meant that he would have to live a hand-to-mouth existence for the rest of his life. Along with many other factors, his revelations forced the tobacco companies to shell out 246 billion dollars as settlement towards various lawsuits. It's worthwhile remembering that none of this money came his way.

It is the hallmark of censorship to punish those who threaten the powers that be. The irony is that the one who performs an extremely valuable public service also comes under tacit or open censorship. She or he is continually harassed; false cases are filed against the person. Often the person is bumped off.

J. Edgar Hoover, director of the FBI, used to snoop not only on his enemies but also on members of the Senate and Congress, not to mention ordinary citizens. President Nixon did that and so did the Stasi (State Security Service) in East Germany. Is that what the future holds for us? The most disheartening factor at the moment is the sheer apathy and indifference of our people. Are we to understand that the possibility of our every movement being constantly watched, our emails opened and our phones tapped does not bother us? In that case, even the good Lord cannot help this beloved and benighted country of ours. Unless we decide that we will not allow sloth, denial and indifference to destroy the values of freedom and democracy enshrined in the Constitution of India.

The Honoraries

ONCE UPON A TIME there was an institution called the honorary system of doctors in public hospitals. Since the majority of patients in India have always been so poor that both medical insurance and good medical care were beyond their reach, the British devised a system whereby doctors of repute in private practice would devote a certain amount of their time to looking after patients in public hospitals, and also to work as part-time faculty in medical colleges. Both MDs and doctors with FRCSs and MRCPs from London, Glasgow and Edinburgh, were recruited as assistant or full professors and worked many hours a week for a token honorarium. The benefits were twofold. Patients in public hospitals now had access to the kind of medical expertise they could never have afforded. And medical students were taught the theory and practice of medicine and surgery by the best minds in the field.

Many of the doctors and their amazing talent, the sheer art and finesse with which they operated, their diagnostic genius, their ability to zero in on the most critical symptoms amongst a plethora of information or the total lack of it (given the fact that many patients could only speak in their own regional language), and their quirks, eccentricities and peccadilloes became the stuff of legend. One could fill tome after tome with these tall-sounding but true tales but here's just a brief sampling. There was this general surgeon who smoked while operating. His students, who revered his skills but dreaded his tantrums, puzzled over the effect of Char Minar cigarette ash against that of imported Marlboros when it was dropped into the cavity of an open abdomen. One famous cardiologist from the Parsi community was so good and therefore so busy, the only way you could see him, they said, was to have a cardiac arrest by appointment three weeks in advance. Who can forget the honorary physician with a sulphurous temper who bit his nails till he drew blood and had to dip them in a solution of iodine every night? He had done only his MD, and yet his diagnostic skills were so remarkable, even the most established MRCPs in Bombay would call him for advice when they encountered a particularly tricky case. He would walk into his outpatient department, draw his registrar close to him and whisper not to admit the ninth patient from the left because she was suffering from galloping TB (this was before the time of streptomycin) and would be dead by the next evening, or he would spot a little boy with fever and while the students debated whether he had malaria, measles or typhoid, he would ask his assistant to admit and isolate the boy immediately in the infectious diseases ward because this was a rare case of nasal diphtheria. He was, as his students will tell you, rarely wrong.

Medicine may have come a long way from those days. Some of those advances, not to mention costs, have been staggering, but those brief anecdotes encapsulate the difference between machine diagnostics and the finely developed diagnostic sense of the human mind. Technology has wrought a crucial change in the way medicine views a human being who is sick. Today the patient is often perceived as the disease he's suffering from and ceases to be an individual with a unique body, mind, past, hopes and aspirations plus a specific ailment. In short, a man, woman or child with his own unique story.

Teachers almost always become role models for their students. The conscientious ones who were punctual, who went to their OPD on the appointed days, did the rounds of their wards and kept track of the progress of their patients, would very likely turn out students with a lively sense of responsibility which made it mandatory that they paid the same attention (though not as much time) to their free patients as they did to the paying ones. On the other hand, those who never or very rarely turned up in OPD but left it to their registrars to take care of it, would usually generate crop after crop of students who, when they passed out, became honoraries who were as callous and uncaring.

The population of Mumbai has grown at an alarming rate. Many new hospitals have come up in the last two or three decades, a great many of them owned by private corporations. While they may have a symbolic free or near-free section, they make no bones about being profit-driven. Half of the population lives on pavements, under bridges or in slums. Obviously they cannot afford to pay for medical treatment or hospitals. Yet despite the disproportionate number of the poor and the borderline poor in the city, the number of public hospitals run by the state government and the municipality has barely kept pace with growing demand.

There is an acute shortage of space, beds, nurses, staff, operating theatres and most of all, medication and money. Forget the most advanced technological equipment and diagnostic aids, even when it comes to critical and commonly used gadgets, most hospitals often have outdated and broken down stomach pumps, ventilators and other life-saving aids.

The government and the municipality are reluctant to invest money in equipment and new hospitals for very sound reasons. Patients, after all, are not vote banks, and as such, there's no return on investment and no quid pro quo. If there is an epidemic, a riot, bomb blasts, many patients have to perforce lie on mattresses on the floor. Conditions of hygiene are primitive when they are not abysmal. The hours the young interns work are often beyond endurance. And yet, by and large, considering the inhuman workload, miserable living conditions and the questionable infrastructure, public hospitals in Bombay have a remarkable record of patient recovery.

Hospital infections, as everybody knows, are amongst the most deadly and intractable. But since the country won independence, doctors in public hospitals have discovered a mysterious new condition. Oddly enough, it strikes only politicians, influential industrialists, scamsters and other high-minded people like mafia bosses who are remanded to police custody. It goes without saying that such cases are extremely rare.

The moment these worthies are incarcerated, they develop a serious heart condition and have to be instantly removed to private rooms in government or municipal hospitals. Seniormost doctors are rushed in to take care of such prestigious patients. The sick person is allowed food from home, a TV set, a cell phone and other life-saving amenities. Naturally, in line with their high standing, the neta gets to hold court in his private suite or room.

The Medical Council of India did away with the honorary system in Mumbai and replaced it with full-time salaried doctors in the pay of the government. The rationale for this was that only full-time employees could do justice to the patients. There's no denying that the honorary system had flaws. (Which system devised by humans doesn't?) Partisan camps, dynastic appointments, a lack of accountability, all of them occasional. But honorary doctors worked under highly unfavourable conditions. More often than not, they had to see at least fifty patients in the OPD within an hour and a half or two at the most. That worked out to two and a half minutes per patient. By any measure that is an absurd time frame in which to diagnose and treat a patient, and simultaneously teach students. But the fact is that despite its flaws and the assembly line speeds at which the patients were examined, especially in Mumbai, in the great majority of cases the patients got well.

There are, broadly speaking, three kinds of doctors who get into public hospitals. The first are the committed lot. They are idealists who believe they must work for the amelioration of society and especially the poor. Many of them are intensely into research even though the facilities are primitive. The second variety are doctors who are good at their job, are ambitious but do not have the wherewithal to set up private practice. All that the third segment wants, not to put too fine an interpretation on it, is to get by without having to work too hard. You get your pay, often quarters to live in (no mean attraction in a city like Mumbai) and a provident fund. Add to that there is hardly any likelihood of being kicked out for incompetence.

The full-time doctor system has been in place for a few decades now. Medical science has splintered into more and more specialized disciplines, and technological advances have taken quantum leaps, but most public hospitals are even more acutely strapped for funds today than ever before. While the salaries of doctors at public hospitals have gone up considerably, there is still a great deal of dissatisfaction with their remuneration package, for the simple reason that since the opening of the market in the early 1990s, the fees charged by private practitioners have shot up into the stratosphere and continue to rise. Ultimately, the poorest patients, it would appear, must continue to make do with government hospitals, and that last resort of both the penurious and the wealthy, none other than the Almighty himself.

Tuesday, Bloody Tuesday

SOMEONE MUST HAVE SWITCHED on the TV in the next room. That's off. Watching TV is usually limited to the evening hours here, never in the mornings, certainly not as early as 8.30 a.m. I drift into the other room. Nobody notices my entry; they are mesmerized by the images on the TV screen.

I seem to be suffering from an acute attack of jet lag. I am disoriented and find myself in some other time frame. I seem to be back in 1993 during the bomb explosions.

A full flank of a compartment from a Mumbai local train has been pried open like the lid of an Amul cheese tin can. The camera is playing coy and shying away every time it comes close to dead bodies. The editor at the studio keeps cutting back to a wet windowpane that's been pulled down all the way and has two red bloodstains at the bottom, then to people walking on the rail tracks lifting hastily covered bodies. Two drenched men gesture angrily at the camera as they escort a baffled friend away from the scene.

Now the camera cuts to the reporter who has miraculously escaped the bomb blasts in another compartment and is about to tell of the impact of the explosion and how for a few stunned moments everybody sat uncertain and paralysed, and then suddenly the train emptied out. But before he launched excitedly, perhaps for the seventh or ninth time, on a paean to the unconquerable spirit of Mumbai and how the commuters of the train got down to help the wounded even before the police or the ambulances turned up, he makes certain that his channel gets a plug by telling us that as usual, his channel will be on the scene 24x7.

President Pervez Musharraf, we are told, has condemned the terrorist attacks. Soon, very soon, railway minister Lalu Prasad and Sonia Gandhi herself will give us their insights on who was responsible for the terrible events of Bloody Tuesday.

By now I am beginning to perceive that I have not segued into the past but am watching that awful, mind-numbing thing called breaking news, the fresh, piping hot, make-my-day, instant transmission of current-in-the-thick-of-disaster TV coverage.

I am close to 9,000 miles away from the seven simultaneous blasts that have shaken Mumbai once again to the roots, but even that vast distance will not safeguard me from what I would rather not know. I am regressing rapidly and asking inane questions: Why this constant need to kill? Will this slaughter of innocents never end? Is it mankind which is bloodthirsty? Or is it their God? Who, in God's name, is doing this? Was it Pakistan? The ISI? Was it SIMI? What was the trigger this time? Is it what we did in Gujarat? Is it because Kashmiri young people have no jobs and no future? Is it because the militants in Kashmir do not want a rapprochement between Pakistan and India? Is it because Musharraf thinks we are pussyfooting the talks on Kashmir? Or is it but one more stopover in the series of explosions that have shattered Madrid, London and now Mumbai?

I want to go lie down. Will someone please shut off the world? I rouse myself from my stupor and try to call a friend who commutes daily from Bandra into town and back again in the evenings, Is he okay? I can't get through. The voice of MTNL tells me: 'All lines on this route are busy.' I try for another half an hour and then give up. Is Naresh all right? Or has the terrorist RDX got him?

I should know a thing or two about terrorism. After all, I am the author of the book called *God's Little Soldier*. I spent close to eight years studying the extremist mind and came to the conclusion that clarity and understanding would come, not from a linear, straightforward approach, but through ambiguity alone. It was important to grasp that in the new arithmetic, right could be both right and wrong, and wrong could also be right.

I learnt that the definition of the enemy had remained the same since the time man began to live in tribes or perhaps even earlier. The identity of the enemy was always clear: he was the 'other', the one who was either a threat of annihilation for the group that called itself 'us' or who had already subjugated 'us'. It was obviously implicit that the opposite side could also view 'us' as the 'other'. When the Muslim invaders arrived in India, they were the 'other' for the Hindu 'us'. Clearly there was no mistaking the Christian Crusaders. They were the villains and the 'other' in Muslim eyes.

But the notion of the enemy changed for the first time in history in the last couple of decades of the 20th century. The enemy no longer had a sharp, unmistakable profile. The enemy was one or hundreds of innocent bystanders in Baghdad, Kabul or Tel Aviv who had never done the 'us' group any harm or were in any way connected to the perceived grievance.

In the transactions of terrorism, the bystanders became nothing more than victims or collateral damage. They are the instruments by which the militants in Iraq, for instance, think they are getting back at President George W. Bush and the so-called coalition headed by America.

At its core, the act of terrorism is a negation of all things that stand for life.

And yet of what use was all this knowledge now? How could I make sense of the madness I was witnessing on the TV screen and the chaos in the mind? The individual tragedies of the seven coordinated blasts had emasculated all the wisdom of my insights, not to mention the fine theories of the great thinkers and scholars. I had no answer to the woman on the screen whose eyes looked uncomprehendingly at the corpse of her dead husband as she aimlessly flipped a corner of the white sheet covering him back and forth.

Mahim, Bandra, Khar ... seven blasts, seven stations in Mumbai alone. Another seven or ten stations in Baghdad, and four in Jerusalem tomorrow or the day after. The agony of Christ ends with fourteen stations. Obviously, mankind is not satisfied with fourteen or 14,000. Nothing, it would seem, will quench man's thirst for blood and murder.

We Are All in Batra Lala-land

INDIA HAS HAD ITS share of man-made calamities since we won independence. The Partition, the Chinese invasions, the repeated terrorist attacks on Mumbai and Delhi, to mention only a few. But none of these posed the danger that we face now. It is from the enemy within, that too from a force that claims to be super-patriotic.

I am referring to the eighty-five-year-old Dina Nath Batra, the former principal of a school and the founder of the Shiksha Bachao Andolan Samiti, who sees himself as the saviour of Hinduism and Hindu culture. This zealous warrior has many victories to his name. He got Penguin to pulp Wendy Doniger's *The Hindus: An Alternative History* and got Aleph to drop her volume, *On Hinduism*. His threats made Orient Blackswan undertake a 'comprehensive assessment' of Megha Kumar's book *Communalism and Sexual Violence: Ahmedabad since 1969* (actually it was a reassessment after the book was out). Now he has won his greatest victory so far. The Gujarat School Textbook Board has approved nine of Batra's books for schoolchildren. We have now decided to wilfully enter the dark ages. Indeed we seem to have declared a blackout on life itself, on the incandescence of verifiable knowledge, history, geography and science, scientific speculation and technology.

Our great saints like Kabir, Lalla, Basawanna, Dnyaneshwar and so many others from as early as Vedic times have warned us against ignorance and superstition as the deadliest enemies of mankind. What we have today are false messiahs who, in the name of venerating our ancient texts, do grave injustice to our past; to its exuberant openness and to the extraordinary powers of observation, analysis and insights that flowered in the great philosophical texts and commentaries like the Upanishads, Panini's Grammar, the Kamasutra, the medical texts, the wonderful Sanskrit imagination and literary works. But how can we airbrush the fact that we also have a parallel history of discrimination, black magic, bigots, babas, gurus and charlatans, and that we invented the caste system which still continues to be the bane of our country.

Batra's take on Indian science, history and culture is familiar: the proof that the very first aeroplane was flown in India is in the epic Ramayana where Rama's plane was called Pushpakviman; western science appropriated the technological discoveries and inventions made by Indian ascetics thousands of years ago; the epic Mahabharata was the first to understand stem cell research; taking care of cows eliminates infertility; the map of Bharat should be redrawn to include Pakistan, Afghanistan, Bhutan, Bangladesh, Tibet, Myanmar and Sri Lanka, amongst other assertions.

Fortunately, many Indian historians, thinkers and scientists have condemned this hokum. But one of the most troubling facts about this is that not only were all the books lauded by the then Gujarat Chief Minister and current Prime Minister Narendra Modi but there is a deliberate silence on the part of BJP elders like L. K. Advani and Jaswant Singh and new converts like M. J. Akbar. What has happened to Arun Shourie who was so brave and articulate in the Emergency days?

That is indeed a matter of grave concern. There are already signs of various forms of censorship at work. Exclusion is nothing but an extension of censorship, and conversely, appointing someone only because she or he belongs to your party is little less than nepotism. Not even two months in power and we find the Centre turning down the collegium's, nomination of a highly respected lawyer like Gopal Subramanyan as a Supreme Court judge. What the current government wants, it appears, is an echo chamber in both Parliament and the judiciary.

If there is one thing that still holds true in India, including Gujarat, it is our belief in education as a universal good. And of course the route to a good job as well as an improver of the quality of life. Sadly, the Batra doctrine subverts the Modi government's own mantra of 'development'. The first prerequisite of any kind of education, whether it is economics, IT, history or science and technology, is truth and integrity. The problems facing the country are humongous. Four examples will suffice: malnutrition amongst the children of the poor that the UN says amounts to genocide; TB is at its peak; we also want to create lakhs of jobs; we need a new and even more productive Green Revolution if we are to feed one and a quarter billion people.

You can't breed the best scientists or economics if they are brought up on a diet of lies and falsehoods and expect them to contribute innovative solutions. How does false history affect science? If you don't know the history of science and the preceding work on a subject, you will not know where to start. But there is an even more urgent matter. This government's idea of development has two premises. Their role model is the unfettered free market economy, and any form of dissent like Green Peace or the anti-nuclear movement has to be scotched. George W. Bush would be happy to learn that we too follow in his steps: 'Either you are with us or you are against us.' Secondly, right now we are hell-bent on ignoring the gravest problem facing the entire human race: climate change. And our only hope is to wake up to it at the earliest and act on it forcefully.

India needs not mere innovation but truly inventive solutions like far more efficient and economical ways of creating and utilizing alternative energy sources. Rigour is of primary importance. Fraudulent solutions like carbon trading and mouthing platitudes and following the Batra model will only make sure that huge chunks of the subcontinent will go under water and others will suffer from appalling droughts. No point depending on developed countries.

Are we up to it? Not if we rear generations on the Batra hokum.

A Hindu Festival Called Christmas: Encounters between a Non-practising Hindu and Roman Catholicism

COME THE FIRST OF December, there's miles and miles of cotton wool snowfall in all the shop windows of Bombay aka Mumbai. The only transportation during this time of blizzards, avalanches and snowdrifts are the reindeers and snow sleds driven by old men in post-office red coats with fur collars and trousers and flowing long fleecy-white beards. Everywhere you see the star of Bethlehem, toy cribs, mangers, the three magi, the shepherds, and the holy couple and their baby. All the fancy stores and the malls (where else but in Bombay will you find multistoreyed malls in the heart of downtown while more than half of the city lives on the pavements and in slums) are twitching with tiny electrical lights draped on stunted or monster Christmas trees. The shiny green nylon fir needles weighed down with trinkets and crackers glitter and glint malevolently.

The temperature hits a chillingly cold thirty-three degrees centigrade during the day on the western littoral of India and occasionally plummets at night all the way to twenty degrees when Bombayites take out their heavy winter woollens: sweaters, jackets, parkas, scarves, monkey caps, mittens, snow boots, not to mention thermal underwear. As the days race past towards the longest day of the year, the tension mounts and the excitement is palpable. The new middle class and the nouveau riche, fat with IT money and new-found prosperity from booming businesses and that very special cornucopia called corruption, will celebrate that secular festival called Christmas by shopping till they have dropped millions in the till every single day in December.

Ah, the wonders of marketing are truly wondrous, for along with cigarettes, GM foods, free trade and uncontrolled consumerism, the West is converting the native idolaters to Christmas, Santa Claus and the mandatory trillion-dollar business of exchanging gifts.

Currently, India has the third-largest population of Muslims in the world, around a 130 million. Along with close to a hundred thousand Parsees (or Zoroastrians), they have been in the country for something like a thousand years, but the rest of India does not celebrate Muharram or Nowroz, the Parsi new year. Christians, on the other hand, number a mere 20 million, most of whom were converted barely three or four hundred years ago. Yet it is their festivals, Christmas, Easter, and now Valentine's Day that the people of India have appropriated as their very own.

Christianity Comes to India

Christianity came to India, according to one theory, with the landing of the apostle, Thomas, the Doubter, on the shores of Kerala at the southern tip of the subcontinent. It is his followers who are known as Syrian Christians. There was, however, a second coming. That was in the year 1498 when Vasco da Gama turned up, oddly enough, once again in Kerala and presented some monumentally tawdry knick-knacks to the king, the Zamorin of Calicut. The Zamorin should have turned him round one-eighty degrees to face the Indian Ocean and kicked him on his butt all the way back to Portugal, but he failed to do so. Instead he welcomed the foreigners, and Roman Catholicism got a foothold in India. The spice trade was the obvious reason for Vasco da Gama's visit, but it was always coupled with saving the heathens.

Once the Portuguese were established in Goa, Jesuits and later other orders began their mission of converting the unwary local population to Christ. The third wave of Christian missionaries came with the British. They were mostly Protestants, and though they had the full support of the Crown, their conversion rates were not a patch on those of the Roman Catholics from Goa.

For a while it looked as if the Portuguese, who were a mercantile power long before the English, would take possession of the western coastline of the peninsula before making inroads into the interior. They rapidly took Goa, Diu, Daman, and Bom Bahia, the Good Bay or Mumbai as it's known today, and then ran out of steam because of lack of funds, support from home and visionary leadership. By the time the British settled down, the only territories left with the Portuguese were Goa, Daman and Diu. But whereas the pursuit of colonization and greed were severely checked, the conquest of souls was vastly successful. Much of Goa became Roman Catholic and parlayed the colonizer's tongue, Portuguese, into a position of power and privilege in government and society. But for sheer prescience, there was nobody who read the future as clearly as the Catholic clergy, who went on a spree to open English-medium schools all over the country.

I Become a Hindu–Catholic

I was given to changing schools with the same alacrity that the Sheikhs of Araby were supposed to change their lady-partners. My father worked in the railways, and one day the wife of one of his Catholic friends, a Mrs Drego, took charge of me and marched me to Don Bosco High School at King's Circle, a suburb of Bombay a couple of miles from my home. She was not a very tall woman, but she had an impressive presence. She wore a saree made from a new-fangled fabric that I had never seen before. It was shiny and slithery, and every now and then it sizzled with charges of electrical static. The saree was blinding white with a broad bottle-green border. But what I kept staring at surreptitiously was that it had stitched-on pleats. Instead of draping it as my mother would, Mrs Drego must have got into it feet first and worn it like a skirt.

We stood in a queue in front of the principal's office for hours, maybe four, perhaps five. I was wise beyond my years and knew that this was a futile exercise. We had already been told several times that all divisions of all classes from grade one to eleven were way beyond full, but Mrs Drego had my hand firmly in hers and she was not about to let go of me. Father Giacomello, the principal, took a break at one in the afternoon, had lunch and came back. We were still there, though I was convinced that I was ready for the last rites that the Catholics called extreme unction. At three o'clock we were ushered in. Father Giacomello looked exhausted, and he quickly set matters to rest. 'If there had been any room, Mrs Drego, I would have admitted the boy. Please go home.' I sprang up from my seat instantly but was firmly shoved back.

'I don't want a room, Father,' Mrs Drego smiled brightly, 'all I want for this clever little boy is a little space. Just two inches is all I am asking for.' Now it was true that I was so thin (already five-eight but barely ninety-six pounds and still shooting up), sometimes you saw me but most of the time you didn't, but two inches? What was Mrs Drego talking about? I was being reduced to Tom Thumb. I had never been so humiliated. But by now the 'clever little boy' was so ravenous and fed up, he was willing to say goodbye to all education and become a shoeshine boy but only after eating Mrs Drego uncooked and whole right then and there.

'Mrs Drego, you understand English? The classes are absolutely full. Listen to me, go home. Try some other school.'

'Two inches, Father. Only two inches.'

The overweight priest who had no neck shook his head in despair and said goodbye to us. Within a month Mrs Drego had got her two inches and I was installed in grade six, division A.

School started every morning with the Lord's Prayer. I was in Don Bosco for six years. Enough time for even a stone or a clod of earth to learn the fine short prayer, but there was something inexplicably perverse and contrary in me. Every single day I mimed and semi-lip-synched the half-familiar words but not once did I recite the prayer. If it was a rebellion of some kind, then it was an extremely childish one. I had no idea what I was rebelling against or what cause I was fighting for. I am ashamed to say that I still don't know all the words.

Above the blackboard in each classroom Christ was nailed all over again to a cross. The patron of the school was the founder of the Salesian order, Don Bosco. But for some odd reason, his portrait did not adorn the walls. Instead we looked at a highly airbrushed Dominic Savio, the boy saint who had doubtless performed some miracle and then ascended to heaven to meet his maker. Dominic was dressed in a jacket and a bow tie, and his eyes were glued to the sky or rather, the ceiling, because like all the super-rich, God has a spiffy loft apartment on the terrace. I was going through a rough patch in my school years and excessively given to bouts of superstition. I grovelled in front of the boy saint and had appallingly abject and servile one-way conversations with him. I had developed a private code for the purpose. If I looked at him in a certain way and prayed desperately, he was supposed to come through for me in my exams. He was far more sensible than I was and gave my frantic entreaties a wide berth.

The faithful in the Catholic school system had Bible class while those that fell outside the pale got moral science. This turgid, mind-numbingly unimaginative and soul-destroying subject was compulsory and came in a question-and-answer format. 'Who made man? God made man.' And so on and so on. The great contribution of Catholic schools to teaching in India is what we called mugging. The idea is that it is a crime to allow young minds, not to mention older ones, to think for themselves. This is, needless to say, a corollary of the 'forbidden fruit' doctrine. Look what happened when our first parents made their own choices: they got kicked out of Eden. The prime example of this school of thinking was the moral science class. Ethical complexity, ambiguity and dilemmas were taboo, a total no-no. If you had any sense, you learnt everything by heart, and you never argued because that might confuse the poor priest and cause him to have a nervous breakdown.

One of the intriguing by-products about being in Don Bosco High School was that I was often taken for a Roman Catholic. Talk about being ambivalent. In my early years there, most if not all my friends were Goan Catholics, most of them from the poorer areas of Parel and Lalbaug. I don't remember whether my speech patterns had become akin to theirs. But I seemed to have drifted away as I moved into the higher grades, and my new companions were mostly non-Catholic. It is difficult to say whether this was because I had become conscious of the differences between our cultures and upbringing.

My family was poor, but I came from reformist stock, and to that extent, from a liberal westernized background that put a premium on education. The school may have had two rather well-fed Italian priests at the helm, but the ones who, I suspect, had a profound influence on the way I looked at Catholics and their clergy, were both Irishmen. Father McFerran was the father-prefect. He was not an imposing figure, but he had to merely walk down the corridor for all the students, teachers and parents to cower. I was certainly petrified of him and made sure that I turned invisible when he was around. To this day, it is a mystery to me why he allowed a boy of whose existence he was unaware, to go on a school trip to Kashmir and then paid half my expenses since my parents could not afford to send me. I would visit him in Madras when he was transferred there and once stayed with him for nearly a fortnight. At this point I am perhaps expected to speak of the abuse I suffered at his hands since it is now the fashion to think of the priesthood as a blighted vocation much given to child molestation and homosexuality. But Father McFerran was an honourable man and beyond reproach. The same with that wonderful pied piper, the great storyteller, Father Dean, who died of blood cancer when he was barely thirty-five. As with most lay people, the good priests still far outnumber the bad ones.

I should have graduated from school in a blaze of glory, but things did not pan out quite that way. I barely managed to get a first division and joined a prestigious Jesuit-run institution called St Xavier's College. It was all downhill from there. I failed in every subject in the mid-terminals and skipped the finals altogether because of a serious illness. Oddly enough what saved me was the moral science paper. (Yes indeed, the Jesuits too were trying to raise the heathens, if not to Christian salvation, to a higher consciousness.) In the mid-term moral science paper there were ten questions which required short answers and one for which you were supposed to write an essay. After staring at the blank answer sheet for an hour, I tried to tackle the essay on Strikes. In what was surely a nadir of inarticulateness, I attempted to unravel the ethical ambiguities and dilemmas of strikes. The bell rang halfway through my answer but at the end of the year when I was advised a change of climate for health reasons and was about to join one of India's oldest colleges in a campus town called Pune, my failure was condoned because of that fumbling, uncertain essay.

Exit the Portuguese

My official Christian education had come to an end. The year was 1961. I was returning to Bombay on the 19th of December (thanks to our British masters we got Christmas vacations in those days), but the train was shunted off to a siding for hours and hours. The liberation of Goa had begun, and the delay was due to heavy troop and ordnance movement. Liberation for whom? There were as many Catholics as Hindus who fought for Goa to become a part of the mother country. But the majority of Goans were bemused, and many in positions of power were deeply upset and dismayed. Some critics in the subcontinent saw this as a betrayal and a lack of patriotism. Somewhere at the back of my mind I too must have felt unhappy about the slow pace of assimilation amongst the Goan population. Superior and supercilious, it would take me years to realize how unfair I was. Regime change, even if one is returning to the fold and to self-rule, is always traumatic. But when the privileged few lose their privileges, then it is bound to breed resentment, even amongst idealists.

Four hundred years is a long time. Konkani may have been the local language but the medium of instruction in schools for hundreds of years was Portuguese. Goan life was deeply permeated with Portuguese culture, cuisine, religion, the spirit of the fado and the carnival. Besides there was prohibition in the rest of India. Little wonder then that there was some trepidation in the Goan mind about joining the motherland.

The Roman Catholic Side of My Writing

I have half-facetiously called this article 'A Hindu Festival called Christmas'. But the other half is not half as risible. The ironies of conversion in India are bemusing, bewildering and fascinating but also tragic. They tell us how deep the roots of the Indian caste system are. You are never a simple Roman Catholic in India. You can only be a Hindu Roman Catholic. Which means you never forget your caste. Brahmin Catholics generally choose their brides from amongst former Brahmin families and that too from the specific Brahmin sub-caste they belong to. Many Goans had settled down in Portugal and some had made it big in government, but even in Lisbon there was no escaping the stranglehold of the caste system. You had better know your place in the pecking order.

The sad fact is that even the clergy is not immune to these prejudices. To write the second section of my novel, *God's Little Soldier*, I lived in a Catholic monastery in America for months. They had recruited the first Indian monk in their order and had found him to be a worthy addition to the group. He was an exceptionally quiet, thoughtful person with a meditative turn of mind. But on the couple of occasions when he spoke to me about some of his brethren from the Catholic community in Bombay, he made disparaging comments about lower-caste Christians and how caste always showed.

My first job in advertising was for a company called MCM. It was the fastest-growing agency in India in the late 1960s and early 1970s. Its fall too was spectacular, and it was dead and buried by 1975. But while it was around, it was one hell of a place to work in. I was in the copy-writing section, and one Sunday Sylvie, the Catholic secretary of the department, asked all of us over for lunch at her home. All I recall of the food was that it was Goan, delicious and plentiful, and we fell on it as if we had got there directly from the famine in Bihar. What stayed with me though was that Sylvie lived in a chawl, a huge complex of tenement buildings with common toilet facilities on each floor. Chawls were not new to me, but this was the first time I was visiting a set-up where the ground floor plus the first four storeys were occupied by Hindus and the top fifth one by Catholics. Those chawls with their parallel Hindu and Catholic worlds would become the location and third protagonist in my novel, *Ravan and Eddie*.

Some debts one can never repay. I don't wish to either. On the contrary may their numbers increase. As you can see, the Roman Catholics have been good to me.

Hallelujah, praise be to God, at the midnight hour of the 24th of December, we will witness the coming of the Hindu god of love and forgiveness, none other than the child Jesus, the latest addition to the overcrowded pantheon of Hindu gods. Which makes him, according to the latest census taken in Swarg, as the Hindu heaven is called, in the year of our Lord, November 2050, god number 33 million and one.

A Rumination on Frauds: The 'Other' and the 'Artist'

On bad days, or perhaps those are really good days, I see myself as a fake and a fraud. I am forced to confront, for instance, how presumptuous it is of me to pretend that I can write. Do I really understand the incredible precision and complexity of words? Have I too fallen prey to the temptation of obfuscating jargon and the desire to impress? What am I doing here at the Freiburg Theatre at its hundredth anniversary posing to be wise and insightful? Who am I trying to fool? Imagine my surprise then when I found that the Nobel Prize winner, J. M. Coetzee had stolen my line. For that's what he said in a BBC interview some years ago: that he felt like a fraud.

My novel, *God's Little Soldier* or *Gottes Kleiner Krieger*, was published in 2006. It told the story of a young extremist who does a stint as a terrorist. Two years later, when I was a Poetikdozent at Tübingen University, Bombay–Mumbai suffered its worst terrorist attack ever on 26/11. More than seventy people were shot dead at the Chhatrapati Shivaji Maharaj Terminus (the former Victoria Terminus), the headquarters of India's Central Railway, alone. The guests in two of Mumbai's most prestigious hotels were held hostage and many lost their lives. The final tally amounted to hundreds dead and many more wounded and crippled.

A few TV stations, newspapers and magazines traced me to Tübingen and interviewed me. I guess the assumption was that I was an expert on the subject, knowledgeable about the ways of extremists, and a man with deep insights into the minds of terrorists. After all, I had spent eight years writing my book on an extremist. It was a salutary experience. I learnt that fiction can never keep pace with reality. At best, if I was any good at it, my work would offer just one take amongst many others on the subject and suggest the complexity of the issues by layering and nuancing them.

If a young artist or anybody was fool enough to come to me for advice, I would tell him two things: one, have faith in yourself, and two, incessantly doubt yourself.

If the imagination is at the centre of an artist's work and not research, moral teachings or some ideological position, then the artist must assume the personae of the full spectrum of characters who figure in his work. From the earliest times when the very first stories were told in words and paintings, an artist had to often get into the mind, body and soul of the alien, the stranger, the enemy, the éminence grise, the ambivalent outsider: in short, the 'other', a concept which became crucial to discussions of literary theory some thirty or forty years ago. The theatre itself has been the site where the 'other' or the intruder has often been explored effectively in plays like Dürrenmatt's *The Visit* (German: *Der Besuch der alten Dame*) or Max Frisch's *Andorra*.

The notion of the 'other' is remarkable in giving us insights into how our minds work, the role of our primal fears about the unfamiliar and the alien. It tells us about the dynamics of dealing with outsiders and others who come from a different culture than ours. It reveals that the archetypal patterns of our behaviour and our responses have not really changed over the millennia.

Let's take just one rather simple example to illustrate the 'other'. It is eventide, the candles have just been lit and the family is about to sit down for dinner when there is a knock on the door. The parents look at each other uneasily. Who could it be at this hour? The man of the house signals to the children to be silent. There is another knock. 'Who is it?' the man asks, but there's no answer. If it was one of the neighbours he would surely have spoken up and hollered his name. The knocking grows more insistent. The man of the house walks up to the door and opens it. There is a stranger at the door. What does he want? Does the outsider mean well or ill? 'I'm on my way to the shrine at Lourdes. I think I've lost my way. I've been riding the whole day, and I was hoping to stay the night in an inn, but my horse needs a new shoe and is limping. Would you be so kind as to allow me to spend the night in your place?'

The woman of the house frowns at her husband. He knows what she's thinking. The stranger is not welcome. He's not sure either. The man looks ordinary enough but so do people who are about to be hanged for murder. The stranger sees the expression on his face and tells him, 'I'll help you with the sowing tomorrow and then leave after the horse has been shod.' The man of the house remembers the time he had gone to the cattle market some 60 kilometres away. On the second night he was so tired he was unable to take another step and knocked on an unknown door. The farmer's family had laid out some straw and thrown a sheet on it and let him sleep in a corner of the house. 'Come on in,' the husband told the outsider, 'and share whatever meagre meal we're about to have.' When the stranger sat at the dining table the man noticed that he was carrying a dagger on his belt.

It's midnight and the man of the house lay awake. Who was this stranger? Was he really going to Lourdes or was it just a story to gull them? He seemed hale and hearty. The healthy don't need to go to Lourdes. And that dagger he had, what was that for? He should have checked the horse to see whether the shoe was really worn out. But his face seemed to be friendly and he had even offered to help with the sowing. But why would anybody leave home when it was sowing time? Maybe he was just a blackguard on the run. Any moment now he would hold the dagger at his throat and ask where the money from the harvest was. Perhaps he knew it had been a good year and would stab him and his family and run away with the money. He should have paid heed to his wife. She had good instincts in these matters. Maybe the only alternative was to kill the man before he murdered his family. Oh God, what should he do? Was the man a villain or an innocent pilgrim? Should he save his family or let the man rest in peace?

Why am I harking back to the concept of the 'other'? As with most buzzwords, loose and lazy usage have trivialized the potential in the notion of the 'other' but there is no gainsaying the relevance and value of the concept, especially in a time when the impulse towards the Balkanization of countries is rampant and the antagonisms amongst religions, races, communities, language groups and tribes are becoming more and more acute.

Even in Death We Cannot Forget the 'Other'

Muslims and Hindus had lived amicably for innumerable decades in the Punjab and the north-western provinces now known as Pakistan. All it took for the two communities to suffer from amnesia and be at each other's throats and kill hundreds of thousands in a few weeks was the partition of India. We didn't stop there – we've fought three wars since Independence.

It is now a cliché to say that India and Pakistan constitute one of the most inflammable regions in the world. But what is truly bizarre and goes mostly unnoticed is that both the 'true believers' of Islam, Shias and Sunnis, are decimating each other in Pakistan, Iraq and many other Muslim countries, with far greater ferocity and animosity than they evince towards India. Even the most peaceful of sects like the

Ahmadiyas in Pakistan or the Bahais in Iran who live quiet lives and mind their own business, are considered heretical and persecuted. Hardly a day goes by when those two dirty words 'Breaking News' are not reporting bombings, arson and terrorist attacks in some part of the world. Is there a dark bloodthirst in us that can only find catharsis and peace when thousands are sacrificed to some primitive and primal urge within us?

Six million Jews killed in the Second World War, half a million of Europe's Roma, some 2 million non-Jewish Poles killed. The tragic truth is that all those deaths have been in vain since we don't seem to have learnt a damn thing. We seek divisions even in death: one Holocaust memorial for the Jews, a belated one for the Roma and a separate one for the Poles. And one of these days the Palestinians will raise a monument to those who died at the hands of Israel, and the Shias will put up one for those massacred by the Sunnis in Iraq, and naturally, the Sunnis will want one all to themselves. And what about the tens of millions who were wiped out by the European invasions and holocausts in the Americas from the 16th century onwards?

Count not the numbers, my friend, for even one man's senseless death is an infinity, and infinity can never be measured.

The 'Other' as Scapegoat

The other is an unknown quantity and hence we do not know his or her intentions. Does he come in peace or to do us harm? Should I as an Indian trust a Pakistani or should you as a German extend a hand of friendship to a Turk? Add to that, if we have had a bad experience with one individual or group from another culture, then the whole community is painted with the same unhappy brush.

Religions and ideologies are like amoebae. They keep dividing and sub-dividing. Some prophet, demagogue or ideologue turns up as the decades or centuries go by and insists that he and his followers are the only true believers, the rest are heretics and should either be excommunicated, burnt at the stake, banished, bumped off, or forgiven if, and only if, they convert to the true path. The Church of England, as we all know, did not come into being because of genuine ecumenical or ideological differences. Henry VIII wanted to divorce Catherine of Aragon who could not give him a male heir. The Pope would not permit him to do so, and that's how Henry VIII became the head of both the state and the Church of England, and in the bargain lopped off the heads of many of his wives and those who opposed him or were no longer of use. It is a moot question whether the common people of England, wanted to break away from the Catholic Church, but the King had decreed it and Rome became anathema. The term 'popery' was invented and now suddenly stood for all that was rotten and reeked of moral turpitude. It also gave licence to the new converts to persecute and murder all those who remained loyal to the older faith.

Those were the dark ages, you may well argue; the populace was illiterate and ignorant. We, on the contrary, live in modern times and in civil society. Our constitutions enshrine the bill of rights or something akin to it. Every citizen has fundamental rights, and in the case of disputes, there are always the courts of law. However, as the French like to say, 'Plus ça change, plus c'est la même chose.' (The more things change, the more they remain the same.) Currently the Knesset in Israel is locked in a bitter battle regarding one of the most controversial subjects in the country: conversion. You would think there would be rejoicing amongst the Jewish community of the world every time someone converted to Judaism. After all, they lost 6 million during the Nazi Holocaust. Think again.

The controversy regarding conversion has a long history but let's just go back to the year 2008 when a rabbi in the city of Ashdod decided with hardly any precedent to annul the conversion of a woman who had embraced the Jewish faith fifteen years earlier on the grounds that she was not observing Orthodox Jewish law. Big deal, you and I might say dismissively. But we would be wrong, dead wrong. It is a very big deal. As J. J. Goldberg points out in his article, *On Conversion, Alienating Israel's Friends*, if your conversion is declared invalid, 'you are caught in a legal limbo, denied normal rights of marriage, burial, adoption and more'. Many immigrants who have been under the impression that they have been following Jewish customs, rituals and practices to the best of their knowledge in their own countries and wish to be recognized officially as Jews in Israel by taking classes in Judaism, discover that Byzantine regulations make conversion nearly impossible.

Clash or Confluence of Civilizations?

At some point in time we must ask ourselves whether it is possible to live with the so-called 'other' peacefully and amicably. I can speak with some confidence about the issue since I come from India. The almost knee-jerk perception in the West about Hindus and Muslims in the subcontinent is that they are mortal enemies. Perhaps the briefest foray into Indian history at this point won't be out of place here.

Rather than staying behind to rule, early Muslim invaders like Mahmud of Ghazni raided the Punjab and north-east India seventeen times between 1001 and 1026 with the express purpose of looting the incredible wealth in the Hindu temples, earning incredible amounts of both lucre and merit, all for doing God's work. Timur, who was the great grandfather of the Mughal Emperor Babur, had heard that the then Muslim rulers of India were lenient to their Hindu subjects and decided to take matters in his own hands. He had a hundred thousand Hindus massacred before he sacked Delhi in 1398 and filled his coffers with gold and precious stones.

Many other plunderers followed in Mahmud Ghazni's and Timur's footsteps, but by and large those Muslims who stayed to rule the country were wise enough to understand that the job of a monarch was to protect and preserve his subjects, whether they be Muslims or Hindus, and not to persecute them. Babur invaded India repeatedly in the 16th century, but it was only on his fourth visit that he defeated Ibrahim Lodi, the Sultan of Delhi, and founded the Mughal dynasty which would rule the country till 1857. Babur was one of the most interesting and intriguing rulers the world has seen. His autobiography *Baburnama* is a masterpiece by any standards and utterly compelling reading. He was a keen observer of nature and a remarkable military strategist and leader. He was also hard on Hindus and destroyed many Hindu temples. It was his grandson, Akbar, who was a visionary under whom the empire expanded rapidly. He was also a great patron of music, architecture, history and the other arts. His grandson, Shahjahan, preserved the integrity of the empire but his greatest claim to fame is the mausoleum he built to his queen, Mumtaz Mahal, the Taj Mahal. His third son, Aurangzeb, killed his eldest brother, imprisoned his father and became emperor. He was an odd mix of qualities: he was power-hungry, a religious fanatic, severely ascetic in temperament and lifestyle. The last of the great Mughals, his successors merely presided over the dissolution of the Mughal empire.

Then the British took over and ruled for nearly two hundred years. By the time the subcontinent got independence in 1947, we were two countries: Pakistan and India. The Partition saw perhaps the worst massacres ever between the two communities. Hundreds of thousands died in a matter of weeks.

Sadly, the record of Hindu–Muslim relations after Independence has been marred by a number of bloody riots and killings, undoubtedly the worst being the violence in Gujarat in 2002.

It's not my intention to gloss over the differences or tensions between the two communities but is Huntington's *Clash of Civilizations* really at work here? It would be salutary to remember that it's over twelve hundred years since Muslims have been in the country. Let the fanatics and the zealots on both sides claim whatever they want, the fact is, there has been so much osmosis, so much unconscious give and take and interaction on both sides, and such a deep subterranean intercourse of cultures that we are now conjoined twins. It is impossible to separate the two strands in our history. Whether it's music, architecture, literature or the languages we speak, you will discover a melding together and a confluence that no amount of cynicism can undermine or deny.

Who can tell what the Muslim or Hindu contribution to a north Indian classical recital is when you hear Kesarbai or Faiyaz Khan sing *Raag Darbari Kanada* or hear Hariprasad Chaurasia seduce you with a flute recital of *Raag Bhimpalas*? We've had Muslim presidents and vice presidents but that could be viewed as mere symbolic gestures. However, cinema, as even foreigners know, is at the very centre of our lives and psyches. For over fifteen years now, the three superstars of India have all been Muslims. You can't fake that. Even more popular than films is film music. Here, too, Muslim music directors are at the very forefront. But let me not labour the point. If only the two communities could let go of their animosities, and our politicians stopped manipulating and exploiting the populace to play electoral politics, the process of healing might get a chance to take place.

'There Is Only One Thing Worse than Intolerance, It Is Intolerance of Intolerance' (Romain Gary)

Let me tell you a story. It is somebody else's real-life story but one that revealed something significant that I had never suspected about myself. It also posed a troubling philosophical problem about human beings: Can we really know ourselves?

But the story first. In 2007 I was invited to the Writers' Workshop Programme in Iowa City. It was a short stint, one that lasted two and a half months. Not enough time to settle down, to get to know the place and the people living there. I was lucky, there was a Professor of Sanskrit teaching at the university who had liked one of my books very much and got in touch with me. It was through him that I met an Indian who was doing his PhD in journalism. Let's call him Anurag Madhok. Madhok was a friendly sort, and in the brief time I was in the programme, invited me to dinner twice or thrice to his place. He had a young and personable flatmate called Abdul who was from Bangalore and was doing a postgraduate course in business management. Like most well-brought-up young Indians, he was always courteous and respectful of the fact that I was old enough to be his father and made it a point to serve me first.

Before I knew it, it was time to leave, and Anurag came to wish me goodbye twenty minutes before I left for the airport. We talked about this and that, all of it inconsequential. We spoke about not losing touch and how far he had come in his PhD thesis. I have no idea how the subject of Abdul came up. Anurag told me that the previous year he had had to move into a new apartment and had been on the lookout for someone to share it. As luck would have it, there were no takers. It was a month into the term when he received a thick envelope marked 'Ref: Apartment-sharing'. He looked at the sender's name and decided to ignore it. The mail was from someone called Abdul Hafeez, clearly a Muslim and hence a non-vegetarian. Anurag had learnt from past experience that if you were not careful about who you chose to share your flat with, you would have a full 365 days to regret your decision.

That night he was listening to music and again noticed the letter from Abdul Hafeez. Normally such letters were a paragraph long, no more. Why was this guy writing half the Bible? He started reading. Abdul wrote about his family. They were devout Muslims. His father was a civil engineer and had worked all his life to make sure his children got the best possible education. Abdul's mother had died of cancer when he was still at school. He had two sisters; one was married and the other doing her master's in paediatric medicine. He also had a younger brother who was studying accountancy. Abdul had done well in college and could have got a job immediately but he had set his mind on getting a degree in business management abroad. He had done well enough to get admission to Iowa City University but not well enough to get a scholarship. So his father had borrowed money to send him to the States. He had asked many people whether they would share their flats with him. American students were upfront and told him they did not want to live with someone whose community was responsible for 9/11. The Indians, and there were many of them in Iowa City, were more polite but just as unequivocal. They never answered.

Six weeks had already gone by. If he didn't get a place soon, Abdul feared he would have to go back to Bangalore. Yes, he said, he and his family kept the *roza* during Ramadan and only ate after sunset and before sunrise during that period. What better reason was there, he asked, to trust him and his family than the fact that they were devout Muslims who were duty-bound to respect all of Allah's creation, the pinnacle of which was man. His sister who was becoming a doctor would never ask whether a child was Hindu, Christian or Muslim, not only because she had taken the Hippocratic Oath but also because God cared for all his creatures.

Anurag Madhok had stated in his advertisement that he was a vegetarian. Abdul would respect that and not eat any meat if he lived with him. He had only one question to ask, would Anurag too refuse to acknowledge the letter and thus avoid saying yes or no to him?

'And to think,' Anurag wondered incredulously, 'that I was not even going to open the envelope, let alone read it.' I sat numb on the flight back to India. I had always considered myself an adamantine secular person; I liked to think that I have an open mind which resists stereotypes and clichés; that I abhorred bigotry and fanaticism of any sort. And yet I could see now that I was as much a victim of prejudices as any fanatic and was blithely unaware of it. I suspected that I too would not have opened the letter. And had I opened it, very likely I would have refused to acknowledge it and thus pretended that I had not received it.

How many dark corners were there in my soul? And would I ever have the courage to confront them and look them straight in the eye? I had no idea that one can be a fraud in so many ways, despite one's best intentions.

The bigots, if they ever get around to it, and not in a moment of weakness but one of great inner strength, will confront their rabid fanaticism and see that the first casualty of extremism of any kind is the truth. And secondly, they will apprehend how casually they have rationalized and justified the use of lies, prestidigitation and chicanery, violence and the deliberate distortion of the 'other'. They might then begin to see that however noble the end, it does not ever justify the means. The last step would be the most difficult one: they would gather the courage to query their own idealism and admit how flawed it was.

The case of the liberals is more complicated. I have good reason to know them from the inside. After all, I am one of them and know at least some, if not all, the sleights of hand by which we claim to be open and tolerant and yet are victims of deep-rooted preconceptions and fears. Since we are sophists, we can wrap our pettiness, anxieties and misdemeanours in fine-sounding words and present ourselves as exceptionally honest people. But while honesty is an absolutely necessary virtue, it can only take us so far and no further. If I may tamper a little with one of Oscar Wilde's wonderfully insightful quotes: 'It is the confession … that gives us absolution.' The question is, are we going to change or are we going to continue in our old devious ways?

I doubt whether Abdul is either a bigot or a liberal. Being a good Muslim for him means being a good, caring human being; that if God is the Creator, then we must all be blood brothers. How many of us can match that wisdom?

The Artist as Intermediary

One cannot ever overemphasize the importance of understanding that we all play a double role. Depending on our perspective, we are both 'us' and 'them', the good guys and the villains or the enemy. Perception is all. There has rarely been a greater need to understand the other than in our times. Every day brings news of new genocides, massacres, bomb blasts, rapes, forced migrations and refugees without refuge. It would seem that mankind no longer knows how to resolve its problems without resorting to violence and the spilling of innocent blood. Gandhiji had said, 'An eye for an eye will make the whole world blind.' It's much worse than that today. If we continue to kill each other, one of these days, all our children will end up as orphans.

This is where the artist can play a critical role. He is not a prophet, proselytizer, apologist or apostle. He has no message.

It is his ability to create a full and rounded universe, to people it with characters that are not black and white but utterly believable in their aspirations, fallibility, compassion, pettiness, over-reaching ambition, vileness and nobility that will transform our stereotype of the 'other' into someone who is as human and real as us.

Remember this speech?

> Hath not a Jew eyes? Hath not a Jew hands, organs, dimensions, senses, affections, passions? Fed with the same food, hurt with the same weapons, subject to the same diseases, healed by the same means, warmed and cooled by the same winter and summer as a Christian is? If you prick us, do we not bleed? If you tickle us, do we not laugh? If you poison us, do we not die? And if you wrong us, shall we not revenge?
>
> *The Merchant Of Venice,* Act 3, Scene 1

I doubt if Shakespeare set out to vindicate the Jewish people. On the contrary, many people suspect that his intention was clearly to portray Shylock as an unmitigated villain. But it is the greatness of Shakespeare that his characters do not pay heed to their creator; they are not his puppets or playthings. They have a mind and a life of their own and are contrary. And hence they become flesh-and-blood human beings who are impulsive and rage and can't hold their tongues when they should be circumspect. Portia will play with words and quibble, and Shylock will be humiliated and the Elizabethan audience and many contemporary audiences too, will go back home feeling good seeing the moneylender get his comeuppance. But Shylock's cri de coeur will also stay in our minds and make us feel uneasy. The power of his speech, the anguish in it and his plea to recognize him as nothing more or less than a human being gives us a glimpse of the artist's unique ability to nuance and empower the other. Shakespeare's portrait of Shylock is one of the most convincing instances of an artist inhabiting the mind of someone deeply loathed by society, in this case Elizabethan society. The bard's understanding of the psyche and plight of Shylock is so compelling that even the most insensitive and antipathetic in the audience will, at the least, see that there is more than a nugget of truth in his utterance, and who knows, might swing in his favour.

Shakespeare may not have talked about the alienation of the 'other', but there are few examples of the phenomenon as vivid and gut-wrenching as Shylock.

God-Bothering

ANTHONY BURGESS, WHO IS remembered mainly as the author of *A Clockwork Orange* and for Stanley Kubrick's movie version of it, did a fairly effective hatchet job on a fellow writer. He dismissed Graham Greene's work by referring to it as so much 'god-bothering'.

Like chewing gum in the hair, the phrase stuck, whatever the facts of the matter. When Greene's *The End of the Affair* was made into a movie some four or five years ago with Ralph Fiennes and Julianne Moore, the director removed the crucial mystical part because of Greene's 'unnecessary' indulgence in god-bothering.

If writers are subject to ups and downs when they are alive, they are even more so after they are dead. Greene's fortunes went into decline rapidly after his demise. For the last ten or fifteen years it has been fashionable to talk of Greene as passé and fuddy-duddy. Much of the credit for this goes to Burgess's poisonous little kindness. Merely as a matter of academic interest, about a couple of years ago, David Lodge wrote an article on Graham Greene in the New York Review of Books where he glancingly exposed Burgess's canard.

Greene wrote over thirty-five novels and what he called entertainments. He also wrote several volumes of short stories, plays, travelogues and essays. Of this massive body of work, only three or four deal with God and the Catholic faith. You cannot mistake a Greene novel. There is amazing humour in them and almost astral prescience, but the overall tone is ironic and that peculiar blend of despair and desperation which is beyond the hopeless.

But to come back to Anthony Burgess. What would he make of the world today? Europe may have ditched God some sixty years ago, but the rest of the world has gone completely bananas with god-bothering. And however reluctantly it may be, even Europe has had perforce to come to terms with it. One third of America is neo-conservative and another third is church going. As for the Islamic world, it is in the grips of a fundamentalist fever that threatens to plunge our world into an old-testament Armageddon. The phenomenon of the jehadis or the holy warriors of Islam affects almost everything we or our governments do, and yet there is not much of an attempt to overcome our stereotypes and no desire on our parts to get under their skin and penetrate their psyches. This is again the result, to a large extent, of the supercilious dismissive attitude exemplified by Burgess and his ilk. Right-wing neo-cons also suffer from this terrible failing and tell the world proudly that they don't do nuance.

If he were alive, Burgess would have most likely to eat his words and start god-bothering in a very big and serious fashion. Christian fundamentalists must decide whether they would rather live in some fantasy world where some Homeland Security department can save them from all future threats or admit that the binary system of 'us and them' and the simplistic demonization of the other is not only barren but self-destructive in that it exacerbates everything and resolves absolutely nothing. Unless we all realize that the other is both different and the mirror of us, unless we stop painting them with the same dark and deadly shade of *Achtung!* and red-hot alerts and probe the wellsprings of so much resentment and violence by nuancing the differences in their aspirations and goals and real grievances, we will continue to live in a fool's paradise.

The problem with Burgess's stance, however, is at the very core of any discussion of art or what is called, amongst theoreticians who prefer jargon to transparent simplicity, the literary project. If the provenance of literature and the other arts is the whole spectrum of life, then how can you exclude anything, especially something that is of moment, perhaps not to you and me but to a great number of people across the world?

My own god-bothering, I must confess, does not spring from some lofty lineage like that of Greene who switched to an uneasy Catholic faith and lived like a good Christian, failing his God often but hanging in there nevertheless. Like a great many of my fellow beings I belong to that tribe of people whom Joyce Carol Oates describes so aptly as people who don't believe in God, in the daytime at least. I suspect in my feckless and faithless fashion, God is that number you call in emergencies: 911 in America. Or 100 in India. And yet despite all my claims that I am heir to Homer and the Mahabharata only in so far as I am a storyteller, I find to my dismay that so much of my writing indulges, surreptitiously or worse, overtly, in god-bothering.

Perhaps I should start with a very brief biographical note. I am a lapsed Hindu. I am told, however, that this state of being is not possible since Hinduism is more a way of life than a religion. Maybe there's some truth to that. My grandfather and parents belonged to a tiny and almost 'disappeared' denomination of monotheistic Hinduism based on the Upanishads. It is called the Prarthana Samaj. A product of Hinduism's intersection with the colonizers' Protestant faith, it revolved around prayer and sermons and shunned idol-worship and polytheism. Perhaps that is the reason why all my life I have disliked visiting temples, but that could also be because I feel unbearably claustrophobic without strong light, and the deity in our temples is usually in the garbhagriha, the sanctum sanctorum, which, as the name suggests, is dark as the womb.

So how come every novel and play I have written deals either head-on or glancingly with religion? That, I am afraid, is as much of a mystery to me as the good Lord himself is. I have no message to deliver and no manifesto. Let me make an odd and not so flattering confession. I know what my books are about only after I have finished them. How I start on a novel is quite banal. Something catches my fancy or intrigues me and occasionally I may instinctively detect the germ of a story. The life around me, and there's plenty of that in India, and my preoccupations filter in randomly as well as by design.

Religions of every hue, whether Islam, Christianity, Buddhism, Jainism, not to mention Hinduism, must certainly be one of my preoccupations. The reason for my fascination with epics, mythology and religion (the three often overlap and the line separating them is indistinct in Hindu texts) comes from my being a sucker for stories from childhood. The other reason is that these texts may be billed as holy books, sometimes as the word of God himself, but what they exhibit is the supreme art of the storyteller.

Let me take just a few examples of the kinds of problems revolving around religion that some of the protagonists in my novels are confronted with.

The Crucifixion is seen through a child's eyes in my novel, *Ravan and Eddie*. Eddie, whose mother is a devout Catholic, has been sent to buy onions but en route he is given a ticket to the film *Rock Around the Clock*. Onions or the film? It's a no-brainer. Eddie sees the film. There's hell to pay when he comes back, and the next day he is sent to see the priest, Father Agnello.

> Far away, above the altar, Jesus Christ continued to haemorrhage silently. His head hung limply to the right. Eddie understood that this was a clay Christ. But each time he looked at him, he had an intense urge to pry out the nails

in his hands and feet and bring him down. Sometimes at night he spent hours struggling with those nails. Exhausted, he would try to pull Jesus off, instead of the nails. One of these days, the nails would stay where they were and Jesus would come crashing down on him.

'Do you have any idea of the consequences of your actions? Let alone your parents, do you realize how you are torturing our Lord Jesus? Even a single sin, a single sinful thought, can cause him unbearable pain and open his wounds again. He has to bleed again and again to wash your sins.' A livid Father D'Souza narrated the far-reaching effects of Eddie's crimes to him in a hoarse whisper.

Eddie was not particularly disturbed by the pain he was causing his parents. If his father had had the slightest feeling or sympathy, he would not have allowed Eddie to starve last night and this morning. As for his mother, they were quits. He was giving her as hard a time as she was giving him. Frankly, he thought she was having a better time of it than he was. But he became terribly restive at the thought that Jesus's wounds were bleeding again because of him. He wanted to break open the hard crust which had formed over the long and throbbing lesion under his chin by hitting it against the back of the bench in front of him. He would keep on bashing his head till the gash reopened and he washed Jesus clean with his blood.

For hundreds of years they had left the Son of God hanging on a cross and now Father D'Souza had the temerity to suggest that he was responsible for Jesus's sufferings. In a fit of temper, Eddie asked, 'And why don't you bring him down and bandage his wounds?'

The blood receded from Father Agnelo's face. He was speechless. It was such a simple and logical thought, it could only have come from the Prince of Darkness, Lucifer himself.

The next quote is from my novel *Cuckold*.

> We were that rarest of couples. Even after years of marriage we were madly in love. I with her and she with somebody else.

That is the central dilemma that confronts the heir apparent of the 16th-century kingdom of Mewar in his personal life in my novel *Cuckold*. On his wedding night, his wife tells him that she is betrothed to somebody else. In time the Maharaj Kumar, or the cuckold of the novel's title, discovers the identity of his rival. The awful irony is that, as the Maharaj Kumar tells us, 'He was my best friend. My confidant and preceptor. The blue god with the flute and the peacock feather stuck in the band around his head.' As you know, the blue god Krishna expounds his philosophy of dharma in the Bhagavad Gita, which is the Maharaj Kumar's constant companion. As a Rajput warrior, the Gita is his dharma, his vocation or if you prefer, his Bible. It is from the Gita that he learns that he must find the purpose of life and its fulfilment in being what he was born to be, a warrior. But he has also been a keen observer of the wily and wise god, Shri Krishna himself. Unlike the Rajputs, for whom bravery is the ultimate value, the prince has no problem putting his tail between his legs and fleeing. He never loses sight of his goal: to go to war only if there's a chance of winning, and that too on the condition that his losses will be kept to the absolute minimum.

The prince's wife, better known as Meerabai, is perhaps the most famous woman in Indian history. As a mystic saint-poet, her verse and words are as much part of our vocabulary as that of the Bible in western countries. But curiously her husband is a hiatus in history. All that we know about him is that he was born, he was married to the princess, and he died. Which meant that the Maharaj Kumar of my novel had to be created from the whole cloth. *Cuckold* is not about her, but she is at the centre of it and the novel is a study of the mystical relationship between a human being and God.

He was returning from a seven-mile walk along the parapet of the fort at eleven at night when he saw his wife sitting at the Flautist's temple. He turned towards the palace but something about her made him go back. She sat still, her eyes closed… There was a strange expression on her face. He knew he wasn't making sense but he could only call it joyous, ecstatic tranquillity. She was no longer of this earth or of this world.

He was sure that the light from the solitary lamp was playing tricks with her face. He drew closer to her. There was a light flowing from her, not just from her eyes which were shut anyway, but from her entire body. He realized that it did not make any difference whether he gave credence to what he saw or didn't. Nothing could touch her. She was a circle and a completeness. All else was without. She was in communion with something that was beyond comprehension. Only someone touched by the divine could be so insensible and self-absorbed. What was she thinking about? That was a silly question. She seemed beyond thought. He would never be able to penetrate the mystery at the centre of her being. But that, he suspected, is the nature of the mystical experience. It is a one-to-one rapport. The rest of the world was, perforce, shut out. To an outsider, the saint's world was quintessentially solipsistic, but that was missing the point. There was no outside for her.

He felt an odd desire. He wanted to cup his hands and gather the light emanating from her.

Who was this woman who, over the centuries, had become the subject of some kitsch that it was well-nigh impossible to cut through the stereotype and see her for what she really was? It's one thing to be worshipped by devotees and quite another to be married to a saint. (Think of how difficult it must have been to be Mrs Mahatma Gandhi or the son of the Mahatma.) What has been forgotten, thanks to the numerous plays and films about Meera and all the hagiographic hogwash written about her, is that saints too are human beings. Greeneyes, or the Little Saint as she's called in *Cuckold,* has a temper. She cheats shamelessly at cards or a game of dice. She will not sleep with her husband, but when he is compelled to marry a second time, she is intensely jealous of the new wife. Some people were offended by my version of the Little Saint but what she showed me in the most unambiguous terms was that she was a feminist five centuries before the word became common currency, but without a label or manifesto: someone who practised what she believed in without giving a damn about what society said of her. Remember she was not only a princess and married to the heir apparent of the most powerful kingdom of the era but was living in extremely orthodox times. Even today if you go to Rajasthan, they will recite verses about how she brought shame on the royal family and the people of Mewar by singing and dancing in public. She was far more complex and greater in stature than those who idolize her will allow.

In 1498, the Portuguese captain Vasco da Gama rounded the Cape of Good Hope and discovered the sea route from Europe to India. What was the encounter between two such diverse civilizations and religions like? Later in *Cuckold* I imagined a scene with one of the Portuguese king's emissaries visiting Mewar a decade or two after da Gama's arrival and offering Rana Sangha, the father of the Maharaj Kumar, a portrait of the Virgin Mary and Jesus.

My attempt was to get inside the head of an Indian prince who has never been exposed to Christian iconography and this is what came of it.

> The mother is thin, long-faced, and unrelievedly morose while her son has an infant's chubby body and mop of curly hair but a bizarre and disconcertingly adult face. In his left hand is a globe with a diamond-studded cross on it. In the top left and right corners are winged creatures called angels. In the background, off-centre to the right, is an echo of the cross motif, but this time it's a wooden one. Impaled on it with thick nails is an emaciated man with every rib in his chest sticking out painfully. The ambassador informed us that this man was none other than the lady's son grown up. His face is even sadder than the mother's. He wears a diadem of thorns and in the middle of his chest is a glowing and ethereal heart. A rather strange concept of god, to say the least. Gods, I have always assumed, are all-powerful. This one, however, needs help and succour desperately. You would need to have a stomach to live with this tearful and gloomy mother and child, apart from a god who is in perpetual pain.

One of the intriguing questions for me about mythology, the epics with gods in them and religious texts has always been who wrote these stories of which we never tire. Admittedly many of the holy books are said to be either the word of God himself or are narrated by an emissary of God like the Prophet Mohammad. While the faithful take them as gospel truth without any human interventions in these texts, scholars believe that a book like Bhagavad Gita in the form in which we know it, is the sum total of accretions that have taken place over centuries. The church approves of four gospels but there are many other gospels which the church fathers decided were heretical and suppressed. They came to be known as the Gnostic Gospels, which were recovered in the last century by sheer accident. Without arguing about the provenance and authenticity of the sacred materials, surely it is likely that some storytellers with wonderful imaginations who go by the name 'Anonymous' were at work on many of these texts?

In the 1970s India witnessed the birth of a brand new goddess when a film called *Jai Santoshi Maa* (Hail, Goddess of Satisfaction) was released. The low-budget film was a freak phenomenon. It was an out-and-out smash hit. *Jai Santoshi Maa* was also responsible for starting a new cult of worship within the Hindu pantheon and the building of temples to this goddess.

I had no thought of inventing a new god or goddess but I did end up writing a little story about the god of time (*Kaal*) which could perhaps throw light on how myths come to be. Unfortunately, my story did not hit the silver screen, and unlike the producer of *Jai Santoshi Maa*, I did not end up making millions. The Maharaj Kumar's father, Rana Sanga, and his two brothers and their uncle wish to know which of the four would inherit the throne. But of course, there's no knowing until the time is ripe. Then the uncle makes an extraordinary suggestion. They could visit the temple of the forbiddingly intimidating Rajasthani goddess, Charani Devi. Her priestess alone would know what the future has in store.

Here's the story of Time or Kaal and Charani Devi.

> Time was suffering from advanced symptoms of megalomania. He was the framework or the boundaries within which everything that happened, happened. The demons, the gods, space and the cosmos were time-bound. Nothing – not even nothingness – existed beyond the limits of time. Little wonder then that Time began to perceive himself as cause and consequence, the begetter

and begotten, as the beginning and the end. It was not just that he had delusions of grandeur, it appeared that he was what he claimed to be: omnipotent, omniscient and omnipresent.

The gods including Brahma, Vishnu and Shiva had seen many crises, they had often been on the verge of defeat or extinction and yet always at the last minute, through imagination, guile, trickery, or the clever use of power, they had pulled back from the edge of chaos and won the day. But Time had been on their side then. Things were a little different now… Time was about to ingest the three worlds when Charani Devi hurried past. She was gathering together the million and one strands of Time here, there, up, below, before, yonder, next. She didn't look to the left or the right. Her hands stretched, foreshortened, her fingers picked up the loose ends and the unbroken threads, endless stretches of pre-history, history-to-be, and the simultaneous present that is the same second multiplied by all the points in space. She must have put glue on the tips of her fingers for not a straggly piece of raveled warp or woof escaped her; she bundled it up helter-skelter, no beginning, no middle, no end, no order, just one monstrously big ball the size of the cosmos. Then the Devi opened her mouth and swallowed all of it in one gulp.

But just as the gods were about to rejoice and celebrate this greatest of victories, they realized they had circumvented one calamity to fall prey to another that was even more devastating. Time had stopped dead. And so had everything else. Because life, as we all know, can only occur on the axis of time with its three sharp and fluid divisions: the past, the present and the future. With Time sitting confused and muddle-headed in the belly of Charani Devi, life would cease to be.

So the gods went into a huddle once again… [Finally] Shiva takes up the challenge…

'You know what I've come for, don't you?' Shiva asked [Charani Devi].

She looked at him with her large limpid eyes. She had always been one of the liveliest and most restless goddesses in the heavens. But the knowledge of her fatc did something strange to her face. It gave her a composure and stillness that wrenched at Shiva's heart. Shiva gently took her hand in his. She held it tightly as if she would never let go of it.

'You want me to unravel the tapeworm of Time. You want the present back.' She spoke after a long time.

'Will you do it?' he asked her. It seemed as if she would never answer.

'It is going to be a long, lonely and loveless vigil,' she said.

'Long and lonely, yes,' Shiva told her, 'but not loveless. No one will ever part us. You have but to think of me and wherever I am I shall return to you.'

And he embraced her forever. For that is what the conjoining of the ling and the yoni is, a timeless union. And so Charani Devi sits in the temple and delicately, oh so delicately, coaxes a fraction of the millimeter of the worm from her mouth. She can never close her mouth for if she does, all mankind and devilkind and all godkind would be forever frozen in suspended animation.

The western calendar, at least the apocalyptic one, as we have all seen, starts with 9/11 in the third millennium. (That's when it became impossible to ignore god-bothering.) But in truth, the Iranian revolution had given us ample notice of Islamic wrath and violence to come when, after Salman Rushdie published *The Satanic Verses* in 1988, Ayatollah Khomeini issued a fatwa demanding the blasphemous author be killed.

Like the rest of the world, I watched in horror as extremist Muslims across the world picked up the gauntlet and hunted for Salman Rushdie. Weeks, months and years passed while Rushdie moved from one hideout to another under police protection. How long would it take before some fanatic chanced upon the whereabouts of the author on the run? What kind of man/woman, I wondered, would take the diktat of the Ayatollah to heart and risk his own future and life, albeit with an assured place in *janaat*/heaven?

Hindsight is not the most reliable of witnesses, but since I had finished *Cuckold*, I suspect my novel, *God's Little Soldier*, must have taken root around this time. One particular decision I had taken even before I started writing. My extremist protagonist would come from a highly cultured Muslim family and not from a madrasa that the template stereotype demanded. The Ayatollah's order to kill Rushdie had triggered a spate of speculation and theorizing, reinforcing stereotypes about Islamic fundamentalism. In the process of writing and rewriting the novel, what became evident to me was that the source of extremism was not limited to brainwashing, or an atmosphere of extreme orthodoxy and aggressive punitive Islam but could also result from a mindset and a susceptible temperament that saw everything in black and white and had no room for doubt or the middle ground. You could convert from Judaism, Hinduism, or any other religion to Christianity or Islam, or from Marxism to capitalism to anarchy, but very likely you would not forsake your extremist stance.

A third of the way in my novel, the protagonist, Zia, abandons Islam in favour of the Catholic faith. The question I had to ask myself was: Why would Zia have a change of heart and faith? I had hinted at Zia's peculiar dilemma in the English text and its German translation but it was only fifteen months after the publication of the original that I wrote a new chapter to highlight the terrible quandary that confronts my protagonist.

Here is a segment from that chapter. After his long stint as a holy warrior of Islam, Zia joins a Trappist abbey as a novice monk and is now called Lucens. This is a conversation that his novice master, Father Paul, who is on his deathbed, has with him.

> 'This is your last chance to come clean, my sad, tortured friend. Why did Zia decide to become Lucens?'
>
> Father Paul never let go. Lucens sensed that he would hound him for an answer even after he was no more.
>
> 'One may occasionally come across Christians who have converted to Islam but I have hardly ever heard of a Muslim who has embraced Christianity. And certainly not a holy warrior like you. At least that's the received wisdom on the subject. So why did a fundamentalist like you break the mould? Was Allah not sufficient for you, Zia?'
>
> The last three sentences were so soft and brittle they disintegrated like mirages on soft desert sands. Lucens was not sure whether he had conjured up Father Paul's words or the priest had actually spoken.
>
> 'You shouldn't be talking so much. It's exhausting you. Would you care for a glass of water?'
>
> 'Last chance, both for you and me. Did you let Him down, Zia? Or did you think it was the other way around?'
>
> 'Who?' Zia deliberately chose to be opaque in the hope that Father Paul would give the interrogation a break.
>
> 'You know well who I mean.'
>
> Lucens realized there was no escaping a dying man. 'It was all such a long time ago, Father.'
>
> 'Yes. As long ago as this very minute, since you can't ever forget what you did there. It was not Christ who beckoned you, was it, Zia? It was your unrelenting remorse, and your need for forgiveness which made you come over.'

It maddened Lucens that this diminishing, receding monk was still trying to provoke him, calling him by his old name, Zia, even though every now and again it seemed as if he had passed out or, perhaps, even died.

'And yet you were caught in a terrible trap. You could not forgive yourself for needing forgiveness. What greater shame could there be for an upright soldier of God who is doing what he imagines is God's bidding and yet is crushed by the weight of the knowledge that his purported good deeds are nothing but heinous acts of the purest evil?'

Lucens was silent…

'Last chance, Zia. Unless you acknowledge the past and your role in it, you will not be at peace with yourself or with God.'

Maybe Father Paul was right. But there were things in Lucens's past that he could not afford to think about even after he was dead.

'The problem with stereotypes, Zia,' Father Paul was not done with him yet, 'is that they trap both the insider as well as the outsider. They are both its victims and yet are unable to break out of them.'

In my last novel, *The Extras*, which is a sequel to *Ravan and Eddie*, there is a mafioso called Three Point One who blackmails the Hindu protagonist, Ravan, into becoming the carrier for illicit goods. Ravan is petrified about working for the man and nearly bungles the delivery in the most visible and excruciating manner possible. Retribution follows instantly in the form of extreme corporal punishment. Ravan is battered so badly that even Three Point One suggests that he should not drive the vehicle back. But Ravan insists on leaving. What's so important that you have to go back, the mafia boss asks him. Ravan tells him he has taken a vow to visit a Hindu holy shrine for twenty-one Tuesdays running. What about the Sufi saint's shrine at Haji Ali, Three Point

One queries him sarcastically. Ravan's answer is revealing. I have already done that, and the nine novenas at St Michael's Church at Mahim too, he says. If there's a holy place, be it a temple, a Sufi saint's tomb or a Catholic church which has a reputation for answering prayers, a Hindu like Ravan will routinely seek blessings in all three places. For all the talk of Hindu–Muslim riots or enmity, many Hindus have no qualms about seeking benediction from any religion or sect so long as it has a reputation for being holy and munificent.

Afterword

A Personal Tribute

Before Kiran and I met, we had discovered each other through our books. It was a discovery that grew into an unexpected and richly rewarding relationship.

We met in 2014 when he came to Dehra Dun to interview me. I asked him why he wanted an interview and he replied, 'So that your views can be archived in a permanent collection at the Chandigarh Literary Festival archives.' Kiran had a high opinion of the Chandigarh festival. He said it was the only one that concentrated on a writer's work and critiques of it. After that first meeting he wrote to me, saying: 'I wish I could have sat with you and listened to you for hours. I am trying to figure out ways to reduce the distance between Mumbai and Dehra Dun to a 20-minute bus ride.' But as there was no such possibility, it happened that we stayed connected by keeping in touch almost every day. Kiran wrote, 'In truth not a day passes when I am not thinking of you. I suspect despite all my cynicism I am an old-fashioned believer in either astral connections or bonds that are beyond the ken of human beings. Life does strange things to us. One of them is our coming to know each other. What can I say but a big thank you.' So we exchanged ideas and feelings, learned of our literary and political like-mindedness and our addiction to the songs of K.L. Saigal, and shared our personal ups and downs.

I came to know Kiran – who had suffered illness, pain and bouts of hospitalization during his childhood, and was never free of life-threatening health problems – as a man with an undiminished zest for life, and one whose novels were famous for their unflagging energy, their ribald riotous humour and their powerful portrayal of the subjugation of women. His own unprivileged background kept him deeply conscious, both in his life and his writing, of those who were marginalized, brutalized or helpless. He reached out to other writers and helped whom he could.

We shared our grief at the assaults being made on the freedom of expression, on the minorities and on the diversity and equality that India had stood for and we made our views public through our non-fiction writing. The changes that were taking place around us, which were destroying the very meaning of India, became our personal as well as political wounds, while the public indifference to the mob lynching and other barbaric events taking place drove Kiran to despair. In a mail to me, he wrote: 'I have had to fight serious depression. I no longer understand the species to which you and I belong. I don't know where we got the notion that mankind belongs to something called civilization. I want us one and a quarter billion Indians to embrace the families of those who have been lynched or butchered, and the murderers brought to fast justice.'

We discussed each other's novels. The power and originality of Kiran's storytelling had given Indian literature a shock that no writer has equalled. I told him that his *Ravan and Eddie* trilogy was our fourth Indian epic – the first three being the Ramayana, the Mahabharata, and India's epic fight for freedom from British rule. The fact that he was bilingual put him in a rare category of writers, and I wished I could have read his haunting novel *Seven Sixes Are Forty-Three* in Marathi. He told me my novels were different from any Indian writing in English. They gave him a picture of the making of modern India, and the secular, democratic values on which it had been built. Together we mourned the tragedy of our multi-religion, multi-culture civilization being shrunk into a one-religion, one-culture identity. The most moving sentences Kiran wrote, which appear at the end of his last published novel, *The Arsonist*, tell us what he meant by religion: 'There is only one God. And her name is life. She's the only one worthy of worship. All else is irrelevant.'

Being half Marathi myself, I shared a Marathi bond with Kiran, and he was delighted that my two recent novellas, which he called 'contemporary classics', had been accepted by a Marathi publisher. One of these, *When the Moon Shines by Day*, I had dedicated to him. Of the next one, *The Fate of Butterflies*, he wrote, 'The thought that you had wanted to dedicate it to me to get me off my third rate health problems gave me a high that just gets higher by the minute' – but in the end I sent him a song – 'Let's face the music and dance' – from an old Hollywood movie that conveyed the spirit of the novel, to use in place of a dedication. Kiran wrote back, 'I love the song, so yes, please put it in place of a dedication, and let's face the music and dance!'

It was our Marathi bond that made me ask him to represent me in Pune to accept, on my behalf, the first Bhai Vaidya Award, as I couldn't go myself. This award, in memory of a distinguished socialist politician, commemorated Bhai Vaidya's lifelong commitment to policies that served human needs, as opposed to those dictated by market value. It was a philosophy we both subscribed to, and Kiran addressed the Pune gathering in addition to my videoed speech.

A fitting tribute to Kiran was the library named after him, built by the Dikshant Global School in Chandigarh. He especially enjoyed his encounters with young readers, and the school, along with himself and all of us invited guests, celebrated the opening of the library a year ago with a rousing programme of music and song.

The Chandigarh festival in particular cherishes the literary achievements of this writer of genius and will create a lasting memorial in his honour. I have offered here a few glimpses of the Kiran Nagarkar I knew, the unusual human being he was, and the many-splendoured relationship we shared.

Nayantara Sahgal
Prize-winning novelist and non-fiction writer

About the Author

Novelist, critic, playwright, Kiran Nagarkar (1942–2019) wrote in both English and his mother tongue, Marathi. Among his notable works are *Saat Sakkam Trechalis* (tr. *Seven Sixes Are Forty-Three*) (1974), *Ravan and Eddie* (1994) and *Cuckold* (1997), for which he received the Sahitya Akademi Award.